# THE SECESSION MOVEMENT, 1860–1861

# THE SECESSION MOVEMENT

## 1860-1861

BY

DWIGHT LOWELL DUMOND, PH.D.

## OCTAGON BOOKS

A DIVISION OF FARRAR, STRAUS AND GIROUX

New York    1973

*Reprinted 1963*
*by special arrangement with Dwight L. Dumond*

*Second Octagon printing 1973*

OCTAGON BOOKS
A DIVISION OF FARRAR, STRAUS & GIROUX, INC.
19 Union Square West
New York, N. Y. 10003

LIBRARY OF CONGRESS CATALOG CARD NUMBER: 63-20889

ISBN 0-374-92375-2

Printed in U.S.A. by
NOBLE OFFSET PRINTERS, INC.
New York, N.Y. 10003

# PREFACE

THIS monograph was submitted originally to the Board of Graduate Studies in the University of Michigan in partial fulfillment of the requirements for the degree of Doctor of Philosophy.

I have attempted to state the premises upon which the several groups of Southerners justified resistance to the federal government, and to trace the process of secession. Such a study, of necessity, emphasizes constitutional interpretations and touches more lightly the important social and economic factors involved. By the same tenets, the question of slavery in the territories, as one phase of the abstract rights of slavery under the Constitution, looms larger than it would in a definitive study of the origins of the war.

It has been my constant concern to detach myself from the tradition that the Civil War was irrepressible. That idea implies that the American people were incapable of solving a difficult problem except by bloodletting, and confuses the designs of party politicians with the arts of statesmanship.

That a twofold revolution was in progress scarcely can be disputed. It is equally clear that the movement at the South was under skillful direction; and, although in no sense a political conspiracy, was well organized from the very first. An exhaustive study of newspaper sources has brought to light material of great value; because news-

v

papers, and not private correspondence, were the sources
of information for the people at large.

I have sought to clarify and to reinterpret without the
use of frequent qualifying phrases, conscious that further
research will bring forth new and sounder interpretations
at many points.

I wish to acknowledge a deep sense of gratitude to
Professor Ulrich Bonnell Phillips and to Professor
Thomas Maitland Marshall. Their contributions in personal inspiration are inseparable; both assisted materially
in criticism and suggestions. I am indebted to many personal friends and archivists who placed at my disposal a
wealth of manuscript material, and who, by their many
courtesies, increased the pleasure of research.

DWIGHT L. DUMOND.

University of Michigan,
    June 1, 1931.

# CONTENTS

# THE SECESSION MOVEMENT, 1860–1861

# CHAPTER I

## CONFLICTING POLITICAL PRINCIPLES, 1860

BEGINNING about the time when Wilmot presented his famous proviso, there developed a divergence of doctrine concerning the aspects of slavery in the territories which, along with other things, was to result in the establishment of the Southern confederacy and in civil war. Was it within the power of Congress to exclude slavery? If not, could the legislature of a territory do so? If such a legislature could not accomplish this directly, could it properly do so by indirection? If not, had Congress any duty to correct the action, or supplement the inaction of the territorial legislature? The compromise measures of the year 1850, the Kansas-Nebraska Act of 1854, and the Dred Scott decision, 1857, were the tangible results of the bitter struggle which involved these questions in state and national politics before 1860. Constitutional interpretations with respect to slavery and the nature of the federal government were expressed in the Georgia and Alabama platforms, in the Freeport and Cooper Union speeches, and in the Davis resolutions. Every individual involved in the controversy reinforced his doctrines by some particular interpretation of the organic act, as previously expressed and variously restated at intervals since its inception.

1

The state-rights men considered the federal government an agent of the sovereign states, entrusted with certain carefully defined powers, for the performance of
specific duties. State governments, they maintained, did
not derive any power whatsoever from the Constitution
or the federal government; on the contrary, whatever
powers the latter possesses were bestowed upon it by the
states through the Constitution. Its powers being deriva-
tive, the state which delegated them might take them
away. Whatever powers had not been delegated to the
federal government nor prohibited the states had been
reserved to the respective states. The fact that a division
of powers had been made confirmed the intention of
limitations, and implied a power capable of enforcing
restrictions. The question was, where did this power of
determining the extent of limitations and reserved powers
reside? Webster and the federal school said that in all
suits in law and equity the Supreme Court was the final
judge, and that in cases not capable of being argued
before that tribunal Congress must judge of, and finally
interpret, the powers of the federal government.[1] Calhoun, Hayne, and the state-rights school held this doctrine
to be a presumption utterly unwarranted either by interpretation of the Constitution itself or the circumstances
of its inception.[2] They regarded the Constitution as an
instrument of union between states which had never surrendered their sovereignty nor agreed to unlimited submission to the government created by the compact. The
states, and not the government so created, were the final

[1] Webster, "Second Speech on Foot's Resolutions," in *Works*, III,
270-342.
[2] Calhoun, "A Discourse on the Constitution and Government of
the United States," in *Works*, I, 111-406; "Letter to Governor Hamilton on the Subject of State Interposition," *ibid.*, 144-193.

judges of the extent of their reserved powers. In case the federal government arrogated authority beyond the limits of the delegation or encroached upon the reservations, each state had the right to determine for itself the nature and extent of remedial measures.[3]

They maintained that it is the nature of all delegated power to increase; that, if the general government were invested with the right to determine the limits of its own powers and enforce its decisions, the Constitution would no longer act as a shield against encroachments upon the vested rights of the people and the independence of the states; that, under the theory of the federal school, there was no real, positive division of powers, since Congress or the Supreme Court, or the two operating harmoniously, might enlarge upon the delegated powers by usurpations; that, therefore, in the last analysis, a government which is the sole judge of the limits of its own powers becomes an absolutism. They contended that the principal justification for the creation of a government by a free people is to afford protection for minorities against the despotism of majorities in cases of internal dissension and sectional disputes; and that, unless some protective power be provided as a restraint upon the will of the many as against the few, the latter, however justifiable their position and sacred their menaced rights, must yield to the stronger party. If, therefore, the majority were invested with definitive rights and unlimited executive powers, the rights of the minority must, of necessity, become subject to the selfish pleasure and unrestrained ambitions of a legislative majority.[4] The Southerners insisted that there

[3] Barksdale, Remarks in House of Representatives, January 23, 1860, *Cong. Globe*, 36 Cong., 1 Sess., IV, Appendix, 171.
[4] *Speech of William L. Yancey of Alabama, delivered in the National Democratic Convention, Charleston, April 28, 1860*, 4.

must be a self-protecting power in the hands of the minority. Limitations placed upon the power of the federal government by the states would no longer restrain, and powers which had never been delegated by the states would be usurped, unless the ultimate source of authority in all cases of dispute rested with the states for whose benefit limitations had been imposed and reservations had been made. It was not in the nature of things for majorities to search constitutions to determine in what respects the rights of minorities were to be observed. These were never safe if protest and remonstrance were the only recourses available. State interposition and secession were, therefore, the only safe and effective measures of resistance, and the right of a state to exercise them was indisputable. They were effective remedies, too long fallen into disuse, in the opinion of the state-rights men, but not completely forgotten nor in any sense discarded.[5]

Not all of the men of the South were state-rights men, nor was the doctrine of state rights confined to that section of the country; but that doctrine was the constitutional refuge of the secessionists; and the fundamental

[5] Yancey took this position in the Charleston convention when he said: "We claim the benefit of the Constitution that was made for the protection of minorities. In the march of events, feeling conscious of your numerical power, you have aggressed upon us. We hold up between us and your advancing columns of numbers that written instrument which your and our fathers made, and by the compact of which, you with your power were to respect us and our rights. Our and your fathers made it that they and their children should forever observe it; that upon all questions affecting the rights of the minority, the majority should not rely upon their voting numbers, but should look, in restraint upon passion, avarice, and lust for power, to the written compact, to see in what the minority was to be respected, and how it was to be protected, and to yield an implicit obedience to that compact. You, in your voting power, are not accustomed to scan its provisions as closely as we, who, less in number, find in the instrument the only peaceable solution of difficulties that otherwise would lead us to defend ourselves with arms." *Ibid.*, 3-4.

cause of secession was the threatened extinction of slavery. After the year 1848 the two were inseparable, state-rights Democrats and state-rights Whigs of pro-slavery bent merging into a Southern-rights association.[6] The Douglas Democrats faithfully adhered to the theory of state rights. It was an essential element of popular sovereignty, and they freely proclaimed it as an argument against congressional intervention for protection.[7] Even the Republicans used the argument of state rights when it suited their purpose to do so,[8] and they wrote a broad declaration of it into their Chicago platform.[9]

As interpreted by the Southern-rights men the Constitution recognized the institution of slavery and provided for its representation, security, and protection. Slavery as an institution preceded the Constitution and was recog-

[6] Phillips, "The Southern Whigs, 1834-1854," in *Essays in American History dedicated to Frederick Jackson Turner* (Guy Stanton Ford, ed.), 216-217.

[7] Pugh said, in the Charleston convention, April 27, 1860: "I believe the Federal Government to be founded upon mutual compact between the States; and as the States entered into that compact of their own sovereign will, so it belongs to each of them, as the arbiter of its own destiny, to decide when the compact has been broken, and the mode and measure of redress." *Proceedings of the Conventions at Charleston and Baltimore* (National Democratic Executive Committee, ed.), 83.

[8] The legislature of Wisconsin, March 19, 1859, in a series of resolutions denouncing the Supreme Court decision in the famous Booth case, said among other things: "*Resolved,* that the Government formed by the Constitution of the United States was not made the exclusive or final judge of the extent of the powers delegated to itself; but that, as in all other cases of compact among parties having no common judge, each has an equal right to judge for itself as well of infractions as of the mode and measure of redress." For an historical treatment of the Booth case see Warren, *The Supreme Court in United States History,* III, 42-80.

[9] The fourth resolution can be regarded in no other light than a concession to state-rights sentiment. Wilmot, temporary chairman of the convention, clearly implied that the resolution was included for that purpose. *Proceedings of the first three Republican National Conventions . . .* (Charles W. Johnson, ed.), 138.

nized, *not established,* by the Constitution where state sovereignty did not prohibit it. They maintained that the institution could not be established or abolished in the territories by Congress. It was established there by the migration of the slave owner with his property. What they demanded was protection for property rights, not laws to establish the institution, because there was no necessity for such laws.[10] The territories were the common possession of equally sovereign states, and to the federal government these states had entrusted, by the Constitution, the duty of administering the common property for the benefit of all. The power to declare what was property was a sovereign power, and could not be exercised except by the people of a state in their organic instrument of government. This right they had never surrendered to the federal government. The eminent domain over the territories resting with the states, a citizen of any state had the right to carry with him into the common territory whatever species of property his state recognized, and look for protection to the agent of the states which had been charged with that specific duty.

All Republicans contended that Congress possessed the constitutional power to exclude slavery from the territories; some few of them maintained that Congress possessed equal power to admit it.[11] They held that the territories were not the common possession of the sovereign states but of the United States; and that as a state might prohibit slavery in its constitution, Congress might do so by the organic act creating a territorial government. This power of Congress, they contended, was established

[10] Smith of North Carolina, Remarks in the House of Representatives, May 2, 1860. *Cong. Globe,* 36 Cong., 1 Sess., IV, Appendix, 277.

[11] Corwin of Ohio, Remarks in the House of Representatives, January 24, 1860, *ibid.,* 143.

by the Constitution and was amply substantiated by precedent and Supreme Court decisions. The Constitution gave to Congress the "power to make all needful rules and regulations concerning the territory and other property of the United States." As interpreted by the Republicans of the federal school, this clause gave to Congress a full and complete authority over the inhabitants of the territories; a power unrestricted by the Constitution, untrammeled by representatives of the governed, almost imperial. They contended that slavery was the creature of local, state, or municipal law, and could not exist in any acquired territory until established by the territorial legislature under express provision by Congress.[12] Slavery, dependent upon local law for its legal existence, possessed no transitory qualities. Congress could, therefore, confine slavery within its existing limits, and prevent the admission of any more slave states.

The Republicans affirmed the right and duty of Congress to exclude slavery from the territories. The Southern-rights men denied it to Congress, to the territorial legislature, and to the people of a territory until they framed an organic law preparatory to admission as a state. The right of the people of a state and of them alone to recognize or abolish the institution of slavery by their constitution was the foundation of their entire constitutional theory. They never denied that, they never claimed more; and when the Republican leaders said that if the Constitution carried slavery into the territories it also carried it into the states, they were reading something into the claims of the Southern-rights men which was not

[12] Corwin of Ohio, Remarks in the House of Representatives, January 23-24, 1860, *ibid.*, 134-150. Corwin, a conservative Republican, would acknowledge the existence of slavery wherever it already existed in territory at the time of acquisition. It was a safe concession in view of the fact that the United States possessed no such territory and was not likely soon to acquire any.

there. They were creating in the minds of the Northern people an impression of Southern claims which never had been, nor ever could be, asserted under the doctrine of state rights.

Both the Southern-rights men and the Republicans, then, advocated congressional intervention, the former for protection where necessary, the latter for exclusion. Legislation for protection where necessary allowed free states if the people so wished at the time of admission. Legislation for exclusion precluded the possibility of slave states. The former would not make all territories slave, the latter would make all territories free. The Southern-rights men were asking for the right to enjoy the use of slaves as property in the territories. The Republicans denied that slaves were property in the ordinary sense of the term. They were persons also liable to criminal jurisdiction and to manumission, and giving, through their character as persons, valuable political rights to others.[13] The Southerners accused the Republicans of failing to make a distinction between slaves as property and slavery as a political institution, which it could only become at the time of the admission of a state.[14] It was utterly impossible for a Republican to think of slaves as being in the same category with other property; and while many of them attempted to justify their attitude toward slavery upon constitutional principles many more subscribed to the doctrine of the higher law.

When Wilmot proposed the exclusion of slavery from the territory to be acquired from Mexico he was opposed by few Northern Democrats. By 1860 practically all

[13] Sedgwick of New York, Remarks in the House of Representatives, *ibid.*, 179.

[14] Keitt of South Carolina, Remarks in the House of Representatives, *ibid.*, 96.

Democrats denied the right of Congress to exclude slavery from the territories. The invalidation of the Missouri restriction and the decision of the Supreme Court in the Dred Scott case had strengthened the Southern-rights position. But, although the Democratic party was a unit in denying the right and power of congressional prohibition, a difference of opinion had developed over the question of the power of the territorial legislatures; and the intensity of the argument threatened the very existence of the party. All Democrats agreed that a territorial legislature possessed the power to protect slave property; some claimed it equally possessed the power to destroy it. The Southern-rights men held that the territorial legislature possessed no sovereign powers. It was created by act of Congress, and Congress might at any time end its existence. Deriving its powers from Congress, there was a limit to the extent of its legislative jurisdiction. The abolition of slavery was an act of sovereignty. No precedent existed for the abolition of slavery by legislative enactment, except where that power had previously been granted by constitutional provision. Congress could not transfer power which it did not possess. That power could be exercised by the people of a territory at the time of framing a constitution for admission as a state, and not before that time. "A territorial government," said Fitch, "derives all its powers from the Constitution through the General Government; it has no original power; it has no reserved power; and it cannot partake of the powers reserved to and by the States, until it becomes a State." [15]

[15] Fitch of Indiana, Remarks in the Senate, February 2, 1860, *ibid.*, 111; see, also, Hardeman of Georgia, Remarks in the House of Representatives, April 12, 1860, *ibid.*, 223; Crittenden of Kentucky, Remarks in the Senate, May 24, 1860, *ibid.*, III, 2341; Singleton of Mississippi, Remarks in the House of Representatives, December 19, 1859, *ibid.*, IV, Appendix, 53.

The Douglas Democrats contended that the territorial legislature could lawfully exclude slavery, either by non-action or unfriendly legislation. This doctrine they derived from the alleged inherent power of self-government existing in every community. They maintained that sovereignty began with the organization of the territorial government by Congress. It was the doctrine of popular sovereignty and not squatter sovereignty.[16] They claimed as an historical basis for this doctrine of popular sovereignty the theory of non-intervention and as precedent for its application the compromise measures of 1850 and the Kansas-Nebraska Act. By 1860 they were denying the demand of the South for congressional protection on the ground that it was an advanced position, the party having previously defined the doctrine of non-intervention as a cardinal principle. The Southern-rights men denied that

[16] Douglas defined the term squatter sovereignty as the exercise of self-government by settlers in a region within the public domain where Congress had made no provision for the exercise of governmental functions, and he denounced it as the assumption of unconstitutional powers. *Ibid.*, III, 2147. The Southern-rights men took exception to this political philosophy of Douglas and exposed its inconsistencies relentlessly. Benjamin said in the Senate: "When the people of this country first go into the wilderness and find there no government whatever, and then exercise that inherent right of self-defense which drives men, under the laws that God has implanted in them, to associate together in self-defense and organize some system of law for their own protection; then, when it would seem to the common sense of universal mankind that no one could say they were wrong in doing that—then it is that the Senator from Illinois says he repudiates and opposes their power. That is the squatter sovereignty that he objects to. But when the sovereign has come in; when the trustee of all the States has taken possession of the common fund; when it has organized a government that suits it in the exercise of its discretion, and when it has committed the administration of the affairs of the Territory, with certain limitations under the Constitution of the United States, to a Territorial Legislature—then, when the sovereign is present, then the people become invested, by some magical process, with an inherent popular sovereignty that rises superior to the author of their being." *Ibid.*, 2237.

the doctrine of non-intervention was ever intended to set aside the right of protection by Congress for slave property in the territories.[17] The term had originated at the time of the acquisition of Mexican territory in 1848. It was a denial by the Democratic and Whig parties of the doctrine of congressional power to exclude as endorsed by the Free-Soil party at the North. It might more correctly have been called incapacity to exclude, for the question of the right to exclude was the only issue before the people.[18]

The compromise measures of 1850 were barely acceptable to the South and created an unprecedented excitement. They were acquiesced in by the majority of that section (1) because they offered a possible conclusion of the slavery controversy, and (2) because the majority was forced to choose between a qualified endorsement of them and a dissolution of the Union.[19] Douglas, at that time, approved of the legislation; but, four years later, he introduced into Congress the Kansas-Nebraska bill, the enactment of which gave birth to the Republican party and created the dissension out of which arose in 1860 the disruption of the Democratic party and the dissolution of

[17] "Address to the Democratic Party of the State of Texas," in *The Daily Delta*, May 10, 1860; *Daily Chronicle and Sentinel*, Augusta, May 5, 1860.

[18] Davis had said at the time: "But what is non-intervention seems to vary as often as the light and shade of every fleeting cloud. It has different meanings in every State, in every county, in every town. If non-intervention means that we shall not have protection for our property in slaves, then I always was, and always shall be, opposed to it." *Cong. Globe*, 31 Cong., 1 Sess., Appendix II, 919. See, also, Brown of Mississippi, Remarks in the Senate, *ibid.*, 33 Cong., 1 Sess., Appendix, 232.

[19] Garner, "The First Struggle over Secession in Mississippi," in the Mississippi Historical Society, *Publications*, IV, 89-105; Du Bose, *The Life and Times of William Lowndes Yancey*, 251; Capers, *The Life and Times of C. G. Memminger*, 187-229; Claiborne, *Life and Correspondence of John A. Quitman*, II, 114-155.

the Union. This act invalidated the Missouri Compromise restriction and, in substance, said that the will of the people in the territory and not the will of the majority of Congress should decide the question whether they should be a slave or a free state at the time of admission. It denied the right of Congress, as was attempted in the case of Missouri, to keep a state out of the Union because it was slave or because it was free. This act did not contain the principle of popular sovereignty, nor did its endorsement by the Democratic party in the Cincinnati platform commit the party to that doctrine. When the bill was framed and discussed in the Democratic caucus, and later, when it was debated in the Senate, Douglas, Cass, and Stuart stood, as they had always done, on the right of the territorial legislature to exclude slavery if it desired to do so. The Southern members of the party maintained, as they had always done, that the people of the territory might exclude slavery at the time of framing a constitution, and not before that time. Unable to reach an agreement on that important point, they so framed the bill as to leave the question of the power of the territorial legislature open to court decision; and, in framing the Cincinnati platform in 1856, the same procedure was followed. All members of the party in 1860 agreed that was true. Both sections of the party agreed to abide by that decision when it should be made.[20]

It was because of this provision rendering all territorial

[20] Speaking of the Kansas-Nebraska Act, Douglas said: "We did not pretend to decide the question whether the Territorial Legislature had the power or not to prohibit slavery, but we did agree to give them all the power we had; and, if they exercised it in such manner as to violate the constitutional rights of any portion of the people, their remedy is to be found in an appeal to the Supreme Court, and not to Congress." *Cong. Globe,* 35 Cong., 2 Sess., II, 1258. Benjamin, referring to the party caucus, maintained that the South had asserted the right of slave owners to migrate to the territories, to be

legislation with regard to slavery subject to the Constitution and to Supreme Court decisions that some Southern-rights men supported the bill. Eventually they realized what the men of clearer thought had told them at the time, that to rely solely upon the judiciary for protection is a surrender of rights; that protection against unconstitutional laws and against violation of constitutional laws may be left to judicial power; but only legislative enactment can afford protection to persons and property, and in case the legislative branch of the government fails to protect, either through evasion of constitutional duties or by neglect, the judiciary has no power to supply the deficiency. The full force of this truism struck them when Douglas said that the territorial legislature could exclude slavery by non-action. They realized that he was correct in that statement; but to his contention that it might lawfully do so, the Southerners never surrendered. They con-

---

protected in their property rights, and had denied that any power could keep them out constitutionally or deprive them of protection until the time of the framing of a constitution. He said further: "Morning after morning we met, for the purpose of coming to some understanding upon that very point; and it was finally understood by all, agreed to by all, made the basis of a compromise by the supporters of that bill, that the Territories should be organized with a delegation by Congress of all the power of Congress in the Territories, and the extent of the power of Congress should be determined by the courts." *Ibid.*, 36 Cong., 1 Sess., III, 1966. Senator Pugh of Ohio, probably the ablest defender of Douglas at the North and a close political ally, admitted that there had been a solemn agreement at the time, that the power of the territorial legislature over slavery should be left to the Supreme Court: "Both parties so understood it, that was the bill. That was the policy of the Democratic party. There might be a difference of opinion as to what the decision would be; there might be a difference of opinion as to the question itself; but as to the bill there was no question. So with the Cincinnati platform. The Cincinnati platform referred that question to judicial determination; and therefore to pretend that the Cincinnati platform is equivocal, or that the Kansas-Nebraska bill is equivocal, is in my judgment eminently absurd." *Ibid.*, 2241; see, also, Green of Missouri, *ibid.*, IV, Appendix, 70; Crawford of Georgia, *ibid.*, 183; Fitch of Indiana, *ibid.*, 112.

tended that protection was the object and the imperative duty of government, and that in places exclusively subject to federal jurisdiction (including territories, since they were the creatures of Congress, and possessed no sovereignty), the states having no power to protect, the federal government could not, nor could any department of that government, abdicate its powers.[21] The right of the slave owner to enter the territories with his property being conceded, and the power of the territorial legislature to exclude being denied, protection was an inevitable sequence.[22]

The Republicans did not deny the power of Congress to abrogate acts of territorial legislatures. They agreed that a territory possessed no sovereignty. They further agreed that, if the slave owner possessed the right to enter the territories with his property, Congress possessed the power to protect him in the enjoyment of that property; that is, if their vote on the Davis resolutions is any criterion by which to judge their attitude, for only Hamlin and Trumbull voted against the fifth resolution.[23] But

[21] Davis of Mississippi, Remarks in the Senate, May 7, 1860, *ibid.*, III, 1940; *The Semi-Weekly Mississippian,* Jackson, August 23, 1859, said: "The right of appeal from the Territorial to the Supreme Court becomes a mockery when Congress is forbidden to enforce the judgment of the latter tribunal. . . . Rights and obligations are reciprocal."

[22] Said the venerable Crittenden: "To assert my right to go there, to carry my property there, and to enjoy that property, and then to say there is anybody stronger or mightier or more sovereign than the Constitution that can take from me that which the Constitution says I shall have and enjoy, or shall expel me from the place where the Constitution says I may go, I can imagine nothing so inconsistent and so contradictory." *Ibid.*, III, 2341.

[23] *Ibid.*, 2344. *"Resolved,* That if experience should at any time prove that the judicial and executive authority does not possess means to insure adequate protection to constitutional rights in a Territory, and if the territorial government should fail or refuse to provide the necessary remedies for that purpose, it will be the duty of Congress to supply such deficiency."

the Republicans denied the constitutional right of Congress or of a territorial legislature to give legal existence to slavery in a territory, and their understanding of the nature of the federal government would not admit a recognition of the Southern claims that slavery was based in the common law and needed no statute law to establish it.

A majority of Congress, therefore, composed of Republicans and Northern Democrats denied the Southerners their claim to federal protection in the territories. Protection was asked for by the slaveholders only in case a majority in a territory, adverse to slavery interests, should pass positive, aggressive legislation against them, or should evade necessary protection. In case of questionable legislation, the popular-sovereignty adherents offered the protection of a court decision. If the territory refused to abide by the decision, Douglas contended that no matter what the courts might decide, the right of exclusion was perfect and complete under the Kansas Act.

If the right of property in a slave was distinctly and expressly affirmed in the Constitution, as the Supreme Court had said in the Dred Scott decision, and its enjoyment could not be interfered with by Congress or a territorial legislature, the logical conclusion followed that the federal government must protect the enjoyment. The only escapes from that conclusion were (1) to claim that the Supreme Court exceeded its jurisdiction in passing upon the question of congressional jurisdiction in the territories; (2) to accept the decision as temporarily binding and seek to have it reversed; or (3) to deny that the legislative and executive branches of the government were necessarily bound by Supreme Court decisions. The Republicans and Douglas Democrats adopted one or another of these theories to escape the force of the decision.

Among the Republicans who supported the thesis that Congress was obligated to conform to the Constitution only in so far as it understood it, was Representative Conkling of New York. Speaking in the House of Representatives, April 17, 1860, he contended that the citizenship of Dred Scott was the essential limit of the court's jurisdiction in that famous case; that opinions rendered beyond that point were without legal force; but that the possibilities presented by the attitude of the court transformed the issue from a struggle between slavery and freedom to a far greater conflict between governmental agencies for prerogatives and power; a conflict in which the Supreme Court was asserting its authority to prescribe the limits of congressional legislation and executive action. Citing a letter of Jefferson to Gallatin, 1810, in which Jefferson rejoiced in the opportunity of obtaining a majority of Republicans in the Supreme Court, he said:

In 1860, sir, we have a chance to go and do likewise, and I trust we shall improve it. A reorganization and reinvigoration of the court, with just regard to commercial and political considerations, is one of the auspicious promises of Republican ascendancy.[24]

Proceeding on the basis of the denial of the authority of the Supreme Court over congressional legislation, and acting upon their interpretation of the right and duty of Congress to exclude slavery from the territories, the Re-

---

[24] *Ibid.,* IV, Appendix, 236. See, also, Gooch of Massachusetts, Remarks in the House of Representatives, May 3, 1860, *ibid.,* 291-295; Vandever of Iowa, Remarks in the House of Representatives, April 27, 1860, *ibid.,* 269; and Wade of Ohio, Remarks in the Senate, March 7, 1860, *ibid.,* 153.

publicans forced through the House of Representatives, May 10, 1860, a bill declaring null and void all territorial acts of the legislature of New Mexico establishing, protecting, or legalizing slavery.[25] The Republicans could not do otherwise than repudiate the authority of the Supreme Court. Its constitutional interpretations in the Dred Scott case were in direct contradiction to the fundamental principle of their party, the right and duty of Congress to exclude slavery from the territories. Had the party adopted any other course, it would have surrendered its right to exist. It was not the denial of the historical data upon which the decision was based, nor the claim that the part of the decision over and above the question of the defendant's citizenship was *obiter dicta,* that constituted a threat against the South. It was the assertion that the will of a majority may destroy the constitutional safeguards of the rights of the minority.[26] It was the declaration that in the future judges should receive appointments to the supreme bench not primarily because of their recognized ability as jurists but because they adhered to the principles

[25] *Ibid.,* III, 2046.

[26] After an extended discussion of the question in the House of Representatives, January 25, 1860, Keitt said: "I know that the lust of avarice and the lust of ambition will never be satisfied while spoils are to be won and power obtained. I know, too, that mere parchment provisions will never stay back the march of a majority; and that its despotism, raised under the mask of law upon the ruins of the Republic, will be more fatal to liberty than the despotism of a victorious captain." *Ibid.,* IV, Appendix, 95. "The right to destroy is not one of the prerogatives of government, but the duty to protect is its chief aim and attribute. Therefore, the right claimed by the Black Republicans, to abolish or exclude slavery from the Territories is not correlative with the duty to protect the same in the Territorial domain of the United States. The former is a gross and tyrannical violation of the first objects of all Government, Federal and State, imperial and Republican; while the latter is fulfilling the mission and design of every just government, which is to throw an ægis over all who live under it." *Nashville Union and American,* September 30, 1860.

of the anti-slavery party. It was no idle threat, in view of the fact that seven of the nine judges were nearing the age of retirement.

The Southern-rights men insisted that to regard the Supreme Court's decisions as binding only upon inferior courts, and limited to the particular matter involved in litigation before it, was a narrow interpretation of its functions. Its functions and duties included the establishment of precedents, the definition of rights, the enforcement of law, and the establishment of a system of jurisprudence for the regulation of society. It is not to be understood that in their whole-hearted endorsement of the decision of the Supreme Court in the Dred Scott case, and in their denial of the Republican interpretation of the functions of that tribunal the Southerners compromised the doctrine of state rights. Members of the Democratic party, Southern-rights men and popular-sovereignty men alike, were few indeed who would have acknowledged the power of the Supreme Court to control the destiny of any state in the last resort. Neither the advocates of congressional protection nor those who supported popular sovereignty could have agreed to give such power to any branch of the federal government; but both groups could consistently regard, and did regard, Supreme Court decisions as binding upon coördinate departments of the federal government.[27]

The Southern-rights men and the Douglas Democrats agreed that the question of the constitutionality of the Missouri compromise line was before the Supreme Court

[27] Exceptionally clear statements from the leaders of the two wings of the party may be found in *Speech of William L. Yancey of Alabama, delivered in the National Democratic Convention, Charleston, April 28, 1860*, 12, and Pugh's reply to Yancey, in *Proceedings of the Convention at Charleston and Baltimore*, 83-84.

in the Dred Scott case, and that the decision in that respect was final. That part of the decision agreed perfectly with the claim of the slave owner to the right of migration to the common territories with his property. It also supported, in the premises, the doctrine of popular sovereignty. In its denial of the right of Congress to exclude the slave owner and his property, both groups were in perfect accord. They differed, however, on that part of the decision which dealt with the power of the territorial legislature.

This question of the power of the territorial legislature, as related to the decision of the Supreme Court in the Dred Scott case, assumed extraordinary importance in 1860. The leaders of the Democratic party, both North and South, had solemnly agreed over a period of ten years to abide by the decision of the court on that point whenever it should be given. The Douglas Democrats could not acknowledge the decision because it was incompatible with the doctrine of popular sovereignty, which was their political capital. The Southern-rights men, on the other hand, dared not surrender to the leadership of Douglas. Any movement in that direction would have been an acknowledgment, to the North, of a willingness to accept his doctrines as the future guide to governmental action, and popular sovereignty was as deadly to the institution of slavery as congressional prohibition.

The Douglas Democrats, cognizant of the gravity of the crisis, sought to evade the force of the decision by denying that it fulfilled the contract as previously agreed upon. Pugh, the recognized spokesman of the Douglas followers, labored faithfully to establish a working basis for the restoration of party harmony; but the inconsistencies into which his chief had been driven rendered his task almost impossible. He acknowledged the solemn compact of the party to abide by the Supreme Court's decision relative to the power of the territorial legislature; but he insisted that the test case must arise out of an attack by a territorial legislature upon the institution of slavery, and that if no such attack were ever made there would be no occasion for controversy.[28] The Dred Scott case had not arisen in a territory; it was begun before the framing of the Kansas-Nebraska bill; it involved other questions; and the power of the territorial legislature had not been argued by counsel. The question before the party was, according to Douglas, What was the Supreme Court decision in the Dred Scott case? The proper procedure, then, was to cease the quarrel over the true interpretation of that decision, wait for another case to arise, and allow the court itself to state what had been its meaning.[29]

To this argument of the Douglas Democrats the Southerners replied that the Supreme Court, with but two judges dissenting, had agreed that the question of the power of the territorial legislature was within the jurisdiction of the court in the Dred Scott case; and that, as the court was then constituted, the decision in any case which might arise in the manner prescribed by the Douglas men was predetermined. In the excitement of the moment, they made no distinction between the announced intention of the Republicans to reorganize the Supreme Court and the assurance of the Douglas Democrats that they would abide by the Dred Scott decision if and when that decision should be affirmed in some future case arising in a different manner. The Republicans were contending that Congress must exclude slavery, and the Douglas

---

[28] *Cong. Globe*, 36 Cong., 1 Sess., III, 2241.
[29] *Ibid.*, 2241-2242.

Democrats were contending that the territorial legislature might do so lawfully, irrespective of the Supreme Court decision in the Dred Scott case. The position of the Douglas Democrats was the more hostile to the slavery interests. The Democracy was about to split into two hostile sections over the issue.

# CHAPTER II

## A PROJECT OF COÖPERATION

SOUTHERN-RIGHTS men had not kept pace with their Northern adversaries in respect to the organization of a sectional political party. Their forces had been divided from the first in an effort to gain control of the Whig and Democratic parties. The Whig party had crumbled in the process, and its successor, the American party, had proved to be an abortive and short-lived organization. The result was that by 1860 there were many Southern-rights men without party affiliations. Some were ready to support the nominees of a united Democracy against the rising tide of Northern sectionalism [1]; others, retaining their ancient prejudices against the Democracy, inclined to a new separate organization. Their ultimate action was profoundly influenced by events of the winter, 1859-1860.

Within the ranks of the Democratic party, Southern-rights men were in control throughout the entire lower South by 1860. The Southern-rights associations in Ala-

---

[1] The following statements from two powerful New Orleans papers are typical of a widely expressed sentiment: "At the time of the meeting of the Charleston Convention, it was regarded as holding the destiny of the nation in its hands. To its nomination every citizen expected to give in his adhesion." *The Daily Picayune,* May 15, 1860. "Up to the time of the meeting of that body [Charleston convention], there was a general disposition on the part of Southern men of all parties to sustain its nominees, if they had given us national, conservative men." *New Orleans Daily Crescent,* May 12, 1860.

bama had assumed the leadership in the movement to purge that party after 1847. Every convention which met in the state during the ensuing thirteen years repudiated the doctrine of territorial sovereignty and demanded protection for slavery in the territories by congressional action. Webster declared, on the eve of the ratification of the treaty of Guadalupe Hidalgo, that the Mexican municipal laws against slavery would prevail in any territory we might acquire. Cass asserted the right of the people in acquired lands to legislate against slavery; and the abolitionists urged antagonistic legislation by Congress. The Democratic convention, which met at Montgomery in February, 1848, demanded that Congress should at once repeal the laws against slavery, either by the treaty provisions or by legislative enactment. They further declared that any one opposing this demand was a traitor to the party and to the "perpetuity of the Union." [2]

In 1856 the state convention passed resolutions consistent with the party's previous position. The platform of that year asserted, as one of the basic principles of the Democratic party, the "unqualified right of the people of the slaveholding states to protection of their property in the States, in the Territories and in the wilderness in which territorial governments are as yet unorganized." That resolution clearly implied the necessity of congressional action for protection since the power of the judiciary did not extend to the territories where governments were not yet organized. The resolutions of that year went further, and denied the right of Congress to interfere for the prohibition of slavery in the territories. Having stated this definition of non-interference, the resolutions endorsed

[2] *Journal of the Democratic State Convention held at Montgomery, Alabama, February 14, 1848*, 10-14.

the principle as incorporated in the Kansas-Nebraska Act.[3]

The leader of the Democratic party in Alabama was William L. Yancey. He was a brilliant orator, prominent in state-rights conventions, and indefatigable in promoting the Southern cause. He had been trying for years to arouse the South to the need of coöperative action in defense of her institutions; but he looked beyond the regularly organized political machinery for an ultimate means to safety. On May 10, 1858, he welcomed the Southern commercial convention to Montgomery as the forerunner of a far more important body which should devise an independent sovereignty for the South in case of further aggression from the North. On June 15 he wrote his famous letter to Joseph S. Slaughter of Atlanta, in which he deprecated further attempts to preserve the rights of the South in the Union, and proposed an organization of Southern men as the nucleus of a later secession movement. One month later at Bethel Church, Montgomery County, Alabama, he organized the "League of United Southerners." The members of this organization were never to become a political party, were never to put candidates into the field. They were to retain their old party affiliations, consult within the organization as to the best

[3] *Official Proceedings of the Democratic and Anti-Know-Nothing State Convention of Alabama, held in the City of Montgomery, January 8th and 9th, 1856*, 9. The American or opposition party of Alabama asserted the Southern-rights platform in even stronger terms. It declared that neither Congress nor a territorial legislature had any power to legislate upon the question of slavery except for its protection; that the power to exclude slavery from a territory could be exercised for the first time at the formation of a constitution; and that squatter sovereigny was "violative of the spirit of the Constitution, and an insidious and dangerous infringement upon the rights of the slave-holding States." "Platform of the Alabama American Party, adopted in February, 1856," in *Important Political Pamphlet for the Campaign of 1860*, 14-15.

means of advancing the interests of the South, and then, in their respective parties, secure the nomination of the purest and best Southern-rights men. It was an attempt to purge the old national parties. More than that, it was an organization of missionaries in every community of the South and West to prepare the groundwork for secession when the moment for it should come. But the organization did not prosper. Not more than six chapters were ever organized, none outside the state of Alabama. Yancey, like Rhett of South Carolina, was regarded as a secessionist *per se;* and his plea for coöperative action produced no tangible results, because conservative men feared that any movement directed by him would lead to disunion. That same fear defeated the only effort ever made by Southern-rights men to effect coöperative state action for the preservation of Southern institutions within the Union and, curiously enough, made possible the organization of a Southern sectional party.

The failure of John Brown's raid into Virginia was ample evidence that the danger from such forays, so far as the slaves were concerned, was slight; but the reaction at the North to the arrest and execution of Brown was regarded by most Southerners as proof of an abiding hatred for the institution of slavery.[4] There was an immediate revival of the agitation for commercial non-intercourse,[5] and a noticeable crystallization of secession sentiment. Positive action for the formulation of a definite

[4] Villard, *John Brown, 1800-1859, A Biography Fifty Years After,* 558-559, is an excellent account of the sentiment at the North. A notable exception to the general Southern attitude was the *Vicksburg Daily Whig,* January 28, 1860, which declared: "The attempt to make the whole North responsible for the acts of a few madmen is so manifestly unjust, as to only render contemptible those who so act."
[5] See *The Daily South Carolinian,* Columbia, January 29, 1860; the *Vicksburg Daily Whig,* January 18, 1860; and the *Daily Chronicle and Sentinel,* Augusta, March 6, 1860.

program, however, centered in the activities of the legislatures of Alabama, Mississippi, South Carolina, and Virginia.

The legislature of South Carolina proposed a convention of delegates from the slaves states, to devise some policy for concurrent action in defense of their interests. The resolutions of December 22, 1859, were written by C. G. Memminger, later Secretary of the Treasury in the Cabinet of Davis. Memminger had been the leader of the conservative South Carolinians since the days of nullification, and had been a consistent opponent of secession as a relief from Northern aggression. The resolutions and the message of Governor Gist recommending them asserted the right of secession and urged immediate coöperative action by all of the slave states as the single alternative for separate state action in defense of Southern institutions. The resolutions provided for a special commissioner to urge the coöperation of Virginia, and Governor Gist assigned the commission to Memminger.

Memminger proceeded at once to Richmond and, by invitation, addressed the general assembly on the nineteenth of January. He described in detail the growth of antagonism between the North and the South over the questions of slavery and the admission of new states into the Union, the struggle over petitions, the circulation of incendiary publications, the separation of the churches, the admission of Texas, the Wilmot Proviso, and the Compromise of 1850. He alluded to the resolutions sent by Virginia to South Carolina in 1851, urging her to refrain from the folly of secession over the compromise measures, and cited the acts of injustice on the part of the North since that time, as evidence of the failure of the policy of submission. The United States, said he, had ceased to be a "more perfect Union"; the Union had failed to "establish justice," had failed to protect the most valuable property of the South, and had failed to "insure the domestic tranquillity." [6]

Still more important is that part of his address which dealt with the purpose of the proposed convention. The Northern press and the opposition press of the South had vigorously denounced the proposed conference as another attempt on the part of South Carolina to precipitate secession.[7] Memminger urged the conference as "the proper step in any contingency." The Union could not go on as it was. Either the South must have constitutional relief or the Union would be dissolved. Various projects had been proposed to relieve the crisis, among which were a dual presidency, a division of the Senate into two classes, equal division of the territories, and commercial independence. A conference would bring together the best minds of the South to discuss and propose measures which the Southern states could demand as the price of continuance in the Union. Only by uniting upon some plan of action, by adopting proposals acceptable to all, and then standing solidly behind them was there hope of getting the North to respond. "South Carolinians," said Memminger, "have no confidence in any paper guarantees, neither do we believe that any measures of restriction or retaliation within the present Union will avail. But with equal frankness we declare that when we propose a conference, we do so with the full understanding that we are but one of the States in that conference, entitled like all others to express our opinions, but willing to respect and abide by

[6] Memminger, "Address to the General Assembly of Virginia, January 19, 1860," in *De Bow's Review*, XXIX, 751-771.
[7] *Richmond Whig and Public Advertiser*, February 2, 1860.

the united judgment of the whole. If our pace be too fast for some, we are content to walk slower; our earnest wish is that all may keep together. We cannot consent to stand still, but would gladly make common cause with all. We are far from expecting or desiring to dictate or lead." [8]

The Virginia legislature took no action relative to the invitation of South Carolina, and after Memminger returned to Charleston he reported by letter to Governor Gist. He ascribed the hesitancy of Virginia to the feeling that Southern rights could be preserved within the Union and the fear that the proposed conference would lead to disunion. He took occasion to say again what he had expressed at Richmond, that if there were still "fraternal feeling enough existing at the North to stay the tide of fanaticism and to do justice to the South, then the apprehension of disunion from a conference becomes, in fact, the very best instrument to assist the supposed fraternal feeling of the North." [9] Meanwhile, the Mississippi legislature adopted a series of resolutions which declared that the prospect of the election of a Republican President by a sectional vote was sufficient justification for a council of the Southern states, with their protection and safety by separation in view; accepted the invitation of South Carolina to such a council and suggested the first Monday in June, at Atlanta, as a desirable time and place; directed the governor to appoint delegates, not to exceed ten in number, to the convention; and provided for a commissioner to Virginia, who should urge her to join in the Atlanta conference. [10]

[8] Memminger, "Address to the General Assembly of Virginia, January 19, 1860," in Capers, *op. cit.*, 276.
[9] Memminger to Gist, February 13, 1860, in *ibid.*, 280-281.
[10] Proclamation of Pettus, February 15, 1860, in Official Correspondence of Governor John J. Pettus, 1859-1860.

Governor Pettus, in compliance with the resolutions, appointed Peter B. Starke, formerly a Whig and afterward a supporter of Bell and Everett, as a commissioner to Virginia. Starke proceeded at once to Richmond and addressed a communication to Governor Letcher. It set forth the view of the Southern-rights school that slavery was a domestic problem in which neither the free states nor the federal government had any concern, except for the protection of the institution by the federal government within the limits of its jurisdiction. It denounced the attitude of the North as having been provocative of the invasion of slave territory for the purpose of "destroying, without their consent, the relation of master and slave." It urged Virginia to send delegates to Atlanta, and declared in plain terms the purpose of that council to be, not the promotion of secession sentiment, but rather to "devise some remedy consistent with their interest and honor in the Union." It just as definitely said, however, that "if, in her sincere desire to be enabled to enjoy all the rights of perfect equality in the Union (as she hopes to do by means of this proposed conference), she shall be disappppointed, then I have no hesitation in saying that she will prefer, and will resort to, independence out of it." [11]

Shortly after his arrival, a joint committee of the two houses of the legislature published a majority report drawn up by A. H. H. Stuart, state senator from Augusta County and former Secretary of the Interior in Fillmore's administration.[12] The report implied the existence of a wholesale conspiracy in sixteen Northern states against the institutions and lives of the Southern people; a situation

[11] Starke to Letcher, February 20, 1860, *Communication from the Hon. Peter B. Starke, as Commissioner to Virginia, to his Excellency, J. J. Pettus, with accompanying Documents,* 8.
[12] Starke to Pettus, July —, 1860, Official Correspondence of Governor John J. Pettus, 1859-1860.

which was doubly dangerous because the conservative people at the North had relapsed into a state of indifference. It recommended that the militia of the state be placed in readiness for service, proposed commercial independence, and recommended coöperative action by the Southern states in the general program.[13] The legislature passed resolutions endorsing the three propositions, but delayed giving definite answer to the waiting commissioner from Mississippi. When it became evident that they were likely to adjourn without taking action, Starke addressed a sharp note to Governor Letcher concerning the delay, and urged that some action be taken by the legislature before adjournment. Citing the report of the joint committee, he said: "Can all these things be true, and yet the time be not actually, now, arrived when we are called upon imperatively, without delay, to confer together and to consult upon the highest duty, What shall we do to be saved?" [14]

In his letter to Governor Letcher, Starke reminded the legislature that the South would never be stronger, relative to the North, than at that time. Already in the minority, they held one of their grievances to be the declaration of the Republican party that there should be no further increase in slave power. "To submit now will be evidence to those who already contemn us that we will never resent or resist. This they will find indeed to be untrue; but tempted by this to increase and aggravate aggression, they will force us to resistance by a bloody civil war, which will be irrepressible and implacable, and in which nothing can or will be saved but by fire and blood."

Starke labored faithfully to convince the legislature that the proposed convention was not a step toward seces-

[13] Starke to Letcher, February 20, 1860, *Communication from the Hon. Peter B. Starke . . . with accompanying Documents*, 10.
[14] Starke to Letcher, March 1, 1860, *ibid.*, 16.

sion, but the only possible way by which dissolution and civil war could be averted. The legislature, however, refused to sanction that program, and resolved that direct legislation by the several states would be more effective than any action by a convention sitting in an advisory capacity.[15] The other states having refused to participate in the conference, the Mississippi delegates wrote to Governor Pettus saying it would be fruitless for them to attend.[16] The conference did not meet and the last hope of coöperative action by the Southern states was gone.

Fear that a conference of Southern states would lead to disunion was responsible in part only for its failure, and can not be construed as a denial of the right of secession. The Richmond *Whig* opposed it on the ground that it would lead to nothing but "increased excitement and a wider national breach." It added, however, that it would support a convention when necessity arose "not for the purpose of patching up a faulty constitution and propping a falling government, but for the purpose of annulling the one and destroying the other." [17]

Those who advocated the convention insisted that it was for the purpose of effecting Southern unity as a means to preserve Southern rights within the Union; and they supported their professions of faith with unanswerable logic. "The folly of rejecting a convention confines the question of disunion to the States, and there some act may, and in our candid opinion will, bring about that result," said the Richmond *Examiner*.[18] Governor Gist of South

---

[15] Virginia Resolutions, March 8, 1860, in *ibid.,* 20-21.
[16] Cassidy to Pettus, May 24, 1860; Harris, Gholson, Hill, and Clayton to Pettus, May 30, 1860, in Official Correspondence of Governor John J. Pettus, 1859-1860.
[17] *Richmond Whig and Public Advertiser,* January 31, 1860.
[18] *Richmond Semi-Weekly Examiner,* February 3, 1860.

Carolina expressed the same opinion, saying that if he desired a dissolution of the Union and wished to effect it, nothing would please him more than the refusal of the Southern states to meet in conference.[19] The very fact that the Democratic legislature of Mississippi, which six months later was unanimous in its call for a secession convention, sent a man of opposite political faith and a devoted Unionist to Virginia, was evidence that it wished to preserve the Union, if possible. The same may be said with respect to South Carolina. Starke and Memminger received their appointments at the hands of Governors Pettus and Gist, respectively, and, as we shall see later, these two officials did more than any others to direct the secession movement at the end of the year. When the attempt at coöperation within the Union failed, they adopted the policy of Alabama, and turned to separate state action; and when, in their judgment, secession became imperative, they adopted separate state secession as the best possible means for success. They then did everything possible to avoid what the more conservative states wanted and had refused, what they had offered and now wanted to avoid, a conference of states for coöperative action.

The failure of the conference proposal was significant in another respect. Its disappointed advocates pointed out that its rejection would serve to paralyze the conservative element at the North, convey a false impression of Southern dissension, inspire anti-slavery men to further aggression, and insure a Republican victory in the presidential election, which Alabama was already pledged to resist by secession.[20]

[19] *Gist to Hicks*, February 3, 1860, in [McCabe], *Facts versus Fancies*, 30.
[20] The *Richmond Enquirer*, January 31, 1860; *The Charleston Mercury*, March 10, 1860.

Alabama had assumed an advanced position in rejecting the South Carolina program. The legislature, February 24, 1860, had passed resolutions directing Governor Moore, in the event of a Republican victory in November, to issue immediately a proclamation for an election of delegates to a state convention. That convention was to have wide discretionary power to do whatever the exigencies of the time demanded for the best interests of the state. The legislature also endorsed the right of secession, refused to participate in a conference, and appropriated two hundred thousand dollars for military purposes.[11]

Meanwhile, Yancey had succeeded in carrying through the state convention a set of resolutions thereafter known as the *Alabama platform*. This platform (1) endorsed those parts of the Cincinnati platform relating to slavery; (2) reëndorsed the resolutions of 1856 demanding protection for slave property in the territories and in unorganized territory; (3) reaffirmed the ninth resolution of the state platform in 1848, which declared it to be the duty of Congress to open all territories to slave owners and to protect them thereafter in their property rights; (4) asserted the principle that the Constitution is a compact among the states; (5) declared the territories to be common property and as such open for immigration by the citizens of every state with all property recognized as such by the Constitution; (6) denied the right of the territorial legislature to prohibit the introduction of slavery; (7) denied the right of Congress to prohibit slavery in the territories; (8) supported the principles enunciated by Chief Justice Taney in his decision in the Dred Scott case; and (9) instructed its delegates to the Charleston convention to vote as a unit, to present the above prin-

[11] Shorter to Brown, January 3, 1861, *Official Records . . . Armies*, Series IV, Vol. I, 16-17.

ciples for the consideration of the convention, and to withdraw unless they were adopted prior to the selection of
candidates.[22]

Nine months before the presidential election, therefore,
South Carolina and Mississippi offered a program of co-
operative action to the other Southern states. The offer
was rejected by all but Alabama as a step toward dissolution of the Union. Alabama rejected it because she chose
to rely upon separate state action in any emergency which
might thereafter arise, and designated the election of a
Republican President as such an emergency. The Democratic party in Alabama outlined a program which was
likely to effect precisely what Yancey and Rhett had long
counseled: a Southern sectional party. That situation in-
sured that the test would be made as to whether the
Union could survive "sectionalism in all parts of the
Republic."

Not slavery alone nor the question of what party was to
administer the government for the conservation of existing
institutions were to constitute the nature of the test. A
Southern political organization was in the making for a
contest before the country against an existing Northern
party organization. In a broad sense each was a revolutionary agent; each regarded the existing government as
having failed to perform its functions. A victory for the
one would be regarded by the successful contestant as a
mandate from the people to institute far-reaching social
reforms, by the other as an exigency requiring sweeping
political reforms or a dissolution of the Union.

[22] *Proceedings of the Democratic State Convention held in the
City of Montgomery, commencing Wednesday, January 11, 1860,*
27-34.

# CHAPTER III

## THE CRISIS IN THE CHARLESTON CONVENTION

SOUTH CAROLINA, Florida, Mississippi, Louisiana, Texas, and Arkansas endorsed the Alabama platform and, rallying behind Yancey, went into the Charleston convention determined to force the issue to a conclusion. They were convinced that the principles for which they were contending constituted the correct interpretation of the Constitution. They were not willing that the Democracy of the North, claiming the right of exclusion for territorial legislatures and not certain to cast an electoral vote for the nominee, should dictate the party platform.[1] They knew

[1] Davis of Mississippi, Remarks in the Senate, May 24, 1860, *Cong. Globe*, 36 Cong., 1 Sess., III, 2341; Curry of Alabama, Remarks in the House of Representatives, March 14, 1860, *ibid.*, II, 1155-1159; *Speech of William L. Yancey of Alabama, delivered in the National Democratic Convention, Charleston, April 28, 1860*, 3. Yancey said in part: "We have come here, then, with the twofold purpose of saving the country and saving the Democracy; and if the Democracy will not lend itself to that high, holy and elevated purpose; if it cannot elevate itself above the mere question of how perfect shall be its personal organization and how widespread shall be its mere voting success, then we say to you, gentlemen, mournfully and regretfully, that in the opinion of the State of Alabama and, I believe, of the whole South, you have failed in your mission, and it will be our duty to go forth and make an appeal to the loyalty of the country to stand by that Constitution which party organizations have deliberately rejected." The *Richmond Semi-Weekly Examiner*, March 6, 1860, stated the issue concisely when it asked: "Shall Democratic minorities in Republican States be allowed to shape the policy of the Democratic party with regard to the institutions of slavery, which exist only in Democratic States? Will the platform, so adopted, be likely to enlist the vote of the Southern States *absolutely necessary* to success?"

that their endorsement of Douglas as the party candidate would be regarded as an irrevocable acceptance of his doctrines, and that the North certainly would unite in acting upon that policy.

The contest between the two sections of the party to secure endorsement of opposing principles was intensified by a feeling of bitter personal animosity between Douglas and the Southern-rights men. The position assumed by Douglas in the senatorial struggle over the admission of Kansas under the Lecompton Constitution had left a bitterness which nothing could efface. It had assumed such proportions by 1860 that Douglas' usual political sagacity failed him, and he refused to accept the nomination if tendered him at Charleston unless the party adopted a platform endorsing popular sovereignty. His *Harper's* article, in which he virtually endorsed the sweeping consolidation theories of Republicanism, was equally fatal.[2]

---

[2] Douglas endorsed Republican doctrine in this article by saying that "if it be the imperative duty of Congress to provide by law for the protection of slave property in the Territories upon the ground that 'slavery exists in Kansas' (and consequently in every other Territory), 'by virtue of the Constitution of the United States,' why is it not also the duty of Congress, for the same reason, to provide similar protection to slave property in all the States of the Union when Legislatures fail to furnish such protection?" Douglas, "The Dividing Line Between Federal and Local Authority," in *Harper's Monthly Magazine,* XIX, 531. In an editorial with the caption "Senator Douglas' Short Cut to Black Republicanism," *The Southern Argus,* Norfolk, August 28, 1860, said: "His dividing line between Federal and Local authority separates Federal power, not from Territorial power, not from State rights, or State authority, but from all authority that is not Federal in its nature. Thus the States and the Territories are placed upon a common level as to their original powers; the difference, if any exists, being in favor of the Territory, since the States, by entering the Union, have renounced the exercise of a portion of their sovereign rights, and delegated others to the General Government, while the Territories remain in full possession of sovereign attributes."

The Southerners seized upon both as further proof that he had broken faith with the party.[3] Benjamin analyzed the opposition to Douglas correctly when he said: "We separated from him because he had denied the bargain that he made when he went home; because after telling us here in the Senate that he was willing that this whole matter should be decided by the Supreme Court, in the face of his people he told them that he had got us by the bill; and that, whether the decision was for us or against us, the practical effect was to be against us; and because he tells us now again that he is ready to make use of Black Republican arguments, which he answers at home, and to put them forth against the Democratic party in the speeches that he uses here in the Senate." [4]

On the other hand, Douglas also denounced all who differed from him as traitors to party principles previously enunciated in the Compromise of 1850, the Kansas-Nebraska Act, and the Cincinnati platform. He was reading into those documents the doctrine of popular sovereignty, claiming for himself alone the virtue of consistency, and defining opposition to his principles and political ambitions as party heresy and disunion sentiment. Moreover, he went into the Charleston convention with sufficient strength to prevent any other candidate from receiving the nomination. His strength was in the Republican states from which few Democratic electoral votes were expected. It is a significant fact that of the fifteen states in which the popular votes for Lincoln exceeded those for Douglas, Breckinridge, and Bell combined,

[3] See Curry, Remarks in the House of Representatives, *Cong. Globe*, 36 Cong., 1 Sess., II, 1159.
[4] *Ibid.*, III, 2241.

twelve sent their delegations to the Democratic national convention instructed for Douglas. They represented one hundred twenty votes on the floor, nineteen more than one third.[5]

The convention assembled at Charleston, South Carolina, April 23, 1860, with full delegations present from every state. From the moment of its temporary organization, disruption impended. No one denied it; none minimized the gravity of the situation. The ablest men of the party, with a seriousness rarely seen in party conventions, sought to avoid a rupture. Day after day the representatives of the Democratic states sought to break through the ranks of the Douglas faction in an effort at compromise. But that section of the party, with the solid delegations of twelve Republican states as a nucleus, would neither recede nor compromise.

The first clash of rival interests emerged in the course of organization. Two full delegations from New York were present in Charleston, each claiming to have been regularly elected and demanding the right to cast the thirty-five votes of that state in the convention. The Douglas faction had secured tickets of admission from the chairman of the national executive committee and was present at the time of temporary organization. The opposing delegation, headed by Mayor Wood, had been less fortunate and was outside demanding admission. After prolonged and bitter debate the New York delegation was allowed to place representatives on the two important committees on credentials and organization, and to par-

[5] Maine, New Hampshire, Vermont, Rhode Island, New York, Ohio, Indiana, Illinois, Michigan, Wisconsin, Minnesota, and Iowa. The remaining three were Pennsylvania, Massachusetts, and Connecticut.

ticipate in the proceedings of the convention until the committee should make its report.[6]

With this disturbing question pending, dissension flared up again on the morning of the second day when the committee on organization presented the following resolution:

> *Resolved,* That the rules and regulations adopted by the National Democratic Conventions of 1852 and 1856 be adopted by this Convention for its government, with this additional rule:
>
> That in any State which had not provided or directed by its State Convention how its vote may be given, the convention will recognize the right of each delegate to cast his individual vote.[7]

Charles Clark, representing the Mississippi delegation, claimed that the resolution had been submitted in committee the previous evening and had been voted down by a majority of the states, the committee having adopted the former rules without change. The proposed rule, he declared, had been adopted since the final adjournment of the committee on Monday evening, and although the chairman was said to have had a majority of the committee together, neither himself, Lubbock of Texas, nor La Seré of Louisiana had been given notice of the meeting nor any previous intimation that the committee would be reassembled.[8]

The Southerners not only charged irregularity in committee procedure, but opposed the proposed rule as contrary to precedent. They claimed that three definite rules

[6] *Proceedings of the Conventions at Charleston and Baltimore,* 3-9. The seats of the Illinois delegation were also contested, but the case of the contestants was a weak one; and although that contest was linked with New York in the debate it was not in fact the question at issue.

[7] *Ibid.,* 11.                    [8] *Ibid.,* 12.

had been followed since the party's first organization, to insure internal harmony and prevent it from degenerating into a mere sectional organization: first, every state was given a representation in the national conventions equal to its electoral vote, regardless of how strong the party might be within the state; second, a two thirds vote was required for nomination in order that a nominee particularly objectionable to any large section might not be presented to the country as the choice of the party; and third, the right of each state delegation to cast its vote as it might choose had been recognized. The practical effect of the last rule was that the majority in each delegation determined the entire vote of the delegation whenever it chose to do so. The proposed rule would prevent the majority in a delegation from controlling its entire vote unless previously instructed to vote as a unit. It was intended, furthermore, to apply to delegations appointed by state conventions which the Southerners claimed would have so instructed their delegations had they realized that such a change was imminent.

The Douglas leaders maintained that in 1852 at Baltimore, and in 1856 at Cincinnati, the right of every delegation to divide its vote was recognized unless the state convention which made the appointment had ordered otherwise. The Southerners admitted this, but denied that the party ever had operated under a rule which prevented the majority of a state delegation from controlling its vote if it wished to do so. The rule was adopted by a vote of 198 to 101.[9] At best it is only possible to obtain an approximate estimate of its effect. It is certain that the Southern-rights men believed it was a cunningly devised trick to circumvent the will of a majority.[10] Davis de-

[9] *Ibid.*, 20.
[10] "Speech of Hon. William L. Yancey of Alabama, at Memphis, Tennessee, August 14, 1860," in *Nashville Union and American, Sup-*

clared in the Senate, May 17, that from "a comparison made by those who had an opportunity to know, it appears that the minority report could not have got a majority of the delegates if each delegate had been permitted to cast his own vote." [11] Butler of Massachusetts said that the rule secured for Douglas fifteen votes from New York, six from Ohio, five from Indiana, and two from Minnesota which were actually opposed to him. Pugh denied in the Senate that a single man in the Ohio delegation would have voted for the Southern platform even if there had been no unit rule. [12] Numerous charges and denials were made, but the essence of the matter seems to be that the scheme was devised to secure the acceptance of Douglas as the nominee upon his own platform, and that, in part at least, it was responsible for the disruption of the party.

The third day of the convention brought no abatement of ill-feeling, for with the morning came the report of the committee on credentials. The majority of the committee reported in favor of the sitting delegation from New York, headed by Dean Richmond. The minority report was signed by the committeemen from Alabama, Mississippi, Georgia, Texas, Arkansas, and California. It recommended that the two delegations each select thirty-five delegates to cast seventeen votes, the odd vote to be cast alternately, the sitting delegates to cast it first. [13] This was the solution of a similar question in the case of New

---

plement, August, 1860; Andrew Ewing, Sam Milligan, and Alfred Robb, "Address to the Democracy of Tennessee," in *Nashville Union and American*, July 1, 1860; Buchanan, "Mr. Buchanan's Administration on the Eve of the Rebellion," in *The Works of James Buchanan, comprising his Speeches, State Papers, and Private Correspondence* (John Bassett Moore, ed.), XII, 56.

[11] *Cong. Globe*, 36 Cong., 1 Sess., III, 2144.
[12] *Ibid.*, 1968.
[13] *Proceedings of the Conventions at Charleston and Baltimore*, 30.

York by the Cincinnati convention four years before. The case was exigent because of the greatness of New York's block of votes; and animosities were intensified by the fact that the sitting delegation consisted of thirty anti-Douglas and forty Douglas delegates, under the unit rule casting the entire vote of the state with Douglas as against the South. The contesting or Wood delegation was solidly against Douglas.

In presenting the minority report, Brooks of Alabama said: "It presents one of the most humiliating aspects it has ever been my misfortune to discover; for in the mass of evidence before the committee I regret to say every fact alleged in the case was susceptible of the clearest proof, and also of the clearest refutation. I wish you to observe that, while I shall endeavor to state to you what the testimony on one side proves, or conduces to prove, the testimony on the other pretty clearly disproves." [14]

Barry, committeeman from Mississippi, reported that "the gentleman from New York [Cochrane] said that he could prove anything by the affidavits of respectable men in the State of New York. I confess, sir, my hair stood on end at that assertion." [15] "You cannot rely upon the testimony," said Brooks, "because, as a gentleman remarked to the committee, in New York they can prove anything; and I tell you they have done it in this case."

From the testimony presented to the committee there appeared to have been no division in the state, except in New York City, until the assembling of the state convention at Syracuse, September 14, 1859. That convention virtually broke up in a riot during the process of organization, Wood testifying that if a thirty-two pounder had

[14] *Ibid.*                    [15] *Ibid.*, 35.

been fired in the convention hall it could not have been heard. "Then the gentlemen whom the sitting members here represent," said Whitely of Delaware, "retired to the back part of the hall, and as I say retired properly; because, however much we are bound to fight for our country, we are not bound enough to be mutilated by a party of shoulder-hitters, in order to show our Democracy." [18] As to what happened thereafter there was disputed testimony. Two conventions were held, each claiming a majority of the regularly elected delegates. That also seems to have been true, because after participating in the Wood convention a large number of the regular delegates went over to the Richmond convention "and participated in its deliberations, undertaking to give themselves two chances; as one of the contestants remarked, they undertook to avail themselves of the benefits, no matter which side 'turned up Jack.' "

The point raised by the minority of the committee was that the Wood faction represented the regular Democracy even though they did sit in two conventions, and that both factions ought to be excluded or else both ought to be admitted as was done at Cincinnati. Any other course would alienate the Wood faction, representing the Democratic city of New York, without which the party could not hope to carry the state. The convention, however, rejected the minority report and allowed the delegation headed by Dean Richmond to retain its seats. The importance of the contest subsequently became apparent when the minority (Douglas) platform was substituted for the majority (Southern rights) platform by a vote of 165 to 138. Had the New York delegation been uninstructed or the Wood delegation seated, the Southern-

[18] *Ibid.*, 33.

rights platform would have been adopted by the convention.

The committee on resolutions reported during the morning of the fifth day, Friday, April 27. A majority report was presented by Avery of North Carolina, a principal minority report by Payne of Ohio, and a second minority report by Butler of Massachusetts. The substantial differences between the two major reports were to be found in the first and third resolutions of the majority report and the first and second resolutions of the minority report. In the majority platform, they were as follows:

1. *Resolved,* That the Democracy of the United States hold these cardinal principles on the subject of slavery in the Territories; first, that Congress has no power to abolish slavery in the Territories; second, that the Territorial Legislature has no power to abolish slavery in any Territory, nor to prohibit the introduction of slaves therein, nor any power to exclude slavery therefrom, nor any power to destroy or impair the right of property in slaves by any legislation whatever.

3. *Resolved,* That it is the duty of the Federal Government to protect, when necessary, the rights of persons and property on the high seas, in the Territories, or wherever else its constitutional authority extends.

The first two resolutions of the minority platform as reported by Payne were:

1. *Resolved,* That we, the Democracy of the Union, in Convention assembled, hereby declare our affirmance of the resolutions unanimously adopted and declared as a platform of principles by the Democratic Convention at Cincinnati, in the year 1856, believing that Democratic principles are unchangeable in their nature, when applied to the same subject-matter; and we recommend as the only further resolutions the following:

2. *Resolved,* That all questions in regard to the rights of property in States or Territories, arising under the Constitution of the United States, are judicial in their character; and

the Democratic party is pledged to abide by and faithfully carry out such determination of these questions as has been or may be made by the Supreme Court of the United States.

Butler presented as a second minority report, signed by himself alone, a resolution merely endorsing the Cincinnati platform of 1856.

Payne, in presenting the minority report, exhibited the sectional alignment by stating that the majority report had been supported in committee by the members from the fifteen slaveholding states, California, and Oregon, representing one hundred sixty-seven electoral votes.

The majority report, said Avery, represented a principle so vital to a great, solidly Democratic section of the nation that it should be given respectful consideration by those delegates from states which would probably not return a Democratic electoral vote, and whose material interests would not be affected by its adoption. It contained "no proposed invasion of the constitutional rights of the North . . . no proposition that you and your property shall be excluded from the Common Territories of the United States." On the other hand "we regard this principle as more important in its ultimate effects than any principle ever discussed before in America, so far as affects the future fate and destiny of the people of the South." [17]

The wrangle in the committee was transferred to the floor of the convention when the principal minority platform was moved as a substitute for the report of the majority. Stripped of its verbiage, this minority report was a simple endorsement of the Cincinnati platform, which in turn, like the Kansas-Nebraska Act, had been an evasion, an attempt to shift to the courts the responsi-

[17] *Proceedings of the Conventions at Charleston and Baltimore,* 50.

bility of deciding a constitutional question upon which the
two sections of the party could not reach an agreement.
The Douglas adherents had emphasized non-intervention
by Congress before their constituents as the cardinal principle of the Cincinnati platform, and had built their doctrine of popular sovereignty upon it. They had won and
held the hearts of the Northern Democracy by eulogies of
the inherent right of self-government. If the territorial
legislature did not possess absolute power to legislate with
regard to slavery, the doctrines of popular sovereignty
and congressional non-intervention became absurdities.
Whether or not the Supreme Court had decided the question, as the South claimed, it had indicated explicitly what
its position would be on any case which might arise. The
only hope for the Northern Democratic leaders was to
cling to the doctrine of non-intervention, secure its endorsement, if possible, and failing in that, to place upon
the Southern-rights men the odium of deserting party
principles. Any other course was political suicide.

"This question of intervention in the Territories," said
Payne, "has been the subject of more misfortune, of more
altercation, of more estrangement, of more heartburnings,
than all other evils combined since the Government commenced. I repeat that, upon this question of congressional non-intervention, we are committed by the acts of
Congress; we are committed by the acts of the National
Democratic Conventions; we cannot recede without personal dishonor; and, so help us God, we never will recede.
. . . The abandonment of that position, the surrender of
that ground, would be attended with the immediate and
inevitable disaster and overthrow of the Democratic party
of the free States." [18]

[18] *Ibid.*, 55.

If the doctrine of non-intervention had any merit, it was that most often advanced by its exponents of eliminating the slavery question from national politics in the hope that public agitation might cease. Non-intervention by Congress as a party platform might win the presidential election and it was certainly the most favorable for party success in the Northwest, but it would never silence agitation in Congress so long as the Republican party existed. The Douglas men were thinking in terms of party necessity, and asking the South to yield to that necessity principles which were their sole defense in the great public arena from which the Republicans refused to let slavery agitation recede. The Southerners were asking the Northern Democrats to yield the possibility of party success in the defense of what they believed to be the constitutional rights of the South. Yancey stated the case clearly when he said:

Ours is the property invaded; ours are the institutions which are at stake; ours is the peace that is to be destroyed; ours is the property that is to be destroyed; ours is the honor at stake—the honor of children, the honor of families, the lives, perhaps, of all—all of which rests upon what your course may ultimately make a great heaving volcano of passion and crime, if you are enabled to consummate your designs. Bear with us, then, if we stand sternly upon what is yet that dormant volcano, and say we yield no position here until we are convinced we are wrong. We are in a position to ask you to yield. What right of yours, gentlemen of the North, have we of the South ever invaded? What institution of yours have we ever assailed, directly or indirectly? What laws have we ever passed that have invaded, or induced others to invade, the sanctity of your homes or to put your lives in jeopardy, or were likely to destroy the fundamental institutions of your States? The wisest, the most learned, and the best amongst you will remain silent, because you cannot say that we have done this thing. If your view is right and ours is not strictly demanded by the compact, still the consequence, in a remote degree, of your proposition may bring this result upon us; and if you have no domestic nor municipal peace at stake, and no property at stake, and no fundamental institutions of your liberties at stake, are we asking any too much of you today when we ask you to yield to us in this manner as brothers, in order to quiet our doubts—for in yielding you lose nothing that is essentially right? [19]

Neither side would yield. On the sixth day of the convention, the Southern-rights men, still hopeful of compromise and reluctant to leave the convention—a step which their constituents had instructed them to take in case of failure to secure an endorsement of their platform, and a step which the Northern delegates had repeatedly defied them to take—managed after the most bitter debate to force a recommitment of the platform by a majority of one vote.

Once again there were three reports. The majority report, supported by the original seventeen states, endorsed the Cincinnati platform with the following explanatory resolutions: [20]

1. That the government of a Territory organized by an act of Congress is provisional and temporary; and during its existence, all citizens of the United States have an equal right to settle with their property in the Territory without their rights, either of persons or property, being destroyed or impaired by congressional or territorial legislation.

2. That it is the duty of the Federal Government, in all its departments, to protect, when necessary, the rights of persons and property in the Territories, and wherever else its constitutional authority extends.

3. That when the settlers in a Territory, having an adequate

[19] *Speech of William L. Yancey of Alabama, delivered in the National Democratic Convention, Charleston, April 28, 1860,* 4.

[20] This platform embodied the resolutions presented by Bayard of Delaware, Bigler of Pennsylvania, and Cochrane of New York.

population, form a State constitution, the right of sovereignty commences, and, being consummated by admission into the Union, they stand on an equal footing with the people of other States; and the State thus organized ought to be admitted into the Federal Union whether its Constitution prohibits or recognizes the institution of slavery.

The minority report presented by Samuels of Iowa was identical with the previous one except that the second resolution was stricken out and the following inserted:

Inasmuch as differences of opinion exist in the Democratic party as to the nature and extent of the powers of a Territorial Legislature, and as to the powers and duties of Congress, under the Constitution of the United States, over the institution of slavery within the Territories:

2. *Resolved,* That the Democratic party will abide by the decisions of the Supreme Court of the United States on the question of constitutional law.

This main minority report was signed by seven states only. Three states had absented themselves from the committee, and New Jersey, Pennsylvania, Indiana, and Minnesota joined with Massachusetts in a simple endorsement of the Cincinnati platform without explanatory resolutions. For the first time the Northern Democracy showed signs of weakening. Great confusion and disorder followed the committee reports, and so bitter did the debate become that Chairman Cushing was not able to restore order until he threatened to vacate the chair. The convention then adjourned until Monday. Sunday only served to consolidate the two opposing forces, and on Monday the rupture came. The vote on Butler's minority platform stood 105 to 198, the Southwest and the Northwest uniting to prevent adoption of the Cincinnati platform without explanation.

The main minority report was then substituted for

that of the majority by a vote of 165 to 138.[21] Every state which was ordinarily Democratic voted against the substitution, including fifteen of the seventeen in which Buchanan had received majorities in 1856. In other words, the majority report from the committee, though it was never voted upon directly, received the support of the entire South, and a majority of all the states. It was rejected by a bare majority of votes, all but twelve of which came from states recognized as free soil and from which the party had no hope of receiving a single electoral vote.[22]

The several resolutions of the minority report were then voted upon separately. The second resolution was swept away by a vote of 138 to 21, Alabama, Louisiana, Arkansas, Georgia, and Florida refusing to vote after the adoption of the first resolution. The followers of Douglas could not endorse the second resolution because they did not believe in the natural law of slavery, nor in the right of the common law and the Constitution to enforce it. To their minds, before slavery could exist in a territory it must be legalized by legislative enactment and thereafter sustained by local police laws. They were free to go before the country, so far as the platform adopted was concerned, unhampered by obligations to abide by Supreme Court decisions. They were free to go back to their constituents without having admitted that they had ever compromised their claims regarding the power of the territorial legislature by agreeing to submit the question to the courts.

[21] Yancey afterward estimated the true alignment of the convention as 159 to 144. "Speech of William L. Yancey at Baltimore, June 23, 1860," in *The Daily Delta*, June 30, 1860.

[22] Pennsylvania voted against the report in the committee, but gave a majority for it in the convention. California and Oregon voted with the South. Democratic National Executive Committee, *Address to the Democracy of the United States, July 18, 1860*, 6.

The Alabama delegates complied with their instructions and promptly withdrew from the convention after the majority platform was rejected. General L. P. Walker announced the reasons for their action. The convention having rejected the Southern demands, there existed a direct issue between it and their own constituents. They were seeking guarantees in pursuance of the Constitution, as they believed, for the stability of an institution which formed the basis of their economic and social life. They believed they were acting for the preservation of their liberties, the honor of their people, and the sacredness of their homes.[23] Members of the convention sat silent as one state delegation after another followed that of Alabama from the convention.

In submitting the communication from the Mississippi delegation, Colonel D. C. Glenn said: "I hold in my hand the solemn act of her delegation upon this floor, and I say to you, gentlemen, that it is not a hasty action; that it is not one conceived in passion, or carried out in caprice or disappointment. It is the firm resolve of the great body of the people whom we represent, which was expressed in the convention that sent us here; and that resolve that people and we, their representatives, will maintain at all costs and at all hazards." [24] The majority of the Charleston convention had announced to them in a most solemn manner, said Beverly Mathews, that their rights could not be recognized; that while the federal government possessed the power to protect all other species of property within its jurisdiction, it possessed no power to protect property in slaves as recognized by fifteen sovereign states;

[23] *Proceedings of the Conventions at Charleston and Baltimore*, 118-120. The written communication was signed by the entire Alabama delegation, but John A. Winston afterward repudiated his action.
[24] *Ibid.*, 121.

that while the Republicans claimed for the federal government the power to destroy, the Douglas Democracy, controlling the convention, denied the power either to destroy or protect; and "this, they assure us, is, and must, and shall be the condition of our coöperation in the next presidential election." [25]

Louisiana, the next state to withdraw, presented no prepared address. Ex-Governor Mouton announced their departure and stated that two members of the delegation, although acting with the majority, did so under protest. [26]

South Carolina followed Louisiana in the order of withdrawal. The action of her delegation was likewise not unanimous, three delegates refusing to sign the communication and two of the three remaining in the convention. There is some evidence that Douglas had counted upon the support of the South Carolina delegation. [27] Reid, however, stated afterward in the meeting at the Military Institute that he did not sign the communication because it was hastily drawn up. South Carolina, he said, had thought of remaining in the convention in hopes of effecting reconciliation, but "where Alabama goes, there the Carolinas will go also." [28] Perry, one of the two delegates remaining in the convention, said that he and Colonel Boozer remained because their constituents asked for nothing more than the ratification of the Cincinnati platform.

[25] *Ibid.*, 122.
[26] *Ibid.*, 120-122, 138. The Louisiana delegation was composed almost entirely of large property holders, there being but one lawyer and one officeholder. It represented several million dollars in sugar and cotton plantation property, eight of its members having average incomes in excess of $25,000, and holding more than sixty slaves each. McHatton and Jones were the two delegates who withdrew under protest. *The Daily Delta*, May 5, 1860.
[27] For a stout denial, see *The Daily South Carolinian*, Columbia, May 10, 1860.
[28] *Proceedings of the Conventions at Charleston and Baltimore*, 120-121, 138.

It was his conviction that, if the remnant of the convention would endorse the Dred Scott decision, those delegates who had withdrawn would return.[29]

Florida and Texas, the next states to withdraw, acted unanimously. The Arkansas delegation did not act as a unit, although the convention at Little Rock had demanded congressional protection for slavery in the territories where such property might otherwise be insecure, and had instructed its delegates to the Charleston convention to withdraw unless this demand was endorsed previous to the nomination of candidates. After six of the Southern states had withdrawn from the convention, Burrows presented a written communication signed by himself, P. Jordan, and Van H. Manning. Those three delegates withdrew immediately, and on the following day Francis Terry, J. P. Johnson, and F. W. Hoadley took similar action.[30] Stirman, one of the two delegates from the state who remained, agreed to accept the platform if a Southern man were given the nomination. Flournoy remained and became the leader of the Douglas faction in Arkansas during the choleric canvass which followed the adjournment to Baltimore.

When Burrows of Arkansas ceased speaking, Bayard of Delaware, prominent statesman and representative of the Democracy of the upper South, announced the withdrawal of himself and his colleague Whiteley. His action was indicative of what might be expected of a large part of the remaining delegations unless some compromise could be agreed upon. Several states had already retired for consultation and the convention adjourned until Tuesday morning.

The next morning twenty-eight of the Georgia dele-

[29] *Ibid.,* 136.        [30] *Ibid.,* 124-125, 129.

gates presented a written communication and withdrew.[81] Four of these had voted in consultation against withdrawing, but agreed to act with the majority. Cohen, one of the eight remaining delegates from that state, state-rights man and in sympathy with the seceders by his own declaration, stated that he remained in the hope of effecting some reunion of the Democracy in order to prevent a Republican victory in November. He contended that the only sense in which the South was divided was in point of time, and made a passionate plea for conciliation.

The rump convention then proceeded to the business of nominating a candidate for the presidency. Chairman Cushing ruled that a vote equal to two thirds of all the electoral votes was necessary for a nomination, and his ruling was sustained by the convention. For fifty-seven ballots, over a period of two days, the Douglas followers sought to force his nomination upon the convention. Maine, New Hampshire, Vermont, Rhode Island, New York, Ohio, Indiana, Illinois, Michigan, Wisconsin, Minnesota, and Iowa, comprising one hundred twenty votes in all, steadfastly refused to compromise on any other candidate, and with but one exception every vote from those states was cast for Douglas on every ballot.[82] Repeated efforts were made to secure the endorsement of Hunter of Virginia, Guthrie of Kentucky, or Lane of Oregon, but to no avail; and on the tenth day of its session the convention adjourned to meet again at Baltimore on the eighteenth of June.

[81] *Ibid.*, 128.
[82] Minnesota gave one vote to Johnson after the ninth ballot. In addition, Douglas received the following votes without change throughout the fifty-seven ballots: Massachusetts 5, Connecticut 3½, Pennsylvania 9½, and Maryland 2.

# CHAPTER IV

## THE DEMOCRACY DIVIDED

It was during the evening session, Monday, April 30, that the delegates of eight states withdrew from the convention. They then assembled at St. Andrew's Hall to determine upon a future course of action. Many members of state delegations which had not withdrawn were present, among whom Snead of Missouri and Fisher of Virginia were appointed on the committee to report permanent officers for the organization.[1] The Wood delegation from New York was also present by invitation from Yancey and Fisher. Desiring to the very last to preserve the unity of their party organization, no one had given thought to the questions that would arise in such an exigency as had occurred. They had followed out the instructions of their state conventions; but the national convention had adopted the Cincinnati platform without explanation. That platform had been given two constructions, one at the South, the other at the North. If in its future action, the convention should nominate upon that platform a man who was in sympathy with the Southern construction, the seceding delegates would be in an embarrassing position. They had first of all to remember their relation to those states which had not withdrawn

[1] *Proceedings of the Delegates who withdrew from the National Democratic Convention at Charleston, in April, 1860, 3.*

but whose interests were coincident with their own; and they had to consider their status with regard to their constituents. They had been instructed to withdraw from the convention if certain contingencies arose, but no provision had been made for their future action. Having withdrawn, were their commissions at an end? If so, then whatever action they might take would be as private citizens, and in no sense binding upon the Democracy of their respective states. Yancey, Bayard, and Mouton concurred in that opinion. It was their conviction that no further action should be taken until the following day, inasmuch as other Southern state delegations would probably join them. They should then perfect their organization and remain in session until the remnant of the regular convention took some definite action. If Douglas should be nominated, the proper procedure would be to adopt the majority platform, make their own nominations, and seek vindication for their action before the country at large. This sentiment prevailed and nothing further was attempted.

The bolting delegates reassembled on Tuesday, May 1, at Military Hall. It had been decided, after more sober reflection that the swiftly moving events of the previous evening had permitted, that the convention should restrict its membership to those delegates who had withdrawn from the regular convention. In compliance with this ruling, the Wood delegation retired from the convention, once more assuring that body of their whole-hearted coöperation. The convention then unanimously adopted a report of the committee nominating Bayard as permanent chairman; and upon assuming that office he urged the members present to rely upon their own consciousness of right as vindication for the course they were pursuing. If the rump convention nominated Douglas, thereby endorsing the popular sovereignty construction of the Cincinnati platform, he was willing to unite in nominating candidates for the presidency and vice presidency. Yancey then submitted a series of resolutions which were in substance the majority platform the regular convention had refused to endorse. These resolutions were referred to a committee of one from each of the nine states represented and the convention adjourned until the following day.[2]

The adjournment of the Democratic convention to Baltimore without having nominated a candidate for the presidency forced the bolting delegates to change their plans. They had, during the three days of their session, confidently expected the nomination of Douglas. They had been unanimous in their determination, in that event, to continue their organization as an opposition party, make nominations, and go before the country as the true national Democratic party. But Douglas had not been nominated; his strength had been barely more than one third of the whole; and, if his opponents remained firm, Hunter or some other man recognized as truly Southern in principle might be nominated. Such a course would give to the platform adopted—the Cincinnati platform—a Southern construction, save the party, and perchance the Union. Had Douglas been nominated, and the convention adjourned *sine die,* the whole course of events might have been changed.

It is doubtful if there were many men in the South but hoped for the preservation of the Union, if what they believed to be their constitutional rights might at the same time be secured. Those who were courageous enough to

---

[2] *Ibid.,* 6. The convention met at the Charleston Theater during the last two days of its session.

declare for secession if a Republican were elected, however, were also the most insistent upon a Southern platform for the Democratic party. It was but natural, therefore, that those men who withdrew from the ranks of the Democracy at Charleston should be branded as disunionists. The Douglas adherents seized the opportunity in an effort to spread dissension in the ranks of the bolters and charged some of them with deliberately disrupting the party in order to further their scheme for disunion. They made the cry of disunion their political capital. They utilized it at Baltimore to exclude delegations from the Southern states which came there honestly seeking to preserve the party; and, when their own intransigence drove the remainder of the slave states and portions of the delegations from six free states from the Baltimore convention, they sought refuge behind the charge that the original Charleston bolters had come to Baltimore in order to complete the disruption of the party. Thereafter the entire membership of the constitutional Democracy was denounced as disunionist; and, although that party carried nine states in the presidential election, polled nearly three hundred thousand votes in the free states, and failed to carry Kentucky, Virginia, and Tennessee by the narrowest of margins, the charge has met little challenge in the subsequent years.

How much outside influence entered into the proceedings of the bolting delegates on that last day at Charleston we will probably never know. Dissension arose over a resolution offered by Judge Meek, that a committee be appointed to prepare an address to the country explaining the bolt. Barry of Mississippi hoped that the platform would be reopened at Baltimore and changed to meet the views of the South. He maintained that they were still delegates to that convention until their constituents released them or filled their places, and that they ought to go there and preserve the party organization, if possible. Hooker, also of Mississippi, opposed Barry's contention because they had separated from the others on matters of principle and would lose the moral effect of their action by going to Baltimore. He argued for immediate nominations and a resolute maintenance of their organization. It was upon this issue that the charge of disunion crept into the proceedings. Jackson of Georgia charged those who were seeking immediate and irrevocable action with an attempt to prevent the possibility of a reunion of the party. Yancey held that in proposing an address they were seeking "neither to preserve nor destroy the Union, but rather to preserve the constitutional rights of the South, and define the position of the Southern States in retiring from the Convention, and their subsequent action." Simons of South Carolina opposed the resolution because he was unwilling to allow a committee to speak for him, unless he could previously examine the address. He was opposed to a reunion of the party and would not go to Baltimore. Bayard likewise opposed the publication of an address. He trusted no one to speak for him and hoped for a reunion of the party at Baltimore. So fearful was he of a disunion movement that he resigned his position and retired from the convention.[3] The united opposition of Texas and Mississippi finally defeated the resolution, and the convention adjourned to meet again at Richmond on the second Monday in June.[4]

Before adjourning at Charleston, the rump convention had recommended that the party organizations in the several states make provision "for supplying all vacancies

[3] *Ibid.*, 9-10.     [4] *Ibid.*, 11-12.

in their respective delegations to this Convention, when it shall reassemble." [8] This recommendation transferred to the constituencies of those delegates who had vacated their seats at Charleston the responsibility of deciding their future relation to the party. Those delegates had done nothing to embarrass their constituencies. The Democratic party organizations in the several states were free to adopt any one of several courses: they might endorse the action of their delegates, accept the division of the party as a fact, and send them to Richmond to complete the organization of the constitutional Democratic party; they might repudiate the action of their delegates and send others to Baltimore to unite with the Douglas Democracy in making nominations on the Cincinnati platform; or they might endorse the action of their delegates, send them to Baltimore in hope of reuniting the party on a revised platform, and also accredit them to Richmond in case the Douglas Democracy refused to compromise.

That permanent disruption of the Democratic party was regarded with apprehension by its Southern leaders is apparent from the remarks of Jefferson Davis in the Senate four days after the adjournment at Charleston. While engaged in debate on his resolutions, he said with reference to the proceedings:

After days of discussion, we saw that party convention broken. We saw the enemies of Democracy waiting to be invited to its funeral, and jestingly looking into the blank faces of those of us to whom the telegraph brought the sad intelligence. I hope this is, however, but the mist of the morning. I have faith in the Democracy, and that it still lives. . . . Thanks to a sanguine temperament, thanks to an abiding faith, thanks to a confidence in the Providence which has so long ruled for good the destiny of my country, I believe

[8] *Proceedings of the Conventions at Charleston and Baltimore*, 152.

it will reunite, and reunite upon sound and acceptable principles. At least, I hope so.[6]

Benjamin predicted that within six weeks the party
would be reunited upon sound principles, and that the
Northern members who had acted on the basis of expediency, although privately agreeing with the South in principle, would openly acknowledge the justice of the cause
of the South. "I do not know when," he said, "in the
whole course of my life, I felt such an utter shrinking
of my whole being; I do not know whether I ever felt my
heart sink within me as it did at the news that the Democratic party was about to break into two sectional divi-
sions."[7] Faith in the ultimate reunion of the party was
not confined to these two leading representatives of the
Democracy of the Southwest. Clingman, non-interven-
tionist senator from North Carolina, relied upon the great
vitality of the party, and upon its "good and true men in
every section of the country," to effect a restoration of
harmony.[8] Acting upon their expressed convictions, a
portion of the senators and representatives from the states
in question united in an address to their constituents urging them to accredit delegates to Baltimore.[9]

Delegations from other Southern states had remained
in the convention at Charleston because they were led to
believe that the platform would be modified by explanatory amendments to suit their demands. Subsequent proceedings of the convention had strengthened the prospect
of such action at Baltimore. A modification of the platform would remove the cause of separation, and a failure

[6] Davis, Remarks in the Senate, May 7, 1860. *Cong. Globe,* 36
Cong., 1 Sess., III, 1939.
[7] Benjamin, Remarks in the Senate, May 8, 1860, *ibid.,* 1967.
[8] Clingman, Remarks in the Senate, May 8, 1860, *ibid.,* 1965.
[9] *Montgomery Advertiser,* May 23, 1860.

to modify it would certainly lead to the withdrawal of the remainder of the Democratic states. United action on the part of all the Democratic states would result in either case. This faith in the reunion of the party at Baltimore had its origin in what was known as the *Tennessee resolution*. After the separation at Charleston, constant conferences were held between the delegates of the slave states who remained in the convention and those who had withdrawn. The purpose of these conferences was to unite the South, and, if possible, reunite the party. The tangible result was the following resolution, offered by Howard of Tennessee in the regular convention:

*Resolved,* That the citizens of the United States have an equal right to settle with their property in the Territories of the United States; and that, under the decision of the Supreme Court of the United States, which we recognize as the correct exposition of the Constitution of the United States, neither the rights of person nor of property can be destroyed by congressional or territorial legislation.[10]

The New York delegation drafted this resolution and sent it to the Tennessee delegation as a compromise which they would support providing no other states withdrew.[11] Russell of Virginia stated at the time that this resolution was approved by every Southern state in the convention, was acceptable to New York, and could be passed as indicated by a poll of the convention delegates. Its adoption either at Charleston or at Baltimore would probably have reunited the party, and the assurance of its adoption if brought to a vote is the one thing which kept the remaining Southern states in the convention at Charleston. In

[10] *Proceedings of the Conventions at Charleston and Baltimore,* 136.

[11] Andrew Ewing, Sam Milligan, Alfred Robb, "Address to the Democracy of Tennessee," in the *Nashville Union and American,* July 1, 1860.

the interval of adjournment it was, more than anything else, the hope which induced the states of the lower South to return delegations to Baltimore, and the main factor in the reluctance of other states to participate in a separate organization movement previous to that convention.

Meanwhile Southern sentiment was adjusting itself to the new situation. The one prevailing idea of the Southern-rights men was to unite the South. When it adjourned at Charleston, the party was committed to the Cincinnati platform and to that alone, with respect to the vital issue of slavery. It was apparent from the proceedings of the convention that the Southern states which remained in the convention would accept the platform if a Southern man were nominated. They refused to accept Douglas because his nomination would place a popular sovereignty interpretation upon that platform. It was believed in all parts of the South that, if his nomination were persisted in again at Baltimore, every Southern state and a portion of the Northern states would leave the convention. The idea, therefore, that the meeting at Richmond, June 11, would be joined by the delegations from all the Southern states in advance of the Baltimore meeting began to wane; and the Democratic press of the upper South strongly urged the states of the lower South to return their delegations to Baltimore.[12]

[12] "We respectfully, but earnestly, appeal to the convention that will assemble in Richmond on the 11th of June next, to take no decided action until they shall be informed of the measures adopted by the Baltimore Convention on the 18th of June. As matters now stand, the question of a platform is still open, and we yet trust that the Democratic Baltimore Convention will see the vital importance of adopting a platform that will meet the views of the Richmond Convention, and thus secure the harmonious and united action of the Democracy of every section of the Confederacy." The *Richmond Enquirer*, May 11, 1860; see, also, the *Daily Courier*, Louisville, May 4, 1860; and the *Richmond Semi-Weekly Examiner*, May 11, 1860.

In opposition to this course there was an interesting combination of those Southern-rights men who had been seeking for years to establish a Southern political party; of the Douglas minority faction who saw an opportunity to purge the Democratic party of its extreme Southern-rights element; and of the unaffiliated Southern-rights Whigs who hoped to reconstruct their former organization on the ruins of a divided Democracy.

The questions at issue were most confusing. Was the Tennessee resolution a sufficient guarantee of Southern rights? Would the bolters at Charleston be readmitted to the Baltimore convention, especially if contesting Douglas delegations were present? Did the resolution requesting the states to return full delegations have reference to vacancies created by the bolters?

The Yancey-Rhett followers were opposed to the Tennessee resolution because, like the Cincinnati platform, it was susceptible of a double interpretation.[18] They had urged the bolters to make nominations at Charleston. They insisted that the Douglas followers would never yield, and that if the Southern delegations should go to Baltimore the result would be a reënactment of the Charleston drama. Upon returning to Alabama, therefore, Yancey exerted all his influence to prevent such

[18] See *The Charleston Mercury*, May 3, 1860. *The Daily Delta*, New Orleans, May 15, 1860, said: "It simply repudiates the right of the Federal Government to impair the rights of person or property in the Territories, thus leaving open the great question whether slaves are property, and as such entitled to the same protection that is extended to all other kinds of property. Even a Black Republican could stand on such a platform as that, and logically deduce from it the power even to prohibit slavery in the Territories! If we cannot have the aid of the Northern Democracy without deceiving them, or being ourselves deceived, we should a thousand times prefer defeat. The time has passed for ambiguous resolutions and fraudulent platforms." For an opposite view, see the *Daily Courier*, Louisville, May 10, 1860.

action. At last, finding the opposition too strong, he bowed to the inevitable and announced that he had been mistaken and would support the program of returning delegates to the convention at Baltimore as "a duty he owed to the Democracy of the States, of the Cotton States, and of the Union." [14] In South Carolina, however, the sentiment prevailed that Southern interests would be served best by the maintenance of an exclusively Southern-rights party, and that state accredited a new delegation to Richmond only.

In Alabama and Louisiana, the two states in which the Douglas followers held conventions and sent contesting delegations to Baltimore, a small minority from the first had denounced the action of their state delegations at Charleston as a movement for disunion. When news of the disruption reached New Orleans, a call was issued through the *Bee* for a "Union Demonstration" meeting in opposition to the "secession action of the State delegation at Charleston." [15] The meeting was held on Tuesday evening, May 8, and was a distinct failure, most of those in attendance being hostile to its purpose. [16] A resolution was adopted by those present pledging their opposition "to all parties or fragments of parties and all aspirants for public office whose claims to public confidence are in any manner identified with disorganization or disunion senti-ment and designs." [17] The action of the state delegation

[14] *Substance of Speech by William L. Yancey in Estella Hall, Montgomery, May 12, 1860;* and Yancey, *Speech in the Democratic Meeting at Marion, Perry County, May 19, 1860.*
[15] *The New Orleans Bee,* May 3, 1860.
[16] *The Daily Delta,* May 9, 1860.
[17] The principal speaker at this meeting was Colonel Isaac E. Morse, late Attorney General of Louisiana. Morse had been a bitter secessionist four years previously during the struggle over Kansas; had delivered what was claimed to have been the only disunion speech ever delivered in New Orleans; and had been defeated later as

at Charleston, however, received the hearty support of nearly the entire New Orleans Democracy. Six hundred business and professional men, representing the commercial and industrial interests of the city, issued a call for a mass meeting on Saturday evening, May 12. The signers designated themselves "friends of the Constitution, impressed with the necessity of upholding, within the Union, the Constitutional Rights of the several States as the only safeguard against a dissolution of the Confederacy." [18] The meeting, one of the largest ever assembled in the city, was enthusiastic and unanimous in its endorsement of the action of the state delegation. General W. R. Miles presided and T. J. Semmes, Attorney General of Louisiana, and Colonel D. C. Glenn of Mississippi were the principal speakers. This was a gathering of business men in the second greatest commercial city of the country. Their interests were indissolubly bound up with those of the planters of nearly every state whose delegations had opposed the doctrine of popular sovereignty to the disruption of the party. They were dependent for their wealth upon permanence and peace for the vested interests of these tributary states, and the phenomenal growth of abolitionism at the North had driven them to the point where they were ready to say, with Miles, that they would have guarantees for their constitutional rights "in the Union if we can; out of the Union if we must." [19]

---

a candidate for representative as a result. He was the leader of the opposition forces in May, 1860, until Pierre Soulé later identified himself with the movement. In this meeting, Morse appeared to be devoted to the Union which less than four years before he had designated a "miserable abstraction" and an "ignominious bondage." See *The Daily Delta*, May 12, 1860, for a comparison of the two speeches.

[18] *The Daily Delta*, May 13, 1860.
[19] *Ibid.*, May 11, 1860.

Semmes spoke of the meeting as having "been convoked to satisfy the nation that New Orleans, the great emporium of slave products, into whose lap is poured a glittering stream of wealth from the seven states which abandoned the convention, is animated by the determination to support and uphold the rural population of the South in their constitutional demands." [20] The assembly then adopted resolutions endorsing the demands of the slavery interests for protection in the territories by every department of the federal government, and commending the Louisiana delegation to Charleston for refusing "to accept temporary success at the price of principles involving the very existence of our institutions." A final resolution stated: "That in view of the prospect of an adjustment of the differences which occurred at Charleston, and considering that harmonious action will strengthen the bond of union, it is expedient and proper to reassemble the late State Convention, which met at Baton Rouge in March last, for the purpose of determining the course to be pursued by the State in reference to the Presidency."

In accordance with the general wish of the Democracy in the state, as expressed by this and similar assemblies elsewhere, the state Democratic executive committee issued a call for the former convention to assemble at Baton Rouge. The theory upon which this was done was that the delegates to Charleston had not resigned, but had simply withdrawn from the convention, which had no power to receive resignations even had they been tendered. The delegates were the representatives of the Democratic party in Louisiana and that organization alone possessed the power to accept their resignations, to censure, or to

[20] *Ibid.,* May 13, 1860.

return them to the adjourned convention. The Baltimore convention was not a new convention, but an adjourned meeting of the Charleston body; and during the interval of adjournment, whatever action might be taken by state organizations should be taken by those conventions which had previously appointed the delegations. There was, therefore, no more necessity for a new convention in Louisiana than in Illinois or any other state.[21]

Meanwhile Pierre Soulé had identified himself with the Douglas forces, and through his influence a second opposition meeting was held in New Orleans on the night of May 19.[22] The entry of Soulé into the controversy altered the prospect, for it marked the beginning of a definite Douglas or popular sovereignty party in the state as opposed to the regular party organization. A resolution was adopted at this second meeting, calling a convention at Donaldsonville, June 6, and delegates were appointed to it. This faction justified its action upon the resolution adopted at Charleston requesting the Democracy of the several states to fill all vacancies. It held that the former

[21] This position was supported by the Democratic press of the upper South. The *Daily Courier*, Louisville, June 9, 1860, said: "Their withdrawal from the Convention then in session certainly cannot be held to have excluded them from any future Democratic Convention to which they may be sent; nor from the adjourned session of the Charleston Convention, particularly if they, on their return to their constituents, be again accredited as representatives. . . . The delegates from Alabama, for instance, were instructed in positive terms to pursue a certain course. Knowing that such instructions had been given by the body which appointed them, they were admitted into the Charleston Convention as Democrats, no voice being raised against their recognition. . . . If they did not represent a Democratic constituency, they were not entitled to seats in the National Convention; if their constituents were Democrats then, they are Democrats now, having committed no offense." For the "Address of the Louisiana Democratic State Central Committee," see *The Daily Delta*, May 15, 1860.

[22] Soulé had been one of the leaders of the resistance party in 1850 and had been denounced at the time as a traitor and disunionist.

delegates had resigned their seats,[23] and that it was the duty of the state Democracy to send a new delegation to Baltimore, or return the same delegation *with new instructions.* The state executive committee had approved the action of the delegates, and had reconvened the old convention which had previously adjourned *sine die.* That procedure would not secure an expression of the sentiments of the party regarding the new issue presented. It was, therefore, the duty of the party, meeting in local assemblies, to send delegates to this new convention at Donaldsonville, that a true expression of the will of the majority might be secured.[24]

The Douglas convention assembled at Donaldsonville, June 6, 1860. It was composed of one hundred forty-nine delegates, representing personally or by proxy only twenty of the thirty-nine parishes in the state, and was as unrepresentative of the state Democracy as it was irregular. Among its members were many former members of the Whig and American parties.[25] The convention adopted

[23] This was the interpretation placed upon that resolution by the extreme Southern-rights wing of the Democratic party and by the opposition press. "The National Convention has already considered their places vacant, and cannot repudiate its own action. It will have before it the applications for admission of those who were chosen in lieu of the Seceders, and it cannot so far stultify itself as to reject the delegates elected at its own request, to receive those who had spurned its authority and disobeyed its fiat." *The New Orleans Bee,* May 24, 1860. "The resolutions adopted inviting Democrats from the seceding States to send Delegates to fill vacancies, could not have looked to vacancies which might occur in the ordinary course of things, for that was provided against by the alternates appointed for every Delegate in the Convention. The invitation, therefore, could have had reference only to the vacancies occasioned by the seceding Delegates." *The Charleston Mercury,* June 30, 1860.

[24] "Proceedings of the Douglas Meeting at Odd Fellows Hall, May 19, 1860," in *The Daily Delta,* May 20, 1860; "Proceedings of the Donaldsonville Convention, June 6, 1860, in *ibid.,* June 8, 1860.

[25] Colonel Preston Pond of East Feliciana had been a candidate for Congress on each ticket, and in each case had been defeated by the Democratic candidate.

a series of resolutions and appointed delegates to represent the state at Baltimore. The resolutions (1) denounced the action of the "seceding delegates as an unwarranted rebellion against that great principle of Democracy and paramount rule of party discipline which pledges the assent and submission of the minority to the will and resolves of the majority"; (2) endorsed the doctrine of popular sovereignty; (3) branded the demand for protection by congressional legislation as the "delusive hallucinations of political dreamers"; and (4) expressed its preference for the nomination of Douglas at Baltimore.[26]

In Alabama, the division in the ranks of the Democracy did not, as in Louisiana, develop after the adjournment of the Charleston convention, but had its beginning in the state elections of 1859. In the state convention of January, 1860, which appointed delegates to Charleston, a further division occurred over the question of federal protection and popular sovereignty with respect to slavery in the territories. The majority, led by Yancey, demanded protection by every department of the federal government, and a small minority under the leadership of Forsyth and Seibels endorsed Douglas and popular sovereignty.[27] The division carried over into the state legislature, Forsyth protesting most vigorously against the action of that body in providing for arming the state and for a state convention in the event of a Republican victory in November.[28] During the debate on these measures, Forsyth declared that the platform adopted by the January state convention

[26] "Proceedings of the Donaldsonville Convention, June 6, 1860," in *The Daily Delta*, June 8, 1860.

[27] *Proceedings of the Democratic State Convention held in the city of Montgomery, commencing Wednesday, January 11, 1860.*

[28] For details of the resolutions passed by the Alabama legislature at this time, see Shorter to Brown, January 3, 1861, in *Official Records . . . Armies*, Series IV, Vol. I, 15-17.

could not be adopted at Charleston without disrupting the national party organization; and when the Alabama delegates withdrew from the latter convention he denounced their action as part of a prearranged plot to disrupt the Union by breaking up the party.

The eleventh resolution of the platform adopted by the convention in January had provided for an executive committee which should, in case the delegation withdrew at Charleston, issue a call for a new convention.[19] In accordance with this instruction, the committee issued a call for a state convention to meet at Montgomery on June 4. Primary meetings were held in forty-four counties, and delegates were appointed to this convention. The procedure was regular, and the convention, so far as any convention could, represented the Democratic party of the state. The convention reaffirmed the state platform adopted in January, approved the action of the delegation at Charleston, and appointed a new delegation, consisting largely of the members of the Charleston delegation, to Richmond and Baltimore.[20]

Meanwhile Ex-Governor Winston had deserted the ranks of the regular Democracy and joined Forsyth in denouncing the action of the state delegation at Charles-

[19] "That should any emergency arise, either by the failure of the Charleston Convention to meet the just expectations of the South, or to erect a platform of principle before the nomination of a candidate for the Presidency as to cause a majority of the Southern delegates to retire from said Convention, then, and in that case, our delegates are instructed to report the same to the executive committee, who shall thereupon proceed to call a State Convention, that such action may be had in the premises as the exigencies of the crisis may demand." *Proceedings of the Democratic State Convention, held in the City of Montgomery, commencing Wednesday, January 11, 1860,* 30.

[20] *Montgomery Daily Mail,* June 5, 1860; *Proceedings of the Conventions at Charleston and Baltimore,* 190; *Address of the Democracy of Alabama to the National Democratic Convention, at Baltimore, June 18, 1860,* 4.

ton as a plot on the part of Yancey to break up the Union. A call was issued by Forsyth, Seibels, and Figures for a state convention of the "National Democracy" to be held at Montgomery, June 4, the same day and place of meeting of the regular state convention. Participation in the movement was not limited to members of the Democratic party. In the Montgomery *Confederation* "all Democrats and all other persons who are in favor of Alabama being represented in the Baltimore Convention" were urged to hold county meetings and send delegates to the convention. The Mobile *Register* extended the invitation to "all those who are in favor of the perpetuity of the institutions of the government, the integrity, power, and authority of the Democratic party." The Hunstville *Advocate* urged all conservatives and friends of Stephen A. Douglas to participate. This convention, consisting of delegates from twenty-eight of the fifty-two counties of the state, endorsed the doctrine of popular sovereignty and appointed delegates to the Baltimore convention.[81]

In Texas and Arkansas, because of the slow means of communication, there was not sufficient time for a state

[81] *The Mobile Register,* June 5, 1860. The report of the delegation sent to Baltimore by the regular convention said in part: "We are advised that in this Forsyth Convention . . . were leading opponents both of the State and National Democracy, who had never voted a Democratic ticket. Among them were Thomas McPrince and Lewis E. Parsons, both leading and prominent Whigs and Know-Nothings. The latter was a candidate upon the electoral Fillmore ticket in 1856, and is a delegate appointed by that body to this National Democratic Convention. Two others, H. W. Hilliard and Alexander White, were recent additions to the Democratic ranks, but ancient leaders in the Whig ranks, the former a candidate on the Fillmore electoral ticket in 1856, for the State at large. Among the Delegates sent here, and who contest our seats, are persons who were members of the State Convention in January, 1860, and were Delegates at Charleston, and who thus are bound by it, as the regular Convention of the Democracy, to wit: J. C. Bradley, P. G. King, William Garrett, Thomas B. Cooper, M. J. Bulger." *Address of the Democracy of Alabama to the National Democratic Convention, at Baltimore, June 18. 1860,* 7.

convention to assemble. The state executive committee of
Texas, therefore, reappointed the former delegation and
accredited it to Richmond and Baltimore. In Arkansas,
conventions of the two congressional districts were in session when the Charleston delegation returned to the state.
These district conventions reappointed the former delegates and accredited them to Baltimore only.[32] In the
northern district, a mass meeting was called at Madison
by an anonymous advertisement in the Memphis newspapers. The meeting was attended by about four hundred
men from twelve of the twenty-seven counties in the district, and a contesting delegation was appointed to the
Baltimore convention.[33]

The Georgia state convention, consisting of approximately four hundred members, and representing every
county in the state, assembled at Milledgeville, reappointed the entire Charleston delegation, and accredited
them to Baltimore and Richmond. Forty-one members
dissented, withdrew from the convention, and appointed a
new delegation to Baltimore only. The Florida state convention reappointed its former delegation and accredited
them to Richmond, with authority to return to the Baltimore convention if a compromise appeared probable.

Whether the party would reunite at Baltimore depended upon the attitude of that convention toward two
fundamental propositions: (1) the admission of the regu-

[32] Democratic National Executive Committee, *Address to the
Democracy of the United States*, July 18, 1860, 11. National Demo-
cratic Executive Committee, "Address to the People of the United
States," in *Arkansas True Democrat*, September 1, 1860.

[33] How poorly this meeting represented the sentiments of the
district may be judged from the fact that Hindman, one of the regular
delegates to Charleston, who was reappointed to Baltimore by the
district convention then in session, represented the district in Congress
and had been elected in 1858 by a majority of 18,000 out of a total
of 25,000 votes.

larly appointed delegations from those states in which there were contesting delegations; and (2) the adoption of the Tennessee resolution. The decision rested with the leaders of those states which held the balance of power. The attitude of Douglas and Pugh toward the vital issues, as indicated in the Senate debates, did not augur well for peace. With regard to the admission of the Southern delegates at Baltimore, Pugh said:

> They have no business there. Their seats are vacant. . . . I will sit and vote until the 4th of March, 1861, against allowing one man of them to come back again, unless he is newly elected as a delegate to that convention. . . . I can tell the gentleman [Benjamin] he is mistaken if he supposes that the men who stood there at Charleston for two weeks in that atmosphere voting down your resolutions again and again, and voting for Stephen A. Douglas, are going to be tired when it comes to Baltimore, which is a much more agreeable atmosphere for them.[34]

This was a clear indication that the test for admission at Baltimore would be the endorsement of Douglas as the party candidate for the presidency.[35]

Likewise Douglas, May 16, virtually ended all possibility of the acceptance of the Tennessee resolution as a compromise platform by indicating the interpretation it would receive by him if adopted. It meant, he said, "that

[34] Pugh, Remarks in the Senate, May 22, 1860, *Cong. Globe*, 36 Cong., 1 Sess., III, 2247.

[35] The extent to which the gravity of the crisis was realized by those seeking to restore harmony may be gathered from the following statement in the *Daily Courier*, Louisville, June 6, 1860: "If factions prevail, and local prejudices control the convention, all will be lost; the last bond of union between the States will be sundered; sectionalism and fanaticism will hold their revels in the Federal Capital; the Constitution and the rights of the States will be disregarded; and disunion, and the establishment of but two separate confederacies, as preferable to anarchy, civil war, and internecine strife, will be the choice of evils."

every citizen of the United States has an equal right in the
Territories; that whatever right the citizens of one State
has, may be enjoyed by the citizens of all the States; that
whatever property the citizens of one State may carry
there, the citizens of all the States may carry; and on whatever terms the citizens of one State can hold it and have it
protected, the citizens of all States can hold it and have it
protected, without deciding what the right is, which still
remains for decision." [36] This was but little removed
from sound Republican doctrine, and Benjamin, who had
previously supported the resolution, now thanked Douglas
for warning the South in advance as to how he would
evade the force of the resolution if it were adopted, and
said: "The South will be fools if they do not take advantage of the warning, and see if something cannot be devised which the astute and practiced ingenuity of the
Senator from Illinois cannot get around, if the English
language can hold him." [37]

In pursuance of the general policy adopted at the South
of attempting to prevent a final division in the ranks of
the Democracy, the Constitutional Democratic Convention
at Richmond did virtually nothing. [38] No platform was
adopted, nor nominations made, and after a two-day session of what could scarcely be termed a convention, the
few delegates present, except for those of South Carolina,
proceeded on to Baltimore. *En route* to that city, Yancey
stopped at Washington where he was approached by

[36] Douglas, Remarks in the Senate, May 16, 1860, *Cong. Globe*,
36 Cong., 1 Sess., IV, Appendix, 316.
[37] Benjamin, Remarks in the Senate, May 22, 1860, *ibid.*, III,
2239.
[38] Delegates in attendance: Alabama 21, South Carolina 32,
Mississippi 6, Louisiana 12, Georgia 5, Texas 5, Tennessee 1, Virginia
1, Florida 6, Arkansas 6. Halstead, *Caucuses of 1860*, 154-159;
"Richmond Convention," in *Important Political Pamphlet for the
Campaign of 1860*, 24-25.

George N. Sanders of the New York delegation with an offer of the vice presidency on the ticket with Douglas. He scorned the offer, and so preposterous did the idea seem to be that the Douglas forces in the ensuing campaign vehemently denied that it had ever been made. There is no evidence that the Douglas forces as a whole were a party to the transaction and it is entirely possible that they were not aware of it at the time. That the offer was made, however, in the presence of Fisher of Virginia, S. S. Baxter of Washington, D. C., and Pugh of Alabama, and that Douglas's illness and probable death at an early date were urged as an inducement, there seems to be little doubt.[39]

[39] William M. Browne (editor of the *Constitution*), to S. S. Baxter, and Baxter to Browne, in the *Richmond Semi-Weekly Examiner,* August 22, 1860; a more complete discussion of the incident is to be found in the *Montgomery Weekly Advertiser,* October 17, 1860. For a denial which in substance was a tacit admission that the offer was seriously made see Sanders to the editor of the *Charleston Courier,* October 22, 1860, in *The Daily True Delta,* New Orleans, October 30, 1860.

# CHAPTER V

## THE DEMOCRATIC CONVENTIONS AT BALTIMORE

THE adjourned Democratic convention reassembled at the Front Street Theater in Baltimore, June 18, 1860. Its membership was the same as it had been at the time of adjournment at Charleston. The chairman, Caleb Cushing, had declined to assume the responsibility of issuing admission tickets to any other delegates. South Carolina had refused to send delegates to Baltimore, and the Florida delegation, although present in the city, refused to apply for admission until definite action by the convention should offer the prospect of compromise. Neither Cushing nor the convention, therefore, was called upon to make any decision respecting those two states. Texas and Mississippi had returned their previous delegations and their seats were uncontested. Alabama, Louisiana, and Georgia had returned delegations composed in large measure of their former membership, but in each case there was a contesting delegation, recruited from the ranks of the Douglas followers in those states. From Arkansas, one full delegation was sent by the congressional nominating conventions, composed of the original Charleston delegates with but two exceptions; and a delegation of three members appointed by the mass meeting in the northern district, claiming one half the votes of the state.

Two members of the Charleston convention from that state, Flournoy and Stirman, had not withdrawn and were present in the convention. Bayard and Whiteley, delegates from the county of Newcastle, Delaware, had withdrawn at Charleston and were seeking admission at Baltimore. There was also a contesting delegation present from Newcastle. In only two other cases were there contests. B. F. Hallett of the fifth Massachusetts congressional district had been prevented from attending the Charleston convention by the death of Mrs. Hallett, and had sent R. L. Chaffee as his substitute. The eighth congressional district of Missouri presented an exactly similar case, John B. Clardy, the regularly appointed delegate, having been represented at Charleston by John O'Fallon. These two cases were important because Cushing had admitted Hallett and Clardy to the exclusion of the substitutes, who had been members of the convention at Charleston.

Cushing, having declined to make any decision with regard to conflicting claims, or to pass upon the authenticity of credentials where no contest was presented, placed that issue squarely before the convention for its decision. Howard of Tennessee, who had introduced the famous Tennessee resolution, moved that tickets of admission be issued to all members of the convention as originally organized at Charleston. Cavanaugh of Minnesota instantly moved to lay the motion on the table and called for the previous question. The Douglas forces evidently had decided beforehand upon the course they intended to pursue. The issue which every one felt was to determine the fate of the party was before the convention and, under the rules, closed to discussion. Church of New York, by unanimous consent, then offered an amendment to the Howard resolution providing (1) that the credentials of all persons claiming seats made vacant by the secession of delegates at Charleston be referred to a committee; and (2) that all such delegates upon being admitted be "bound in honor and good faith to abide by the action of this convention, and support its nominees." [1] Cavanaugh, still determined that there should be no debate, immediately withdrew his motion to lay upon the table and called for the previous question upon the amendment. These tactics irritated the already tense situation. To force delegations whose seats were uncontested to submit their credentials to a committee and to propose a pledge as a prerequisite for admission were not conducive to the restoration of harmony. A counter-proposal was then offered by Gilmore of Pennsylvania, providing that the delegates from Florida, Arkansas, and Mississippi be admitted to the convention, and that a committee be appointed to examine the credentials of contesting delegations from Delaware, Georgia, Alabama, and Louisiana. [2] The convention then voted, one hundred forty and one half to one hundred eight and one half, to allow debate upon the subjects under consideration, New York and Rhode Island deserting the Douglas ranks and voting in the affirmative.

Randall of Pennsylvania spoke against the amendment of Church, denying the power of the convention to impose a condition of admission upon the delegations of the seven states. He held that their constituencies possessed an unqualified right to send delegations to the convention "without qualification, without condition, or without limitation from any other power but the supreme power of the people." The convention possessed only a delegated power to perform certain functions for the Democ-

[1] *Proceedings of the Conventions at Charleston and Baltimore*, 160.
[2] *Ibid.*, 163.

racy of the nation. No Southern representative would submit to the test oath, and he doubted very much if it were intended that they should.[3]

Russell of Virginia, who had labored faithfully to restore party harmony, then indicated the position that state intended to occupy. He stated that the convention had adopted at Charleston a voting rule which the Virginia delegation thought contrary to the fundamental constitution of the party; and it had voted down the platform which they wished to have adopted. They remained in the convention after eight states with whom they were in perfect accord had withdrawn, in order to save the party; but, he added, "We mean to see that there shall be fair play at least toward Southern Democrats." The Virginia delegation believed with the representatives of Tennessee that the right of every previous delegate to the Charleston convention to admission into the convention at Baltimore was beyond dispute; but they were prepared to support the Gilmore amendment, if by so doing they could restore harmony in the convention.[4] Ewing of Tennessee likewise supported the Gilmore amendment and pleaded for harmony and conciliation. He explained that the delegations seeking admission had been induced to do so by assurances that a compromise satisfactory to all parties would be arranged. They came to restore harmony not to increase party disorganization, but no man among them ever would submit to a qualified admission.[5]

The Northwest still refused to yield and the debate became bitter. The question was, Did the withdrawal of the

[3] *Ibid.*, 164. Randall's speech was eminently fair and moderate in tone, but was hissed throughout both by members of the convention and visitors in the galleries.
[4] *Ibid.*, 167.
[5] *Ibid.*, 171.

several delegations from the Charleston convention constitute a resignation? The supporters of the Howard resolution and Gilmore amendment held that it did not. The delegates seeking admission had no power to resign their rights to the convention. They were the delegates of sovereign states, and were answerable to those states. The convention had no power to accept resignations; no power to expel or retain; and the members of the former session of the convention needed no reaccrediting. Those members present were there by virtue of that fact, and those seeking admission possessed the same right and were entitled to exercise it.

The nearest the convention could come to harmonizing was an agreement to adjourn. That evening, after adjournment, a compromise was reached between opposing factions. Church was to withdraw that part of his resolution requiring a pledge to support the nominations made by the convention, and Gilmore was to withdraw his resolution entirely. This procedure was followed in convention the next morning, and the credentials of all delegates seeking admission were submitted to a committee for consideration. The committee sat for two days, the convention adjourning from time to time without any attempt to transact business. Finally, on the fourth day of the convention, the committee report was ready. Every one seems to have been aware that a dramatic session was pending and the floors and galleries were densely packed with spectators. As the committee was about to make its report the center section of the floor broke through, and about one hundred fifty of the delegates, including the New York delegation, went down through the stage. There was no basement under the theater and no one was injured. In the midst of the din, Captain Rynders of New York said:

"Mr. President, the platform has not broken down—only one plank got loose." "I hope the convention will repair the platform," said Cochrane, and another remarked, "New York and Pennsylvania have gone down together." Evidently the substance of the committee report was already known, and when the request was made for an hour's recess to allow the repairing of the floor, Captain Rynders requested that they "at the same time repair the injury done to the Democratic party." [6]

The majority report was signed in its entirety by fourteen states; and was based upon the Douglas construction of the resolution of May 3, recommending that the Democratic party of the several states make provision for filling all vacancies. It held that the seats of the delegates from Alabama, Louisiana, Texas, and Mississippi became entirely vacant when those delegates withdrew at Charleston, and that the same was true in part for Georgia, Arkansas, and Delaware. No contesting delegations had appeared from Mississippi and Texas, but there were such from Alabama, Louisiana, Georgia, Arkansas, and Delaware, and for individual seats in Massachusetts and Missouri. The one delegate present from Arkansas (Flournoy) represented one vote. The seats representing the three remaining votes from that state had become vacant by the withdrawal of the original delegates. These seats were claimed by one delegation of six and by another of three persons. [7] The report recommended that all from Arkansas be admitted; the delegation of six to have two

[7] The former were those appointed by the district conventions, the later those appointed by the Madison mass meeting in the Northern district. No mention was made in this report of Van H. Manning, F. W. Hoadley, and John Stirman, who had agreed to unite with the six appointed by the district conventions. They were held to have violated their rights by withdrawing at Charleston.

votes and the delegation of three to have one vote. If either delegation refused to take its seats in the convention, the other was to cast the three votes. Hallett of Massachusetts and Clardy of Missouri were to be unseated and their seats given to Chaffee and O'Fallon who had substituted for them at Charleston.[8] The Mississippi and Texas delegations were to be admitted, there being no contesting delegations from those states. The delegation headed by Pierre Soulé from Louisiana and the Forsyth delegation from Alabama were to be admitted, to the exclusion of those appointed by the regular Democratic conventions of those states. James A. Bayard and William G. Whiteley were to be admitted from the county of Newcastle, Delaware.[9] The two contesting delegations from Georgia were to be admitted, each given one half of the votes, and in case either delegation refused its seats the other was to cast the entire vote of the state.

The minority report was supported by nine states in its entirety, ten states with regard to Georgia, Missouri, and Massachusetts, and eleven states with regard to Alabama.[10] It was based on a different interpretation of the Charleston resolution. When the state delegations withdrew, and stated their reasons for withdrawing, they were still representatives of the Democratic party in their respective states. Their withdrawal was not a resignation, and was not so regarded by the convention at the time. The resolution had reference to vacancies which might occur from a

[8] Hallett was the author of the Cincinnati platform, which was the platform adopted by the convention.

[9] Original delegates to Charleston who had withdrawn and participated in the organization of the Democratic Constitutional party.

[10] Oregon, New Jersey, Pennsylvania, Delaware, Virginia, North Carolina, Tennessee, Kentucky, California, New Hampshire agreed with respect to Georgia, Alabama, Missouri, and Massachusetts; and Maryland agreed with respect to Alabama.

variety of reasons before time for reassembling. Resignations must be made to the appointing power, and the
appointing power must accept them before they were complete and final. The resolution, by requesting that vacancies be filled, had referred the matter to the various state
constituencies. The delegates who had withdrawn at
Charleston had consulted their constituencies as to their
future action and had been sent to Baltimore to restore
harmony in the party.[11] The report said further:

> The fact that delegations are not contested does not
> establish the right to seats in the Convention. There may be
> irregular delegates without contest, and there may be a con-
> test between two sets of irregular delegates. The right of per-
> sons to seats as delegates is to be determined by the fact as to
> whether they were appointed according to the usage of said
> constituency. Wanting these essential prerequisites, they are
> not entitled to seats, even if there be no contestants; and
> having these, their right to seats is not impaired or affected
> by contestants.[12]

This minority report held, therefore, that the committee
had done rightly in deciding, by a vote of 23 to 2, to admit
the Mississippi delegation, because they were members
of the Charleston convention, had never resigned, and
had been instructed to return to Baltimore by a state convention called by the state executive committee. The committee had likewise rightly recommended, by a vote of 19
to 6, the admission of the delegation from Texas, where
no convention had been called, but where the Charleston
delegates had been sent back to Baltimore by the state
executive committee. The minority report pointed out
that exactly the same procedure had been followed by

[11] *Proceedings of the Conventions at Charleston and Baltimore,*
190.
[12] *Ibid.,* 189.

the party in Louisiana, Alabama, and Georgia as in Mississippi. The delegates withdrew at Charleston but did not resign. The state executive committee in each case called a convention, and the convention continued the powers of the delegates and sent them back to the national convention at Baltimore. The committee, however, had voted, 16 to 9, to admit the irregular delegates from Louisiana; 14 to 11, to admit the irregular delegates from Alabama; and 13 to 10, to admit one half of the regular and irregular delegates respectively from Georgia. It had voted to admit the irregular delegates from Arkansas and to reject a portion of the regular Charleston delegation as modified by the filling of vacancies; and had repudiated the principle followed in previous cases by voting to admit the original Charleston delegation from Delaware and to reject the irregular delegation.[18] The minority report maintained also that any substitute delegate received his appointment simply to act in the absence of his principal and that when the principal appeared and took his seat the authority of the substitute ceased. Hallett and Clardy were, therefore, entitled to the seats they occupied.

Immediately after the reading of the two reports New York requested an adjournment for the purpose of consultation before voting. The convention was in an uproar. Cleverly printed bogus tickets had been scattered broadcast and the floor of the convention hall was densely packed with spectators. Butler said that he had not come five hundred miles to attend a mass meeting, and demanded that the floor be cleared of spectators. Realizing the futility of debate under prevailing conditions, the convention adjourned.

On the following morning the minority report was

[18] *Ibid.*, 190-191.

rejected by a vote of 150 to 100½, New York, as in every previous important case, holding the balance of power and voting with the Douglas forces.[14]

The majority report was then ruled divisible and every provision accepted by the convention with the exception of the one relative to Georgia. In the case of Georgia the New York delegation voted with the Southern-rights men to admit the regular delegates as recommended by the minority report.[15]

The convention then adjourned until evening, with a motion pending to reconsider the minority report. In the interval some votes were gained for its reconsideration; but they were not sufficient, and all hope of reconciliation was defeated by a vote of 113 to 139. As the vote neared its conclusion, Russell of Virginia, who had labored earnestly to save the party, announced that the Virginia delegates could no longer participate in the deliberations of the convention. Mingled hisses and applause greeted the announcement, and amid the wildest confusion Cushing ordered the galleries cleared. "I hope," said a Virginia delegate, "the chair will not clear the galleries, and I hope, as we retire from this grave of Democracy, that we may be heard to our heart's content."[16]

Word had just been received, continued Russell, that those delegates to whom tickets of admission had been issued, and who were truly representative of the Democracy of their states, would decline to take their seats.

---

[14] See Appendix B.

[15] *Proceedings of the Conventions at Charleston and Baltimore,* 203. The vote on the various sections of the report was as follows: Mississippi, 250–2½; Louisiana, 158–98; Arkansas, (1) 182–69; (2) 150–100½; Texas, 250–2½; Alabama, 148–101½; Massachusetts, 138–112½; Missouri, 138½–112; Georgia rejected, 106½–145.

[16] *Proceedings of the Conventions at Charleston and Baltimore,* 212.

Twenty-five of the thirty delegates from Virginia then retired from the convention. They were followed by sixteen of the twenty delegates from North Carolina, and by nineteen of the twenty-four from Tennessee. Kentucky asked for permission to retire for consultation, but Stuart of Michigan objected. His objections had been so frequent and his baitings of the Southern delegates so numerous, that on this occasion a member of the Kentucky delegation called out in a stentorian voice, "I wish to know whether the gentleman from Michigan is the manager of this theater." Every delegation which retired was greeted with hisses from the Douglas forces. Smith of California, evidently enraged by the demonstrations of censure, announced the withdrawal of his delegation: "Whilst I cannot say with the gentleman from Tennessee that my Democracy dates back to the time I have no knowledge of it,[17] yet I can say, that it is as unspotted as the azure of heaven. . . . California stands here with a lacerated heart, bleeding over the downfall and destruction of the Democratic party . . . stabbed by assassins, now grinning upon this floor." A dozen men called him to order; the chairman suggested that he use different language; but amid a torrent of hisses, ironical laughter, and finally threats of physical violence, he denounced the Douglas faction in true frontier fashion and retired with his delegation from the convention. California was followed by Oregon, Stevens stating that, being far from the controversy, they had no motive to act in the disturbing question except devotion to the Constitution and to sovereign states, which had been grievously wronged.

Other delegations withdrew when the convention as-

[17] Jones of Tennessee had said he had been a Democrat since he "first drew milk from his mother's breasts."

sembled the following morning. Kentucky presented a written communication asserting that the convention had disregarded all the established usages of the Democratic party, violated every principle of justice and fairness, and destroyed the equal rights of the several states. It had suppressed, by its voting rule, the voice of the Democracy in several states, had denied admission to representative delegations from others, and by such tactics had forced still others to withdraw. It had finally ceased to be a national convention of the Democratic party, and fifteen of the twenty-four delegates from Kentucky would no longer be party to its transactions.[18] Chairman Cushing then resigned his position, and David Tod of Ohio was elected chairman.[19] Butler of Massachusetts tried repeatedly to gain the floor in order to present a written communication from the delegation of that state. He was ruled out of order again and again, and finally read the document without permission. It was a protest signed by fourteen of the twenty-six delegates against the expulsion of Hallett, "an old, faithful, and most efficient servant of the Democratic cause—a regularly commissioned delegate. . . ."[20] The fourteen Massachusetts delegates then

[18] This was the general interpretation placed upon the proceedings of the Baltimore convention by the conservative press which had urged the Southern delegations to return to Baltimore. The *Richmond Semi-Weekly Examiner,* July 3, 1860, said: "His [Douglas's] friends sacrificed him in Baltimore before they nominated him. They violated usages, they destroyed representations, they offended Southern sentiment, they excluded Southern Democracies from their counsels and made delegations for some of them, . . . and then they presented him, a Northern man, on a Northern platform, as they construed it, as the nominee of a Convention first severed by their action and then remodeled and recreated by themselves." See, also, *The Wilmington Journal,* June 28, 1860.

[19] *Official Proceedings of the Democratic National Convention held in 1860, at Charleston and Baltimore* (John G. Parkhurst, Recording Secretary, ed.), 155.

[20] *Ibid.,* 157.

withdrew from the convention. This completed the secessions, and the convention was converted into a testimonial meeting for Douglas. Stevens of Massachusetts, Dickinson of North Carolina, Soulé of Louisiana, and Flournoy of Arkansas were the speakers.

Thirteen states only were represented by full delegations when the balloting for the presidential nominee began,[21] and two of those, Alabama and Louisiana, were represented by irregular delegations which in no sense represented the Democracy of their states. Seven states were wholly unrepresented,[22] and seven others were represented by less than half the members of their delegations.[23] Delegates representing one hundred eighty-two and one half votes remained as participants in the convention. Deducting the sixteen votes represented by the irregular delegates from Louisiana, Arkansas, and Alabama, there were actually in the convention but one hundred sixty-six and one half votes represented by delegates regularly chosen by and representative of the Democracy in the several states.[24]

The rump convention then proceeded to the election of a presidential nominee. The first ballot produced a total of only one hundred ninety and one half votes, and it was obvious that the two thirds rule must be changed if a nomination were to be made. Any change, however, would require a delay of one more day under the rules of the convention. Chairman Tod suggested that he was

[21] Maine, New Hampshire, Vermont, Rhode Island, New York, Alabama, Louisiana, Ohio, Indiana, Illinois, Michigan, Wisconsin, and Iowa.

[22] Florida, South Carolina, Georgia, Mississippi, Texas, Delaware, North Carolina.

[23] Massachusetts, Maryland, New Jersey, Virginia, Kentucky, Tennessee, Arkansas.

[24] See Appendix C.

willing to interpret the two thirds rule to mean two thirds of the delegates in the convention rather than two thirds of the total electoral vote, but numerous objections were made. It was then announced that several delegates who had withdrawn from the convention were still within the hall as spectators, and that if all were counted a total of two hundred twelve and one half votes were present. A second ballot was taken with the express understanding that all votes present but not given would be counted for Douglas by a motion to make the nomination unanimous. That motion was eventually made and the question was put and declared adopted while pandemonium made the voice of protesting delegates inaudible. The nomination for the vice presidency was tendered Fitzpatrick of Alabama, but that gentleman declined the honor and the national executive committee placed Herschel V. Johnson of Georgia upon the ticket.

On the last day of the Baltimore convention, Saturday, June 23, two hundred thirty-one delegates who had either been regularly elected to the convention and had not applied for admission, had been refused admission, or had withdrawn, assembled in Maryland Institute for consultation.[25] Caleb Cushing resumed his seat as permanent chairman, and it was decided to continue as the Democratic national convention, adopt a platform, and nominate candidates for the presidency and vice presidency. No individual was allowed to participate in the proceedings of the convention unless possessing credentials as a regularly elected delegate. Each delegate was permitted

[25] Delegates present: Virginia 24, Georgia 30, New York 2, California 11, Maryland 9, Pennsylvania 12, Louisiana 11, Mississippi 14, Oregon 6, Minnesota 1, North Carolina 15, Florida 7, Tennessee 19, Massachusetts 16, Arkansas 9, Kentucky 10, Alabama 28, Texas 6, Missouri 2.

to cast only the vote to which he was entitled, and no state was allowed a vote in excess of that to which it was entitled by actual representation.[20] The platform included in the second majority report at Charleston was adopted unanimously, and John C. Breckinridge and Joseph Lane were nominated as candidates for the presidency and vice presidency respectively.

[20] *Proceedings of the Conventions at Charleston and Baltimore,* 243.

# CHAPTER VI

## THE CONSTITUTIONAL UNION CONVENTION
## AND THE CAMPAIGN

THE National Constitutional Union convention assembled at Baltimore, May 9, 1860. Its members were survivors of the Whigs with the American element especially prominent. Twenty-four states only were represented by delegates. Ohio, Indiana, and Illinois were the only Northwestern states represented, and from none of them was there a full delegation.[1] California and Oregon were not represented, nor were Louisiana, New Hampshire, and Rhode Island.[2] Former Governor Washington Hunt of New York was permanent chairman of the convention which had been organized with Crittenden of Kentucky temporarily presiding. In his opening address, Hunt referred to the question of slavery in the territories as a "miserable abstraction," and sounded the keynote of the convention deliberations when he said: "I trust we shall not be *very much embarrassed in the construction of a platform. We ought not* to endeavor

[1] Halstead, *Caucuses of 1860*, 104-105; *Important Political Pamphlet for the Campaign of 1860*, 23.
[2] By reference to the table of statistics, Appendix C, it will be observed that Bell polled, in the subsequent election, but 14,404 votes in the seven states of the Northwest, and but 7,000 votes in the two Pacific coast states.

strongly to *establish uniformity of opinion on a question* which we all know and understand—a question that every man will at least *think and feel according to his own judgment.*" [3]

The question of slavery was avoided and national patriotism was emphasized in the convention. A newspaper correspondent observed that the delegates believed the country was weary of the whole theme of slavery and irrepressible conflict, and would rally to the standard of a party which rigorously avoided any mention of them.[4] But there was a more cogent reason for their evasive attitude. They sought by silence in their national platform to leave the way open for state organizations to adopt platforms suitable to their respective constituencies. In substance, it was exactly what the Douglas Democrats desired at Charleston. The only difference was, that the Douglas Democrats wanted an ambiguous platform which could be interpreted one way at the South and another at the North, while the Constitutional Unionists wished to leave each section unhampered by the necessity of interpretation. They adopted, therefore, a platform which recognized no principles other than "The Constitution of the country, the Union of the States, and the enforcement of the laws"; but that was not the entire platform nor, in the light of the subsequent election, was it the most important part. The platform continued: "As the representatives of the Constitutional Union men of the country in National Convention assembled, we here pledge ourselves to maintain, protect, and defend, separately and unitedly, those great principles of public liberty and national safety against all enemies, at home and abroad,

[3] *Important Political Pamphlet for the Campaign of 1860*, 24.
[4] Halstead, *Caucuses of 1860*, 108-109.

believing that thereby peace may once more be restored to the country, and the *just rights of the people and of the States reëstablished, and the Government again placed in that condition of justice, fraternity, and equality* which, under the example and Constitution of our fathers, has solemnly bound every citizen of the United States to maintain 'a more perfect union, establish justice, insure domestic tranquillity, provide for the common defense, promote the general welfare, and secure the blessings of liberty to ourselves and our posterity.' " [8]

This was a distinctly Southern platform. It did not pledge its endorsers to support the union of states at all hazards. It pledged them to reëstablish the rights of the people and of the states, and to restore the principles of justice and fraternity and equality as fundamental principles in governmental action, because those were the terms and the conditions of the Constitution (the written compact) by which men were bound faithfully to support the union of states. It was not an endorsement of federal supremacy, nor of majority rule, but rather of state rights and constitutional protection for the rights of the minorities. The men who framed it did not renounce their allegiance to their states, nor did they surrender the right to demand congressional legislation and executive action for the protection of the slaveholder in the enjoyment of his property in the territories. The convention was dominated by men from the slave states, particularly from Tennessee, Kentucky, Virginia, and North Carolina. The party in Alabama at a later date adopted a platform which stated "that the territories are the common property of all the States, and therefore, the people of all the States have the right to enter upon and occupy any Terri-

[8] *Ibid.,* 112.

tory with their slaves, as well as other property, and are protected by the Constitution and flag of the country; that Congress has no right to legislate slavery into, nor exclude it from, a Territory, and that neither Congress, nor a Territorial Legislature has any right or power to legislate on the subject, except so far as may be necessary to protect the citizens of the Territory in the possession and enjoyment of their slave property." [6]

The party managers denounced the doctrine of popular sovereignty; they asserted the duty of protection by the federal government and in the subsequent election they polled but 2 per cent of the vote in the free states, representing 13 per cent of the total vote cast for their candidate.[7] They denounced the Breckinridge Democrats as attempting to precipitate disunion, but they did not deny the right of ultimate resistance by secession or revolution. They emphasized the fact that although Lincoln might be elected, the Supreme Court and Congress would be against him and that the states of the South should await some

[6] "Platform of the Constitutional Union Party of Alabama, adopted at Selma, June 28, 1860," in *Important Political Pamphlet for the Campaign of 1860*, 16-18.

[7] The attitude of the Constitutional Unionists toward the territorial question is clearly indicated in the following statements from two of their leading journals: "The trouble is that the Bell and Breckinridge men hold that, subject to the Constitution, the Territories have no *lawful authority* to *exclude* slavery nor slaveholders, while Mr. Douglas and his Northern supporters hold that the Territories *have* such lawful authority. . . . To the doctrine of Judge Douglas we, of the Bell party and the Breckinridge party, can never, and will never, assent, as a fundamental principle of party organization, or a fundamental rule of practice in the administration of the Government." *Daily Chronicle and Sentinel*, Augusta, October 10, 1860. "The editor of the Democrat takes the organs of the Union party to task after his rather sharp fashion. He thinks that the friends of Mr. Bell are very inconsistent in holding that it is the duty of Congress to protect the adjudicated rights of slave owners in the Territories and yet refusing to say that they will be for dissolving the Union if the duty shall not be done." *Louisville Daily Journal*, August 27, 1860.

positive overt act before resorting to resistance. They were standing upon the *Georgia platform,* and they polled 34 per cent of the vote in the lower South and 45 per cent of the vote in the upper South. They sought the defeat of Lincoln and the election of a compromise candidate by the Electoral College or the House of Representatives; and after Lincoln's election they sought compromise and coöperation rather than immediate separate state secession. Neill S. Brown of Tennessee said in the national convention: "I would not give up the Union of States for all the negroes and all the manufacturers, all the railroads, and all the ships that sail the ocean," but, when the question of acquiescing in coercion faced him, he cast his lot with the Southern confederacy, and his attitude was a perfectly consistent one throughout.

The Republican platform, adopted at Chicago, May 17, was an embodiment of sound Republican doctrine. It denied that slavery was based in the common law, denied the right of Congress or of a territorial legislature to establish it in any of the territories, denounced the principles of non-intervention and popular sovereignty as deceptions and frauds, and defined the doctrine of the right of secession as treason.[8] A further provision demanded the passage by Congress of "the complete and satisfactory Homestead measure which has already passed the House." In one sense this was the most anti-slavery clause of the platform. The bill referred to had been passed by the Republican House of Representatives as a free-soil measure, with the avowed object of facilitating the formation of numerous free states. It had provided for granting to individuals above the age of twenty-one a

[8] *Proceedings of the first three Republican National Conventions,* 131-133.

quarter section of land as a homestead if occupied for a period of five years. It had been brought to a vote in the Senate where Douglas voted with Seward, Sumner, Wilson, and other Republican senators in favor of it.[9]

This platform, together with the nomination of Lincoln, has been regarded as a repudiation by the party of radical anti-slavery sentiment. They were not so received at the South. The circulation of Sumner's *Barbarism of Slavery* and Helpers' *Impending Crisis* as campaign documents by the Republicans counteracted whatever claims to conservatism the party derived from its platform.[10] The nomination of Lincoln was not regarded as a repudiation of Seward's Rochester speech, but due to Lincoln's greater popularity in the Northwest.[11] What historians have interpreted as a trend toward conservatism, the Southerners viewed as the acts of astute politicians who sought to counteract the effects of John Brown's raid by adopting "a conciliatory tone, 'sinking the nigger' as much as possible from his unpopular eminence in their platform and cunningly resuscitating old questions that now have

[9] The bill was defeated in the Senate by the narrow margin of 31 to 26. For the text of the bill and the vote in the Senate, see *Cong. Globe*, 36 Cong., 1 Sess., III, 1999.

[10] "Both have been disclaimed by a portion of the party for whose service they were sent forth. But it is the dictate of common caution to note how far the principles are sustained of which the expression is disavowed; and to watch for the indication of a coming time when both may be taken up again and set forth as the exponents of a successful party." *The Daily Picayune*, June 10, 1860. "The Republican journals, such as the New York *Tribune* and *Times*, disavow the sentiments of Sumner, and are very desirous to convince the world that they are not the sentiments of the Republican party. . . . The fact is, Sumner has spoken too truly . . . Greeley and Raymond are afraid, just at this moment, to speak the whole truth. They dare not let the conservative portion of the people at the North know that it is the design of the party with which they are associated to make uncompromising war upon the South." *The Richmond Dispatch*, June 9, 1860. See, also, *The Charleston Mercury*, July 3, 1860.

[11] The *Richmond Enquirer*, May 22, 1860.

scarcely the importance of side issues." [12]   Others denounced the Chicago platform as "a rebuke to Southern morality, and a gross insult to Southern intelligence." [13]

Four candidates were thus presented to the people in a campaign in which discussion centered about the question of the abolition of slavery in the territories, but in which men were thinking in terms of the ultimate abolition of slavery in the states.

At the South, the members of all political parties were dedicated to the preservation of the institution of slavery. Douglas and his doctrine were recognized as hostile to the institution, with the result that he received but 7 per cent of the vote in the lower South, constituting but 3 per cent of his total vote. He did only slightly better in the states in the upper South, with but 8 per cent of the vote, representing 5 per cent of his total vote. Lincoln received no support whatever in the lower South, and only 3 per cent of the total vote in the states of the upper South.

The South was determined to resist any attempt on the part of a Republican administration to interfere with the institution of slavery in the states where it existed. The majority in the states of the lower South believed that the election of a Republican President would in itself constitute sufficient cause for resistance. The majority in the states of the upper South believed that resistance should be delayed until some overt act had been committed. [14]

[12] *New Orleans Daily Crescent*, March 16, 1860; see, also, *Breckinridge and Lane Campaign Documents*, No. 6, 6; and *The Daily Picayune*, New Orleans, September 11, 1860.

[13] *The Southern Argus*, Norfolk, October 22, 1860.

[14] An overt act did not necessarily mean an act of violence. In general the exclusion of slavery from the territories by congressional action or the refusal to admit a slave state into the Union were included in that term. The *Daily Chronicle and Sentinel*, April 14,

The former, in the main, were supporters of Breckinridge, the latter of Bell. Every governor but one [15] and virtually every senator and representative in Congress from the seven states of the lower South was on record as favoring secession in event of Republican victory. Three state legislatures had already made provision for arming their states, and had advised the calling of state conventions to determine what course should be pursued. The presidential campaign at the South, therefore, assumed the nature of a preliminary struggle over the question of resistance to Republican rule with the Breckinridge forces upon the defensive.[16] They were upon the defensive because their leading men were charged by the Douglas Democrats and by the Constitutional Unionists with having broken up the Democratic party as one act in a prearranged conspiracy to disrupt the Union.

Those parties presented three principal lines of argument in support of their assertions. The first centered in Yancey and his organization of the *Leaguers of the South;* the second presented the various resolutions adopted by the legislatures of Alabama, Mississippi, and South Carolina, counseling some form of resistance to a Republican

---

1860, said: "If it has come to this, that the General Government, under neither Democratic nor Republican Rule, is able to secure the just rights of the States and the citizens thereof in the common Territory, but that we must either be excluded by our common government or, in the last resort, take what the first-comers may give us, then is the Union a failure, and we of the South must look for new safeguards. If either the Republican *policy* or the policy of the Popular Sovereignty-Freesoil Democracy is to be the settled policy of this government of ours, then we are no longer equals in the Union our fathers framed, and we would as soon *submit* to one as the other, but counsel always no submission to either." See, also, *Republican Banner,* February 10, 1861.

[15] Houston of Texas.

[16] The author does not mean to imply by this statement that the opponents of the Constitutional Democrats were Unionists in the sense of submissionists as that term was understood at the North.

administration; and the third quoted the many utterances
of leading constitutional Democrats in favor of secession
if a Republican President were elected. As to the *Leaguers
of the South* or *League of United Southerners,* as the
organization was variously known, there can be no doubt
that it had been launched, but we have the statements of
Yancey and of Davis that it did not prosper. Davis said
in the Senate, when Douglas first presented the argument
of the Slaughter letter, that so far as he knew there was
never a lodge outside of Alabama, and that not more than
seventy-five men ever joined it in that state.[17] Yancey
himself stated, in the Alabama Democratic convention in
January, 1860, that the league was not organized to further the cause of disunion, but as an organization to secure
the nomination of Southern-rights men in all parties at
the South and thereby preserve the principles of the Constitution within the Union. He further admitted that the
movement had failed utterly, because "the political managers frowned us down for fear of our disturbing the
usual selfish routine of the ambitious leaders of parties,
who feared the ascendancy of the statesman over the wiles
of the politicians." [18]    In spite of these and other continued denials, however, the charges were kept alive by
the Douglas forces at Charleston and in the Senate; were
published in the newspapers of both the Douglas and Bell
forces, and were scattered broadcast in pamphlet form
throughout the South during the presidential campaign.[19]

Basing their arguments upon the assumption that the

[17] Remarks of Davis of Mississippi in the Senate, May 17, 1860,
*Cong. Globe,* 36 Cong., 1 Sess., III, 2156.

[18] *Speech of William L. Yancey delivered in the Democratic
State Convention, of the State of Alabama, held at Montgomery on
the 11th, 12th, 13th, 14th of January, 1860,* 10.

[19] See the *National Union,* August 4, 1860; the *Republican Banner,* Nashville, July 28, 1860; and *The Conspiracy to Break Up the
Union,* consisting of extracts from the *Daily Nashville Patriot* and
published in pamphlet form by the Douglas campaign committee.

lodges of the *Leaguers of the South* were fully organized in all the Southern states and engaged in missionary activities for the dissemination of secession doctrine, the Constitutional Unionists and Douglas Democrats turned to the Slaughter letter again for explanation of the various statements of public men, legislative resolutions, and state party platforms. They contended that the details of the conspiracy to "influence parties, legislatures, and statesmen," and "to precipitate the Cotton States into a revolution," had been worked out in private consultation at Montgomery during the Southern commercial convention of 1858, at a time when no specific cause for separation existed. The plot, therefore, was, in its inception, the work of disunionists *per se,* who sought to arouse the South to their support by introducing the question of reopening the African slave trade into the Montgomery convention, and again in the Vicksburg convention of 1859.[20] Finding the opposition to the reopening of the trade too strong, they next turned to the doctrine of congressional protection as first endorsed by the New Orleans *Delta,* the Montgomery *Advertiser,* and the Richmond *Enquirer,* in September, 1858.[21] In thus bringing forward this doctrine, the leaders of the conspiracy knew that it would never be accepted by the Democratic party, and never desired that it should be accepted; but brought it forward for the sole purpose of disrupting the party and procuring a united North against a united South.

The next step in the evolution of the movement, they

[20] Spratt of South Carolina introduced the resolution into the Montgomery convention, Yancey carried the burden of the debate favoring their adoption, and Roger A. Pryor of Virginia was the leader of the opposition forces. At Vicksburg, Spratt of South Carolina led the debates in favor of the reopening of the trade and Foote of Mississippi the opposition.

[21] The *National Union,* August 4, 1860.

declared, was that of educating the masses to the support of the doctrines of congressional protection and resistance to the inauguration of a Republican President, which had been accomplished through the medium of the newspapers during the year 1859.

The public utterances of many Breckinridge Democrats were displayed as evidence that Southern party leaders had rallied to the support of the conspiracy to bring about the disruption of the union of states and the formation of a Southern confederacy. Virtually every public official in the lower South had at some time counseled resistance to a Republican administration. Governor Pettus of Mississippi had stated, during the campaign of 1859, that he would retire from the canvass if he thought the people "would not sustain him in resistance to the inauguration of a Black Republican President." Ex-Governor McRae of that state, representative in Congress in 1860, had taken a similar position in resolutions sent to the Vicksburg convention in 1859; and, on the eve of his departure for Washington in September of that year, had said at Jackson, that in event of a Republican victory, "Mississippi, separately or in concert with other Southern States as she might elect, ought at once to discontinue her connection with the Abolition States." [22] Jefferson Davis had likewise stated at Jackson, July 6, 1859, that "in the contingency of the election of a President on the platform of Mr. Seward's Rochester speech, let the Union be dissolved.[23]

Other representatives and senators openly declared for secession in event of a Republican victory, some for immediate action, and others in event an overt act should be

[22] The *Weekly Mississippian,* November 20, 1859.
[23] *Ibid.,* July 7, 1859.

committed against the South.[24] The conspirators, it was charged, having carried out their program of education, having secured the endorsement of men in public office, and having placed three states on record as favoring their designs, had then proceeded to the final preliminary act of the drama, the disruption of the Democratic party at Charleston and at Baltimore. It followed, said the Douglas Democrats and Constitutional Unionists, that Breckinridge and Lane were the candidates of a disunion party; and the Douglas campaign committee thanked God that no disunionist supported their candidates.

In answer to the slogan of the Douglas Democrats, "Thank God no disunionist sustains Stephen A. Douglas and Herschel V. Johnson," written by Miles Taylor of Louisiana, chairman of the Douglas campaign committee, the Constitutional Democrats quoted that gentleman's remarks and those of his friend and colaborer in the Douglas cause, Pierre Soulé, in Congress during the struggles over the compromise measures of 1850 and over the admission of Kansas.[25] Both had been fire-eaters of the fiercest sort too recently to have had a complete change of heart. In fact, so little did any one suspect the position that Soulé would adopt in the campaign that, at the New Orleans mass meeting of May 12, his political theories were quoted time and again; and the remark was made by D. C. Glenn of Mississippi: "Let Democrats now in battling for Southern rights say that they learned their political doctrines from the lips of Pierre Soulé." [26] Alexander H. Stephens, Douglas elector at large from Georgia,

[24] See remarks by the following congressmen: S. Moore of Alabama, December 8, 1859, *Cong. Globe*, 36 Cong., 1 Sess., IV, Appendix, 38; J. L. M. Curry of Alabama, December 19, 1859, *ibid.*, 50.
[25] *Ibid.*, 31 Cong., 1 Sess., Appendix, II, 1520; *ibid.*, 34 Cong., 1 Sess., Appendix, 187.
[26] *The Daily True Delta*, May 13, 1860.

had said in the House of Representatives: "Whenever this Government is brought in hostile array against me and mine, I am for disunion—openly, boldly, and fearlessly for revolution." [27] Hiram Warner of the same state, a leading Douglas supporter, had delivered in Congress a most able speech in favor of disunion if Congress refused protection to slave property in the territories. [28] E. C. Cabell, a Douglas supporter in Missouri, freely denounced the Constitutional Democrats as disunionists, but formerly, as congressman from Florida, he had said: "We can only remain in the Union as your equals. . . . We have resolved to resist at every hazard, and to the last extremity, what is called the 'spirit of the age,' which would array the powers of the Government against the interests of our section."

Quoting these former speeches of leading Douglas supporters to show that they *had been* disunionists, the startling disclosure was then made that the Atlanta *Confederacy,* a leading Douglas newspaper of Georgia, was raising the standard of resistance; boldly proclaiming during the campaign: "Let the consequences be what they may—whether the Potomac is crimsoned in human gore, and Pennsylvania Avenue is paved ten fathoms in depth with mangled bodies or whether the last vestige of liberty is swept from the face of the American Continent, the South will never submit to such humiliation and degradation as the inauguration of Abraham Lincoln." The Constitutional Democrats contended, therefore, that the disunionists of Georgia under their old leader, Herschel V. Johnson, and the old disunionists all over the South, were supporting Douglas as part of a well-planned conspiracy

[27] *Cong. Globe,* 31 Cong., 1 Sess., Appendix, II, 1083.
[28] *Ibid.,* 34 Cong., 1 Sess., Appendix, 297, 300.

to elect Lincoln and succeed in disunion where they had failed in 1850.[29]

The Constitutional Unionists and Douglas Democrats seized upon a letter of Lawrence M. Keitt of South Carolina, published in the Columbia *South Carolinian* and in the Charleston *Mercury*, July 20, 1860. In this letter Keitt said:

> Under the teachings of the Abolitionists, the North is about to be consolidated against the South. It is futile to deny, unless all the signs around us betray, that the Federal Government is about to pass into the hands of the majority section, and that all its powers will be used to cripple, and ultimately to destroy, the institution of slavery as it exists among us. . . . It has been said that if the Republican party succeeds in the pending Presidential Campaign, it will succeed through the forms of the Constitution, and that we must wait for an overt act. It is immaterial to a free people, whether they are oppressed under the forms of a Constitution or over and against its forms; they resist oppression itself, and not the form in which it comes. . . . And how can the South be saved from injury if the Republican party succeeds in the coming presidential election? I answer, only by dissolving the Government immediately. If this party succeeds, loyalty to the Union will be treason to the South. The South now stands upon the Constitution, and her standard is in the hands of Breckinridge and Lane; let her sons rally to it, and, under it, move on to equality in the Union.[30]

This was treason, said the Constitutional Unionist press, and only those would support Breckinridge who were willing to sacrifice the country upon the altar of party.

Many Constitutional Unionists had declared, on pre-

[29] *Breckinridge and Lane Campaign Document, No. 16*, 5.
[30] L. M. Keitt to A. G. Sailey, Henry Ellis, and others, July 16, 1860, *Republican Banner*, July 28, 1860; *Daily Missouri Republican*, St. Louis, July 27, 1860.

vious occasions, in favor of separation if Northern aggression continued. Among others were W. L. Underwood of Kentucky,[31] H. W. Hilliard of Alabama,[32] Leander M. Cox of Kentucky,[33] Jeremiah Morton of Virginia,[34] and J. P. Campbell of Kentucky.[35] Benjamin H. Hill of Georgia, leading Bell and Everett elector at large in that state, said at Macon, Georgia, June 30, 1860, after arguing strongly for protection in the territories:

> If the experiment is forced, the fact will turn out to be, in my humble judgment, that this Government and Black Republicanism cannot live together. . . . At no period of the world's history have four thousand millions of property debated whether it ought to submit to the rule of an enemy.[36]

The Constitutional Unionist newspapers of the lower South adopted a similar attitude against submission to further aggression. The New Orleans *Crescent* said, as early as July 21, 1860:

> When the occasion serves it *will* denounce them [Union-at-any-price men]. The *Crescent* has not followed the Democratic journals that support Douglas in proclaiming Breckinridge, Yancey, Slidell, and Company as Disunionists, because these gentlemen themselves deny that such is the case, and we do not believe it of them even if they had not denied it. There are very few Disunionists *per se* in the country. But

---

[31] *Cong. Globe,* 34 Cong., 1 Sess., Appendix, 1166.

[32] *Ibid.,* 31 Cong., 1 Sess., I, 359. Hilliard took an active part in securing a fusion ticket in New York in order to defeat Lincoln; see H. W. Hilliard to Millard Fillmore, August 30, 1860, *Daily Missouri Republican,* September 10, 1860. He was later entrusted by the Confederate government with the important mission of securing a military alliance with Tennessee; see "Convention between the State of Tennessee and the Confederate States of America," in *Official Records . . . Armies,* Series IV, Vol. I, 297-298.

[33] *Cong. Globe,* 34 Cong., 1 Sess., Appendix, 32.

[34] *Ibid.,* 31 Cong., 1 Sess., Appendix, I, 113, 115.

[35] *Ibid.,* 34 Cong., 1 Sess., I, 56.

[36] Quoted in *Breckinridge and Lane Campaign Document, No. 16,* 7.

there are plenty of people, of all shades of political opinion, who will prefer disunion to oppression and injustice *within* the Union. If any politician, no matter to what party he belongs, avows his readiness to remain in the Union and submit patiently to every indignity that may be offered, we shall be as ready to oppose him, and even to denounce him as we ever were.[37]

What is the answer? It is simply this: That the South was a unit in its determination to resist a Republican administration conducted along the lines outlined by Seward, Giddings, and others in their many public utterances. Men might differ as to the question of who was responsible for the disruption of the Democratic party, and as to the motives underlying that action; they might differ as to the questions of the benefits to be derived by the South from an endorsement of the principle of popular sovereignty; they might differ as to the nature which resistance should assume; separate state secession, coöperative action, or revolution *en masse;* they might differ as to the question of time with reference to resistance; but with regard to ultimate resistance in defense of their institutions, they did not differ at all. The South was interested in defeating the Republicans; the Breckinridge Democrats, because from a Republican victory they anticipated death to the institution of slavery; the Constitutional Unionists, because they saw beyond a Republican victory certain disruption of the union of states and civil war.

The Breckinridge Democrats contended that a heavy Southern vote for Bell or Douglas would be understood in the North "as an abandonment of all thought of ever using state authority to stay federal oppression"; and that if the Northern people could be convinced that a dissolu-

[37] See, also, *The New Orleans Bee,* July 27, 1860.

tion of the Union would follow Lincoln's election he would be defeated.[38] The Constitutional Unionists believed that a heavy vote for Breckinridge would embolden the advocates of disunion and a light vote cause them to hesitate before urging extreme measures of resistance.[39]

That neither Douglas nor Breckinridge could win the election was generally conceded. Two possibilities were open for the Constitutional Unionists to save the Union, and each depended upon preventing the Republicans from securing a majority in the Electoral College. If they could be prevented from doing so, a compromise could possibly be secured in that body, or failing there, in the House of Representatives.[40] Few of them indeed, even during the campaign, would have been willing to deny the necessity of the separation of the states in all possible contingencies. They were determined to exhaust every possible effort under the Constitution for a redress of grievances before deserting the Union. They were unionists, it is true, who hoped for peace and harmony; but they were Southern-rights men, and the protection and security of Southern interests was the object of the course they pursued. They opposed the Breckinridge Democrats in the election because the members of that party indicated a

[38] *Richmond Semi-Weekly Examiner,* November 6, 1860; *The Charleston Mercury,* August 4, 1860, said: "That the Union is stronger than slavery in the South, is an axiom of the Black Republican party, their success, in grasping the power of the General Government rests upon it. All movements in the South tending to show that their axiom is true, is a most efficient coöperation with them, and nerves and stimulates their progress and power at the North."

[39] *Daily Nashville Patriot,* October 2, 1860.

[40] The attitude of the Southern-rights men on this point was clearly indicated by the *Richmond Semi-Weekly Examiner,* June 19, 1860, when it said that "those who please may talk about going before a Black Republican Congress for an election; everybody knows what that means—to take the chance of buying a vote, or make a corrupt arrangement, and to ensure what is the certain, final result, absolute submission to anti-slavery domination."

policy which would not allow time for compromise; but, unless compromise could be effected along lines satisfactory to the South, they favored peaceable separation.

As early as July 1, 1860, Governor Isham G. Harris of Tennessee indicated the extremes to which the Breckinridge forces were willing to go to prevent a Republican victory. He had been a delegate to the Baltimore convention, had withdrawn, and had participated in the nomination of Breckinridge in the Constitutional Democratic convention. A meeting of the Davidson County Democracy was held at Nashville, June 30, to ratify the action of the Tennessee delegation in withdrawing at Baltimore. Governor Harris said at that meeting that the Tennessee delegation had "used every means of conciliation, and had offered to make every concession consistent with the maintenance of the Constitution, the equality of the States, and the protection of the rights of the citizen"; and that the movement was not a disunion movement, because "the purely national principles asserted in the platform, as well as the antecedents and present position of our candidates, brand this charge as an unmitigated slander and falsehood." More important, however, than his defense of the action taken at Baltimore, was his advice as to the future conduct of the party. Predicting a certain disruption of the union of states if Lincoln should be elected, he advised that the Tennessee electoral delegates, after the election was over, should support Douglas in the Electoral College, if by so doing Lincoln might be defeated.[41]

As the campaign progressed and it became evident that Lincoln would be elected unless New York or Pennsylvania could be secured by an opposing candidate, an effort was made to perfect a fusion ticket of the opposing

[41] *Nashville Union and American*, July 1, 1860.

parties in those states. On July 6, Mayor Wood published a manifesto in favor of a fusion ticket. Douglas should leave the South to Breckinridge and no Breckinridge ticket should be placed against Douglas in the North. Such procedure would prevent Lincoln from securing a majority of the Electoral College.[42] Following this public statement the Mozart Hall Democratic Club of New York City, of which Wood was president, published a series of resolutions which had been adopted by a vote of 86 to 10, urging all parties to support the Douglas electoral ticket in the election. Eventually the fusion ticket was arranged throughout the state, as well as in New Jersey and Rhode Island. Southern men of all parties came North in an effort to arouse the masses to the danger of the situation. Yancey, because of the prominence given by the Republicans and Douglas Democrats to the Slaughter letter and the League of United Southerners in the campaign, was prevailed upon to make an extended campaign which began at Memphis, Tennessee, and ended at Boston, Massachusetts. Henry S. Foote (Constitutional Unionist) of Tennessee and others did likewise. Yancey made no recession from his original position. He denied that he was a disunionist *per se;* but declared that in the event of a Republican victory, "I hope to God there will be some man or set of men, whom Providence will rear in our midst . . . that there will be some great Washington arise who will be able to scourge them from the temple of freedom, even if he is called a traitor—an agitator, or a rebel during the glorious process."[43] Foote

[42] Fernando Wood to John Van Allen, Watkins, Schuyler and Co., July 6, 1860, in *The Daily Delta,* New Orleans, July 12, 1860.
[43] "Speech of the Hon. William L. Yancey of Alabama at Memphis, Tennessee, August 14, 1860," in the *Nashville Union and American,* Supplement, August, 1860.

was not so emphatic in his statements, but he made it perfectly clear that if once the alternative were presented to the states of the upper South of going with the states of the lower South or remaining as a hopeless minority in a disrupted Union, they would not hesitate to withdraw.[44]

Meanwhile, Herschel V. Johnson, candidate for vice president on the Douglas ticket, was taking a position with regard to resistance to Republican supremacy which was the farthest possible from unionism as that term was understood at the North. He maintained that, not being a disunionist *per se,* he patriotically wished the Union to be preserved. He believed the South was unwise in the course it was pursuing; but "if the doctrine of non-intervention must at last be repudiated; if the national Democratic party cannot be preserved; if the South shall persist in the policy which she has inaugurated . . . until the country shall be forced into two great antagonistic sectional organizations, based on sectional issues and bounded by sectional lines, I shall be recreant to the instincts of my heart if I do not link my destiny with hers, and follow her fortunes for weal or woe." [45]

[44] "Speech of Henry S. Foote of Tennessee at Harrisburg, Pennsylvania, August 14, 1860," in the *Daily Missouri Republican,* St. Louis, August 21, 1860.

[45] "Speech of Herschel V. Johnson delivered in Atlanta and Macon, Georgia, June 28 and 29, 1860," in *ibid.,* July 19, 1860. There was a distinct trend toward Southern unity as the campaign neared its close. Amid all the lip service for the Union, there was an evident consciousness of greater devotion to the security of Southern institutions. The rank and file of the Douglas and Bell parties never subscribed to the extravagant professions of loyalty from their candidates. Typical of many statements was that of *The Daily Constitutionalist,* leading Douglas organ of the lower South, November 3, 1860: "If this threatened danger to our homes, our property, our people, and our honor be averted by the kindness of merciful God; if, again, we become great in the councils of our country, and Abolition preachers and fools become as of yore, the petitioners of Congress for disunion, let us learn a lesson by the solemn and eventful

The popular vote in the election was 1,857,610 for Lincoln, 1,365,976 for Douglas, 847,953 for Breckinridge, and 590,631 for Bell. Although elected by a minority vote, it was not the division of the opposition which gave Lincoln the victory. If every vote cast for Douglas, Breckinridge, and Bell had been given to any one of the three, Lincoln would still have had a majority of seventeen and one half votes in the Electoral College.[46] Before the election returns were fully in, it was evident that Lincoln had been elected, and the secession of the lower South was assured.

---

past, and never divide our forces on the eve of battle." See, also, *Speech of Hon. Albert G. Brown, delivered at Crystal Springs, Copiah Co., Miss., September 6, 1860, 3.*

[46] See Appendix D.

# CHAPTER VII

## THE BASIS FOR IMMEDIATE SOUTHERN INDEPENDENCE

THE election of Lincoln to the presidency marks the beginning of active measures for separation. When the movement began, there was in every state a great diversity of sentiment, according as men believed that a way could or could not be found for insuring the rights of the South against further aggression without disrupting the Union. Three courses were open to the South: (1) recognition of the Lincoln administration, and resistance to any overt act which might be committed; (2) coöperative action to obtain a redress of grievances; and (3) separate state secession, and the formation of a Southern confederacy. The possibility of mere submission in any and all contingencies may be passed over with but slight notice. There were some who subscribed to the doctrine, notably in eastern Tennessee, but nowhere were they of sufficient number to be regarded as constituting a party, save in those districts contiguous to free states, which may rightfully be considered a part of the North in all questions of sectional dispute. In every Southern state the contest was decided according as a majority subscribed to one or another of these policies; but in every case majorities were determined from time to time by the attitude of Northern governors, state legislatures, and congressmen toward the proposed compromises and the question of peaceable separation or coercion. Men differed in November, 1860, over the question of immediate separation or coöperative action for a redress of grievances; but they differed according as they believed or did not believe the election of Lincoln represented the verdict of a Northern majority on the question of ultimate abolition of slavery in the Southern states; and, in spite of this diversity of sentiment, the South was united upon the fundamental issues involved. To understand that unity of sentiment, it is necessary to remember the increasing manifestations of hostility to slavery, on the part of a minority at the North, over a period of a quarter of a century. A long sequence of events had caused to accumulate, upon the statute books of the Northern states, a series of acts known as personal liberty laws. These laws varied from state to state, but in general they forbade the use of all state and county jails for the detention of fugitive slaves; provided for their defense by the public attorneys and at the expense of the public treasury; imposed heavy penalties upon any citizen and state and local official who assisted in the execution of the federal fugitive slave law; granted freedom to any slave brought within the limits of the state, and provided fines of from one thousand to five thousand dollars and prison sentences up to fifteen years for any master who thereafter attempted to exercise control over the same; and extended the benefits of habeas corpus and trial by jury to apprehended fugitives.[1]

[1] A complete analysis of the personal liberty laws of the sixteen Northern states may be found in the "Report of the Committee on the Harper's Ferry Outrage, to the Legislature of Virginia" in [McCabe], *Facts versus Fancies*, 23-28.

It was not the personal liberty laws in themselves, however, nor the denial of the right of slave owners to the protection of their property in the common territories which precipitated the people of the South to effect the separation of the states. These were grievances in the sense that they represented anti-slavery sentiment at the North, and Southerners differed only in the extent to which they believed these aggressions represented the attitude of the Northern majority. Those who favored immediate separation were convinced that there was a deep and abiding hatred in the hearts of the Northern people for Southern institutions. Those who counseled deliberation, proposed compromises, and arranged conferences did so because they felt there was still conservative sentiment enough left at the North to join them and relieve the crisis. Just as rapidly as they became convinced that they were wrong in their estimate of the Northern attitude, they became separationists.

Northern antipathy for the Southern people and their institutions had manifested itself in various and more or less active forms, in addition to those already mentioned. Through the three most powerful institutions for the dissemination of propaganda—the churches, the schools, and the press—the rising generation was being taught that slavery was a barbaric institution, degrading alike to master and slave, and a national dishonor. The separation of the churches had especially tended to alienate the two sections. Speaking before the Virginia convention, John S. Preston of South Carolina said:

This diversity at this moment is appearing not in forms of denominational polemics, but in shapes as bloody and terrible as religion has ever assumed since Christ came to earth. Its representative, the Church, has bared her arm for the conflict—her sword is already flashing in the glare of the torch of fanaticism—and the history of the world tells us that when that sword cleaves asunder, no human surgery can heal the wound. There is not one Christian slaveholder here, no matter how near he may be to his meek and lowly master, who does not feel in his heart that from the point of that sword is now dripping the last drop of sympathy which bound him to his brethren at the North. With demoniac rage they have set the Lamb of God between their seed and our seed.[2]

Denunciations of slavery and slaveholders in the name of Christian morality were not confined to public forums at the North. They were frequent occurrences in Congress, where such prominent members as Sumner, Lovejoy, and Giddings lost no opportunity to annoy and humiliate Southern representatives. The South did not discriminate between the spirit of the Republican slavery repression policy, supported by a veritable flood of hostile oratory and journalistic endeavor, and the open and avowed purpose of the abolitionists. They made no distinction between abolition societies which sent armed bands to the territories to exclude forcibly the slave owner with his property, and a political party which purposed to exclude them by legislative enactment. They did not discriminate between mobs which violently rescued fugitive slaves from government officials, and a political party which had by statutory enactments virtually abrogated the fugitive slave law and denied the right of transit to the slave owner in many Northern states. They did not distinguish between those who eulogized John Brown's band as martyrs, and the governors who refused to surrender the fugitives from justice. Those who favored immediate

[2] *Addresses delivered before the Virginia State Convention by Hon. Fulton Anderson, Commissioner from Mississippi, Hon. Henry L. Benning, Commissioner from Georgia, and Hon. John S. Preston, Commissioner from South Carolina, February, 1861, 61.*

separation made no distinction between men who favored violent methods and the political party they supported; and they regarded the election of Lincoln by substantial majorities as the crowning offence of a party which had for years waged an unrelenting war upon slavery through the media of their literature, schools, legislative halls, and courts.

Those who favored immediate separation did not do so because they expected overt acts from the incoming administration. What they did fear was a subtle campaign to divide the South; an ever increasing effort, in one fashion or another, to array the non-slaveholder against the slaveholder.[a]

They regarded, therefore, a policy of delay until the incoming administration should commit an overt act as the very quintessence of insipidity. They expected the states of the upper South to become divested rapidly of slaves. Increased activity of the underground railway and the uncertain future value of slave property would suffice to influence slaveholders in those states to dispose of their property in the markets of the lower South. The corresponding increase of slave population in some states would only serve to render the horrors of eventual eman-

---

[a] "We have been fighting against abolitionism at the North; and, as a contest of sections within the Union, we have lost the battle. Let us beware of the day when the struggle shall be transferred to our own soil; when the slavery question shall cease to be a sectional question, and shall become a domestic question; when the armies of our enemies will be recruited from our own forces." *The Daily Delta*, New Orleans, November 1, 1860. "The great lever by which the abolitionists hope to extirpate slavery in the States is the aid of non-slaveholding citizens in the South. They hope and propose to array one class of our citizens against the other, limit the defense of slavery to those pecuniarily interested and thereby eradiate it." *The Kentucky Statesman*, Lexington, October 5, 1860. See, also, *Richmond Enquirer*, July 10, 1860; and the *Daily Courier*, Louisville, October 5, 1860.

cipation more terrible; and the abolitionizing of the states of the upper South, coupled with the admission of new free states in the West, would hasten the evil day. Ways were innumerable for sowing dissension, distracting the counsels of the Southern people, and eventually paralyzing resistance to emancipation.[4]

The immediate secessionists admitted that the election of any man to the presidency by constitutional methods did not constitute just cause for resistance; but they contended that the success of the Republican party constituted more than a change of administration. It represented the triumph of new governmental principles, new constitutional interpretations; and the success of a party which purposed the direction of all the agencies of the federal government to the ultimate extinction of slavery.[5] It represented the triumph of a party which regarded the United States as a consolidated nation; and which, acting upon that theory, purposed to proceed to the centralization of power in the federal government, and in one branch of that government, Congress, which was regarded as the judge of the limits of its own powers. Its

[4] The *Frankfort Commonwealth,* January 23, 1861; *Richmond Semi-Weekly Examiner,* November 16, 1860; *New Orleans Daily Crescent,* December 14, 1860; the *Daily Courier,* Louisville, October 12, 1860; Benjamin, Remarks in the Senate, December 31, 1860, *Cong. Globe,* 36 Cong., 2 Sess., I, 217; *The Review,* Charlottesville, January 4, 1861.

[5] There is abundant evidence that it was so regarded by the Republicans themselves. See Doolittle to Selleck, November 16, 1860, quoted by Lane, December 5, 1860, *Cong. Globe,* 36 Cong., 2 Sess., I, 9; Hale, Remarks in the Senate, December 5, 1860, *ibid.,* 10. For the Southern attitude, see Curry to Hicks, December 28, 1860, in Smith, *The History and Debates of the Convention of the People of Alabama . . . 1861,* 404; Wigfall, Remarks in the Senate, December 12, 1860, *Cong. Globe,* 36 Cong., 2 Sess., I, 73; *Richmond Semi-weekly Examiner,* December 4, 1860; *The Kentucky Statesman,* January 6, 1860; *Daily Chronicle and Sentinel,* Augusta, March 8, 1860; *Nashville Union and American,* September 30, 1860; *The Daily True Delta,* New Orleans, October 12, 1860.

political principles were such as to render a majority in power equivalent to the whole. Its numerical superiority would give it power to annoy and abuse the weaker section continually.[6]

The immediate separationists did not believe that the Republican party would be disposed to grant concessions;[7] nor did they believe Northern sentiment would be changed by congressional action or constitutional amendments. They were not inclined, therefore, to accept mere paper guarantees unless supported by substantial proof of a change of heart among the masses. They wanted the statesmanship of the country freed from its thraldom of intolerance and fanaticism.[8] They were disposed to reject any compromises granted as measures of expediency which might be thrust aside when the emergency had passed.[9] They demanded a cessation of the perpetual agitation and the insulting taunts to which slaveholders had been subjected. Finally, at no time after the election of Lincoln would they have agreed to less than a self-protecting power in the control of minority interests. Exactly

[6] "The government will be the minister of the orders of a numerical majority of the whole people, not the agent of the States. . . . No change can be effected in the action of the Government, except by an appeal to this majority at the elections held for Federal officers. . . . The supreme despotism of numbers will know no restraint but its own will, use no ministers but its own appointees, have no policy but that devised by its own agents dependent for bread and place on its pleasure. The reign of national demagogues will be inaugurated." *Richmond Semi-Weekly Examiner,* November 9, 1860; see, also, *The Daily South Carolinian,* Columbia, December 24, 1860.

[7] *The Daily Herald,* Wilmington, February 6, 1861; *The New Orleans Bee,* April 21, 1860; *The Daily Picayune,* New Orleans, January 19, 1861; *Richmond Enquirer,* December 18, 1860; the *Daily Courier,* Louisville, December 19, 1860.

[8] *The Daily Picayune,* New Orleans, December 4, 1860; *Nashville Daily Patriot,* February 19, 1861.

[9] *The Daily Herald,* Wilmington, January 7, 1861; *New Orleans Daily Crescent,* February 14, 1861; *The Daily Picayune,* November 25, 1860.

what they would have been satisfied with in that respect is not clear; but some new governmental machinery certainly, along the lines of Calhoun's doctrine of concurrent majority.[10]

The separationists based their right of action upon the theory of state sovereignty. They believed the federal government to have been created by a voluntary union of states, conceived in a spirit of mutual confidence and respect, and inspired by the desire to insure domestic tranquillity by a recognition of equal rights and privileges relative to the diverse interests and institutions of the several sovereign states. Some agreed with President Buchanan that a state had no constitutional right to withdraw from the Union; and they doubted whether that action could be justified on the claim of reserved rights. They regarded secession as revolution, undertaken by the state at its peril; and leaving to the remaining states the decision as to whether policy and expediency justified coercion by their federal government.[11] Others based their right to act upon constitutional grounds. They maintained that certain states had expressly reserved, in their articles of ratification, the right to resume all powers of government at their own discretion; and that those reservations were a part of the Constitution, their benefits inuring equally to all the states.[12] This interpretation, they contended, gave to each state the right,

[10] *Richmond Semi-Weekly Examiner*, November 13, 1860; *The New Orleans Bee*, November 19, 1860; *The Daily Picayune*, December 20, 1860; *The Daily South Carolinian*, Columbia, December 24, 1860.

[11] Buchanan, "Fourth Annual Message," in *A Compilation of the Papers of the Presidents, 1789-1897* (James D. Richardson, ed.), V, 623-659; Iverson, Remarks in the Senate, December 5, 1860, *Cong. Globe*, 36 Cong., 2 Sess., I, 10-12.

[12] Wigfall of Texas, Remarks in the Senate, December 5, 1860, *Cong. Globe*, 36 Cong., 2 Sess., 13.

with or without cause, to withdraw from the Union. Others, and by far the great majority, based their action upon what they chose to regard as eternal principles of human rights as expressed in the Declaration of Independence; that the people are the source of all political power, and possess the inalienable right to alter their form of government when it ceases to promote the objects of its creation. All united in denying the existence of a consolidated nation. They believed that sovereign and independent states had fought the Revolutionary War for the right to determine their own social and political institutions. They contended that the sacrifices of that war, in treasure and human life, were expended, not in the interest of a federal government, but "to vindicate and to establish community independence, and the great American idea that all governments rest on the consent of the governed, and that the people may, at their will, alter or abolish their government, however and by whomsoever instituted." [13] As one editor put it, "The right to change a government, or to utterly abolish it and to establish a new government, is the inherent right of a free people; and when they are deprived of that right they are no longer free—not a whit more so than the serfs of Russia or the down-trodden millions of Austria." [14]

Advocates of prompt separation included both those who favored separate state action and one group of coöperationists. During the early phases of the secession movement, up to and including the first week of January, 1861, those who opposed separate state secession were generally known as coöperationists. The term is a most confusing one, and requires explanation to be intelligible.

[13] Davis of Mississippi, Remarks in the Senate, December 10, 1860, *ibid.,* 29.
[14] *New Orleans Daily Crescent,* November 13, 1860.

In the aggregate, coöperationists desired a convention of delegates from all the Southern states to discuss the existing crisis and agree upon some line of action which would be acceptable to all; but in the motives which prompted their assumed position, there were at least three distinct groups, and it is not always possible to classify properly a particular individual. The first group was heartily in favor of immediate separation from the North, but honestly believed that a conference of all the slave states, followed by concerted action along definite and predetermined lines, held the possibility of greater success than did separate state action. "We intend to resist," said Posey in the Alabama convention. "It is not our purpose to submit to the doctrines asserted at Chicago; but our resistance is based upon consultation, and in unity of action, with the other slave states." [15] They believed that separate state action would give rise to a disunited South, and ultimately end in the destruction of the rights they sought to preserve; and that the only way to prevent civil war was to forestall attempted coercion by the demonstration of a united South.

The second group of coöperationists opposed immediate separation because they were more sanguine of the Northern attitude, and refused to relinquish hope of preserving the Union until the sentiment of the Northern people could be tested by presenting guarantees of Southern rights for their endorsement. They desired a conference of Southern states for the purpose of presenting a final ultimatum to the Northern states, to be followed by immediate separation unless satisfactory guarantees were given. Their plan was (1) for each state to hold a convention, draw up a compendium of grievances and pro-

[15] Smith, *op. cit.,* 27; see, also, Remarks by Clemens, *ibid.,* 28-29.

posed remedies, and send it to the governor of each state; (2) for the delegates of the Southern states to meet in convention, prepare an ultimatum, and send it to the governor of each Northern state, with the request that it be taken under consideration by a convention of the people; and (3) if the Northern people deliberately refused the demands thus made upon them, arrangements for a Southern confederacy should be completed, and separation consummated.[16]

A third group of coöperationists, although advocating a determined effort to secure a redress of grievances and guarantees against future aggression, would submit to the administration of the federal government by the Republican party until a positive act of aggression should be committed. Some in reality were in favor of no action whatever until the incoming administration should commit an overt act; but they realized the weakness of their position and advocated coöperative action in the hope that the delay necessary to effect concurrent action would permit sufficient time to elapse to prevent the entire movement.

Each of these positions was supported in part by the same arguments against immediate separate state secession, and for that reason only by the most careful analysis of the public utterances and subsequent action of any man can his proper position be determined. The important fact must be remembered, that actually men differed from each other only in the point of time and the conditions on which they would be willing to resort to arms in defense of Southern rights.[17]

[16] "Speech of Joseph W. Taylor at Eutaw, Alabama, December 1, 1860," in the *Republican Banner*, Nashville, December 25, 1860; Magoffin to Hale, December 28, 1860, in Smith, *op. cit.*, 384-389.
[17] This fact is clearly indicated by the following statements

Foremost among the arguments presented in support of a conference of Southern states was, that by no other procedure could Southern unity be preserved. The Southern states and the Southern people were united by a community of interests arising from the institution of slavery; not because all classes shared in the social and economic benefits of the institution, but because they dreaded the social equality and racial conflict which would immediately follow emancipation. On the other hand, every one realized that the establishment of an independent Southern confederacy, while insuring the perpetuation of the institution of slavery, would give rise to other questions of public policy with regard to which there was no such unanimity of sentiment. A feeling existed in the states of the upper South, without substantial evidence, that the planting interests intended to force the reopening of the

from leading newspapers of each of the three political parties: "The parties in the South were contending with one another for possession of the Government. They were not contending about Lincoln's government. . . . The mass of the supporters of Bell and Douglas never did sanction the ultra federal doctrines, and the idea of submission to a sectional government, whatever some of the leaders may have done." *Richmond Semi-Weekly Examiner*, November 16, 1860. "We began our career with the recommendation of Breckinridge or Hunter for the Presidency; defended Douglas from falsehood, supported him and our own Johnson from a sense of duty and party obligation . . . never endorsed the Territorial views of Douglas or doubted the right of secession; stood pledged to abide by the vote of our section. . . . Why should not Southern rights men of 1850 and Douglas men of 1860 rally now to this movement which looks to independence out of the Union?" *The Daily Constitutionalist*, Augusta, December 5, 1860. "We regret to see any attempt to create the impression that there is a division of opinion at the South. The Union ought to be preserved, if possible. Every opportunity ought to be given the misguided men of the North to recede from their intention to put the South under the ban of political and social inferiority. . . . If they still persist, and the issue is precipitated upon us, Governor Moore ought to know that the Southern supporters of Bell and Everett will be as true as his own party in their own defense." *New Orleans Daily Crescent*, October 18, 1860.

African slave trade. The reopening of that trade, it was estimated, would reduce the value of slaves by one third to one half and ruin the slave-producing business of the upper South. The loss would fall heaviest, of course, upon the slave owner; but in a state such as Tennessee, where the taxable value of slave property exceeded $100,000,000, it did not require a shrewd economist to see that ultimately this loss in the aggregate wealth of the state must be distributed, by taxation and the increased difficulty of earning a living, among the poorer, non-slaveholding classes as well.

There was also a diversity of sentiment over the question of free trade; and in this instance the division was not upon social lines. Free trade, while no doubt beneficial to the cotton planter, would be injurious to the sugar planter of Louisiana, to the infant industries of Georgia, Louisiana, Tennessee, and Virginia; and would necessitate the raising of revenue by direct taxation, which in some sections would increase the taxes as much as an estimated five hundred per cent.[18] Aside from these questions of future public policy, there was the question of possible war with the North. In case the incoming administration refused to acknowledge the independence of those states which might withdraw from the Union and attempted to assert its authority over them, armed conflict was an absolute certainty. The states of the upper South would suffer most from a civil war, and they urged that, if they were to fight for Southern independence, they must first be heard. Louisiana was in the midst of a period of prosperity never before equaled in the history of the state. Before 1860, the commerce of New Orleans

[18] The *Republican Banner*, Nashville, December 4, 1860; *The Daily True Delta*, New Orleans, November 20, 1860; Edwin H. Ewing to Alexander H. Stephens, November 28, 1860, in the *Republican Banner*, November 29, 1860.

had steadily increased, doubling regularly every ten years, until one half of the total exports of the Union passed yearly through that port; including $100,000,000 in cotton, $25,000,000 in sugar, and $40,000,000 in other raw products. Economic interests indissolubly bound that state to those of the West and North. From those states, Louisiana dreaded to sever her political connections, and whatever else was done, the Mississippi River must be kept open to free and unrestricted commerce. Conscious of the value of their geographical location, they feared that, in a confederacy of Southern states, they would be forced to contribute toward the elevation of the cities of the Atlantic coast to an artificial rivalry with New York. Furthermore, if the federal government attempted to coerce the South by forcible collection of the revenue, New Orleans would be the first to suffer, being open to attack by no less than five routes from the Gulf and from the upper Mississippi.

What was true of Louisiana was equally true of virtually every other Southern state in some degree; and justice and prudence alike demanded that all the states possessing a community of interests should be consulted in whatever action might be taken.[19] Accordingly, those who believed that the Southern states must eventually assert their independence but opposed separate state action, opposed it because they wished to combine every possible element of strength on the side of the South, and because they wished to prevent individual states from adopting an isolated position.

In the second place, they favored coöperative action in

[19] "Speech of Joseph W. Taylor at Eutaw, Alabama," in the *Republican Banner*, Nashville, December 25, 1860; Edwin H. Ewing to Alexander H. Stephens, December 3, 1860, in *ibid.*, December 4, 1860; Magoffin to Hale, December 28, 1860, in Smith, *op. cit.*, 386; Houston to Calhoun, January 7, 1861, *Official Records . . . Armies*, Series IV, Vol. I, 72-76.

order that a Southern confederacy, when formed, might be respectable in numbers and resources and fully able to take care of itself. Slavery was peculiar to the South, and the only hope of its preservation against the assaults of Northern and foreign foes alike lay in the fact that fifteen states sanctioned it and were willing to assert their combined power for its protection. No one state, separate and independent of the rest, would long be able to preserve its institutions.[20] The Southerners were well aware that hostility to slavery was not confined within the limits of the Northern states. It is true that some of them hoped for a recognition of their independence by Great Britain, but they hoped for it in spite of her pronounced anti-slavery proclivities, and because they expected her material needs to overcome her humanitarian ideals.

Not all Southerners were hopeful of cotton being the determining factor in foreign relationships. The triumph of anti-slavery sentiment in England over the cherished ideal of colonial self-determination and in the face of subsequent ruin and desolation in the West Indies, stood as immutable evidence that no single Southern state which set itself up as the champion of slavery need expect any assistance from that quarter. Secretary of War Floyd, writing to Nathaniel Tyler, editor of the Richmond *Enquirer,* December 1, 1860, said:

[20] "The Constitution of the United States recognizes and protects slavery. . . . Hence, for years, the Abolitionists have hated and cursed the Constitution of the United States, because that alone stood in the way of their fiendish purposes. . . . Dissolve this Union on the slave line, let all the Northern States become a united anti-slavery power, aiding and abetting instead of restraining and overawing the abolitionism of Europe, and where would American slavery be?" *Louisville Daily Journal,* January 26, 1861. See, also, *Republican Banner,* Nashville, January 26, 1861; *The Daily Picayune,* October 31, 1860; and Speech of Joseph W. Taylor at Eutaw, Alabama, in *Republican Banner,* December 25, 1860.

The South can never count upon the friendship of England and of her tolerating evils not her own; once within the reach of her power, she will fix upon us forever the very badge of inferiority which we are ready to destroy the Union for. To sacrifice the interests of a class, or even to starve to death a few hundred thousand of her subjects in what she considers a laudable task, will constitute a very small obstacle in her policy. It is a fatal error to suppose that the interests of England would prompt her to foster the planting interests of the South. It is known that the Prince Consort sat silently by and witnessed the deliberate insult of the American Minister, Mr. Dallas, by a British Peer, before the congregated intelligence of all Christendom, simply because slavery existed in the United States. There is not an Englishman who does not in his heart abhor slavery, if he does not also abhor the country where it exists. England will have margin enough to supply her wants in cotton.[11]

The second group of coöperationists were in favor of delaying secession until every possible hope of preserving their constitutional rights within the Union was exhausted. They agreed with the immediate separationists in refusing to acknowledge a federal administration along the lines of the Chicago platform, and consequently scorned the idea of quietly acknowledging Republican control of the federal government until some positive act of aggression should be committed. They denied, however, that the immediate resumption of independence by separate state action would be any remedy for past grievances. Separation from the Northern states would not blot out remem-

[11] Floyd to Tyler, December 1, 1860, in the *Republican Banner,* Nashville, December 8, 1860. How substantially correct this prophecy was may be seen from the confidential letter of Yancey, who, while in London as the agent of the Confederate States, gave as one of the reasons for his failure to secure recognition, "The anti-slavery sentiment is universal. 'Uncle Tom's Cabin' has been read and believed." Yancey to Reid, July 3, 1861, in Letters and Papers of William L. Yancey.

brance of the long-continued campaign of vilification and the often repeated imputations of moral turpitude, nor bring about a change in the hearts of the Northern people; it would not remove the personal liberty laws from the statute books, nor render more certain the return of fugitive slaves; it would not open the territories to the slaveholder, nor provide any other relief from the danger of relative slave increase. On the contrary, the disruption of the Union would relieve the exponents of anti-slavery fanaticism of all constitutional restraints, and give rise to a continued crusade against the institution. Separation was not resistance to the control of the federal government by the Republican party, but simply withdrawal from its consequences. In the last analysis, it would be submission to that party, and a surrender without a struggle of Southern equity in the territories, navy, and other more intangible but none the less valuable interests; and that was a sacrifice which this group of coöperationists was not prepared to make. They favored, therefore, a convention of delegates from each of the Southern states, for the formulation of specific guarantees which they would be willing to accept in the nature of amendments to the federal constitution. If, after having exhausted every possible method of securing guarantees of their constitutional rights, the Northern people continued adamant, they favored immediate Southern independence.[22]

Governor Magoffin of Kentucky sent to the governors of the slave states on December 9, 1860, an urgent request for a conference of Southern states, and the following

[22] Claiborne F. Jackson to General Shields, December –, 1860, in Smith, *op. cit.*, 406-408; R. M. Stewart to A. B. Moore, December 30, 1860, *ibid.*, 411-412; Magoffin to Hale, December 28, 1860, *ibid.*, 386-387; Governor Letcher to Virginia Legislature, January 7, 1861, in *The New Orleans Bee*, January 12, 1861; *The Daily Picayune*, New Orleans, October 31, 1860.

propositions as a possible basis for constitutional amendments: (1) the repeal of all laws in the free states which nullified or otherwise obstructed the execution of the fugitive slave law; (2) compensation to slave owners for slaves lost through obstruction placed in the way of their recovery; (3) the forced surrender by one state to another of fugitives from justice; (4) the division of the territories on the 37th parallel; all south of that line to eventually be created into slave states and all north into free states; (5) a guarantee of the free navigation of the Mississippi River to every state; and (6) power to be given to the South in the Senate to protect itself from oppressive anti-slavery legislation.[23] Other men spoke of additional and slightly different guarantees, of which non-interference with slavery in the District of Columbia, the right of the slaveholder to pass through all states and territories with his slaves, and non-interference with the interstate slave trade were most frequent.

The third group of coöperationists, those who opposed secession until some further act of aggression should be committed, contended that no immediate danger threatened the South. They argued that Lincoln was not an abolitionist; that he was not in harmony with the extremists of his party; and that, if he possessed the courage to abide by his expressed convictions, no serious consequences would follow his inauguration. They further maintained that even if he wished to encroach upon the South, he would be unable to do so, because majorities in both branches of Congress would be against him.[24] By

[23] Magoffin, "Letter to the Governors of the Slave States," in the *Nashville Union and American*, December 16, 1860.
[24] Ex-Governor Neill S. Brown to A. Milman, A. C. Beech, E. Cunningham, W. S. Cheatam, and others, December 10, 1860, in the *Republican Banner*, Nashville, December 13, 1860; Robert

an analysis of the Lincoln vote they arrived at the conclusion that the political success of the Republican party
would not be repeated. One third of his vote they held to
have come from men who would welcome the immediate
cessation of the slavery agitation, but had been influenced
in the previous election by their opposition to the Democracy. Of the remaining two thirds, they declared, not
more than one half were so anti-slavery in sentiment as
to be willing to adhere to their avowed purposes when
presented with the probable disruption of the Union.[25]

They claimed that the South had many friends at the
North who had steadfastly defended their constitutional
rights at all times; that the conservative reaction, then in
progress, would add to this number a great class of people
represented by the Everetts, the Cushings, the Winthrops,
the Dickinsons, the Douglases, and others; and that hasty
action, in the nature of secession or retaliatory legislation,
would force these people, through self-preservation, to
unite with those who favored coercive action in maintaining the integrity of the federal Union.[26]

---

A. Barrow to William Creevy, H. E. Castellanos, J. Dunlap, and
others, December 10, 1860, in *The Daily True Delta*, December 16,
1860. The estimated strength of the Republican and combined opposition parties in the Thirty-seventh Congress, as compiled by the
opponents of immediate secession, was as follows:

|  | Senate | | House | |
|---|---|---|---|---|
|  | Republi-cans | Opposi-tion | Republi-cans | Opposi-tion |
| Elected ........... | 24 | 30 | 99 | 54 |
| To be elected....... | 5 | 7 | 9 | 75 |
| Opposition majority.. | 8 | | 21 | |

[25] Bell to Burwell, December 6, 1860, in the *Republican Banner*, Nashville, December 8, 1860; "Speech of Joseph W. Taylor at
Eutaw, Alabama," in *ibid.*, December 25, 1860.

[26] Magoffin to Hale, December 28, 1860, in Smith, *op. cit.*, 386-
387; Edwin H. Ewing to Alexander H. Stephens, December 3,
1860, in the *Republican Banner*, Nashville, December 4, 1860; Houston to Calhoun, January 7, 1861; *Official Records . . . Armies*, Series
IV, Vol. I, 72-76.

To this argument, the immediate separationists replied that Lincoln was a politician, who had by his reticence and mental reservations successfully disguised his true position; that he would be unable to resist the pressure of the extremists, even though he might wish to do so; and that, although temporarily handicapped by opposition majorities in Congress, the defeat for reëlection of at least six conservative senators at the North, including Pugh of Ohio and Fitch of Indiana, did not augur well for the future. They acknowledged the existence of many conservative Northern men, but said Hale, "They are utterly powerless, as the late Presidential election unequivocally shows, to breast the tide of fanaticism that threatens to roll over and crush us. With them it is a question of principle, and we award to them all honor for their loyalty to the Constitution of our fathers. But their defeat is not their ruin. With us it is a question of self-preservation—our lives, our property, the safety of our homes and hearthstones—all that men hold dear on earth is involved in the issue." [27]

Believing, however, that the election of Lincoln was not a true indication of the sentiments of the Northern people on the slavery question, and that the elevation of the Republicans to power in the federal government was but temporary, the most conservative group of Southern men sought to delay the disruption of the Union until future events should justify revolutionary action. They did not believe that secession was a constitutional right, nor that it was a reserved right of the states. They may, however, be properly regarded as members of the state-

[27] Hale to Magoffin, December 27, 1860, in Smith, *op. cit.*, 380; see, also, Remarks by Brown of Mississippi, Benjamin, and Pugh in the Senate, December 10, 1860, *Cong. Globe*, 36 Cong., 2 Session, I, 33–44; and *The Daily Picayune*, New Orleans, January 19, 1861.

rights school of political thought. They agreed that, in case of dispute between a state government and the federal government, neither Congress nor the Supreme Court was the final arbiter. They endorsed the exercise of state interposition; but they did not concede to the state the right of determining its own measures of redress. Neither Congress nor a state, but the people of the United States, speaking through their delegates to a national convention, should render the ultimate decision in case of dispute. Here was a case where the Republican party, recently elevated to power in the federal government, claimed the right to Congress of abolishing slavery in the territories. That claim was denied by every slaveholding state in the Union. Where was the remedy? They held that Congress must abandon its claims or secure their confirmation by constitutional amendments; and that by no other means could despotism on the one hand, or hopeless confusion and a disruption of the Union on the other, be avoided. They regarded it as the solemn duty of Congress, therefore, in December, 1860, or of the several state legislatures, to provide for a national convention as soon as it became apparent that amendments of such nature as to relieve the situation could not be secured in the usual manner. The Union, to them, was too precious to be sacrificed at the altar of fanaticism, passion, or prejudice. It was not a partnership in a material sense alone, and its dissolution would be accompanied by evils commensurate with the blessings it had dispensed. Civil war, if not immediate, would eventually follow dissolution; and civil war would mean fraternal strife, servile insurrection, destruction of life and property, business depression, oppressive taxation, misrule, and military tyranny. "It would wrench apart the tenderly entwined affections of millions of hearts, making it a crime in the North to have been born in the South, and a crime in the South to have been born in the North," and destroy a spiritual heritage obtained through many generations which rightfully belonged to the millions yet to be born.[28]

Among those who favored separate state action, the Alabama commissioners expressed a fortright opinion that the Constitution forbade united action but did not prohibit separate state secession.[29] Others—Yancey, Pettus, and Rhett followers—believed separation absolutely essential for the preservation of Southern institutions, and chose separate state action as the plan most likely to succeed. Coöperation necessitated delay; and the more complete the Southern organization by March 4, the less the possibility of attempted coercion. South Carolina and Mississippi had tried, early in 1860, to bring the states into line for coöperative action and had failed. They now planned to secure immediate separate state secession in one or more states, following which the remaining states would be forced to choose between seceding with friendly states or remaining under a hostile government, and perchance, assisting in coercion.[30] The latter contingency

[28] *North Carolina Standard,* Raleigh, July 11, 1860; *Republican Banner,* Nashville, December 18, 1860; *The Daily Herald,* Wilmington, December 11, 1860; *Richmond Semi-Weekly Examiner,* December 14, 1860; *The Daily True Delta,* New Orleans, November 23, 1860.

[29] Curry to Hicks, December 28, 1860, in Smith, *op. cit.,* 401; A. B. Moore to Elmore, Phelan, Pettus, and others, November 14, 1860, in *ibid.,* 409-411; Clopton to Burton, January 1, 1861, *Official Records . . . Armies,* Series IV, Vol. I, 34-38.

[30] The work of the interstate commissioners presents unmistakable evidence that the leaders of the movement had so analyzed the situation. See Elmore to Moore, January 5, 1861, *Official Records . . . Armies,* Series IV, Vol. I, 20. Curry and Pugh to Brooks, January 10, 1861, *ibid.,* 46-47; Harris to Pettus, December 31, 1860, *Journal of the Mississippi State Convention . . . 1861,* 197.

would be certain to minimize opposition in the states of the upper South.

This policy, however, presented one major difficulty. Southern unity must be preserved and jealousies and mistrust among the states avoided. The problem was how to proceed on the basis of separate state secession, yet at the same time secure concurrent action and a free interchange of opinion. The governors of Alabama and Mississippi solved the problem by the appointment of interstate commissioners and, when the practical value of the plan became apparent, conventions in other states followed their example.[11]

These commissioners received their appointments previous to the assembling of any convention in a Southern state and, together with those from South Carolina and Georgia, constituted the diplomatic service of the secession movement. They went to every slave state to urge governors to convene extra sessions of the legislatures, to influence legislatures to provide for conventions, to advocate secession before conventions and, where necessary, before the people in state-wide canvasses. They supplied the governors of their respective states with valuable information on the status of public opinion in those states to which they were accredited. They received dispatches from headquarters concerning the general state of affairs elsewhere, and presented them to the authorities of those

[11] The legislature of Mississippi, November 30, 1860, instructed Governor Pettus to send commissioners to each slave state, using his own judgment as to the number to be sent. Governor Moore appointed commissioners to each slave state upon his own responsibility, but with the knowledge and urgent request of many prominent men of the state. See Legislature of the State of Mississippi, "Resolutions providing for the Appointment of Commissioners," in *Journal of the Public and Secret Proceedings of the Convention of the People of Georgia . . . 1861*, 318; and Commission of John Gill Shorter as State Commissioner from Alabama, in *ibid.*, 308.

states in which they were working. Briefly, while many men were urging a conference of states for coöperative action, the commissioners were effecting coöperation without conference and its attendant danger of delay. Through their efforts, each state was able to secede as soon as public opinion was ready for it; and public officials and conventions were constantly aware of conditions in other states. In the seven states of the lower South, they were largely bearers of dispatches and organizers of a confederacy. They added to those important functions, in the states of the upper South, a final effort to convince the people that the preservation of Southern institutions and Southern independence were inseparable.

Alabama and Mississippi were prevented by untoward circumstances from initiating the secession movement, and by the same circumstances South Carolina was thrust into the position of nominal leadership. This situation was generally recognized in the South at the time.[32] Following the Harper's Ferry incident, the legislatures in these two states had appropriated funds for military purposes.[33] Alabama, anticipating by nearly a year the election of a Republican President, had instructed Governor Moore in that event to order an election of delegates to a state con-

[32] Shorter to Brown, January 3, 1861, *Official Records . . . Armies,* Series IV, Vol. I, 16; McQueen, "Address Before the Texas Secession Convention, February 1, 1861," in *Journal of the Secession Convention of Texas,* 50-52; A. P. Calhoun, "Address to the Alabama Convention, January 8, 1861," in Smith, *op. cit.,* 31.
[33] In his message to the legislature, January 14, 1861, Moore reported that during the year he had purchased with the appropriation 9,000 stand of small arms, 10 brass rifled cannon, 2 columbiads, 20,000 pounds of lead, 20,000 pounds of powder, and 1,500,000 caps. Moore to House of Representatives, *Official Records . . . Armies,* Series IV, Vol. I, 47-52. Sixty-five companies of militia were organized in Mississippi during the ensuing year, but few arms were purchased. Attorney General Sykes to Governor Pettus, January 18, 1861, *ibid.,* 61-68.

vention.[34] Governor Moore was an ardent secessionist but a tenacious constitutionalist, and he withheld his proclamation until after a majority of the electoral votes had been cast for Lincoln, thus delaying action in that state by nearly a month.[35] Doubtless, his devotion to constitutional form, like that of the Alabama commissioners, was strengthened by the exigencies of the secession program. A few weeks' delay did much to soften the bitterness of the presidential canvass and, considering the rapidity with which secession sentiment gained ground, may have been the determining factor in the ultimate action of the state convention.

Unlike Alabama, Mississippi had attempted, in conjunction with South Carolina, to secure a conference of Southern states following the Harper's Ferry incident; and had made no provision for a state convention. The next regular session of the state legislature was to begin on the first Monday of January, 1861. It was necessary, therefore, for Governor Pettus to convene an extra session of that body in order to secure authorization for a convention. He had received meanwhile an admonition from Governor Gist of South Carolina not to ask "for a Southern Council, as the Border and non-acting States would outvote us and thereby defeat action." [36] At his invitation, the Mississippi congressmen met with him at Jackson, recommended the immediate secession of the state,

[34] "Joint Resolutions of the Alabama Legislature, February 24, 1860," in Smith, *op. cit.,* 9-10; Shorter to Brown, January 3, 1861, *Official Records . . . Armies,* Series IV, Vol. I, 15-17; *Weekly Mississippian,* Jackson, November 7, 1860.

[35] In his proclamation as eventually issued he named December 24 as the date for the election and January 7, 1861, for the assembling of the convention. See Moore to Elmore, Phelan, Pettus, and others, in Smith, *op. cit.,* 13-17.

[36] Gist to Pettus, November 8, 1860, *Official Correspondence of Governor John J. Pettus, 1859-1860.*

and requested that South Carolina be urged to make her ordinance of secession effective immediately upon passage.[37] An immense mass meeting of men from all political parties met at Jackson, November 13, and adopted a series of resolutions endorsing the proclamation of Governor Pettus, advocating resistance to the administration of the federal government by the Republican party, and pledging support to any state against which coercive measures might be attempted.[38] The legislature passed, unanimously and without debate, a bill providing for a convention on January 7, 1861,[39] and a series of resolutions urging separate state secession by all slave states.[40]

Of all the states in 1860, South Carolina was the only one in which the presidential electors were still chosen by vote of the legislature. That body, having cast the vote of the state for Breckinridge, decided to remain in session until the result of the election should become known. The action was regarded by all as an indication that a state convention would be called in event of Lincoln's election, and an attempt was made by the conservative members to postpone action by adjourning to the next regular session. Public sentiment, however, was too strong, and the first, in fact the only, show of resistance met defeat. The night preceding this decision by the legislature, a great mass meeting was held at Charleston. Senator Chestnut, Barnwell Rhett, Ex-Governor Adams, and Governor Gist spoke, and each advocated immediate

[37] Davis, *Recollections of Mississippi and Mississippians*, 390-392.
[38] "A Union of Parties in Mississippi for the Sake of the South," in *Weekly Mississippian*, November 21, 1860.
[39] "Mississippi Convention Bill, November 29, 1860," in *Journal of the . . . Proceedings of the Convention of the People of Georgia . . . 1861*, 312-314.
[40] "Resolutions of the State of Mississippi, declaring Secession to be the proper Remedy for the Southern States," in *Weekly Mississippian*, December 5, 1860.

separate state secession. The populace was enthusiastic, and apparently there were few conservative men in the state. Writing to Governor Pettus the following day, Gist said: "If your Legislature gives us the least assurance that you will go with us, there will not be the *slightest difficulty,* and I think we will go out at any rate." [41] It was the desire of the South Carolina leaders that Mississippi should secede first, but the legislature was not in session in that state and could not act for some time. In the meantime anything might happen, with the conservative men both North and South grasping at every possible hope of compromise. South Carolina's legislature was in session, a convention could be called quickly, and the movement would be under way. The situation was ideal, and from every side South Carolina was urged to act at once. The legislature, therefore, ordered an election for December 6. The delegates were to assemble in convention at Columbia on December 17. During the interval, the Mississippi and Alabama commissioners received their appointments.

Three days before the South Carolina convention assembled, John A. Elmore, commissioner from Alabama, arrived at Columbia. He was followed the next day by C. E. Hooker, commissioner from Mississippi, and shortly thereafter by Henry Dickinson, commissioner from Mississippi to Delaware, J. W. Garrott, commissioner from Alabama to North Carolina, by Governor Perry of Florida, and by many other men of prominence from all parts of the South. Elmore and Hooker had both been instructed to advise secession on the part of South Carolina without waiting for other states to act. Their headquarters at the

[41] Gist to Pettus, November 6, 1860, Official Correspondence of Governor John J. Pettus, 1859-1860.

hotel became the meeting place for a free interchange of opinion. They interviewed practically every man of prominence in the legislature and the assembling convention. They freely guaranteed the secession of Mississippi and Alabama, and disseminated the already widely accepted opinion "that the only course to unite the Southern States in any plan of coöperation which could promise safety was for South Carolina to take the lead and secede at once from the Federal Union without delay or hesitation. . . ." [42] On the evening of the first day of the convention, Hooker and Elmore addressed the body in public session. Hooker declared the right of the people to abolish a government which had exceeded its authority as beyond dispute. The issue had passed the stage of argument as indicated by the calm and unanimous manner in which the Mississippi legislature had provided for her convention and for commissioners to other states. Formerly, the leaders of Mississippi had hoped that South Carolina, Texas, Louisiana, Mississippi, Georgia, and Alabama might act simultaneously, but since accidental circumstances had caused South Carolina's convention to assemble in advance of the other states, to delay action now would "have a tendency to throw a damper upon the South and Southwest." [43]

An epidemic of smallpox having broken out in Columbia, the convention adjourned to Charleston; and on Thursday, December 20, the ordinance of secession was passed by a unanimous vote. There was nothing elaborate about the ordinance itself; it simply repealed the act

[42] E. W. Pettus to A. B. Moore, December 12, 1860, in Smith, op. cit., 420-422; Elmore to A. B. Moore, January 5, 1861, Official Records . . . Armies, Series IV, Vol. I, 19-22.
[43] Hooker, "Address before the South Carolina Convention, December 17, 1860," Journal of the Mississippi State Convention . . . 1861, 174; The Charleston Mercury, December 19, 1860.

of May 23, 1788, by which South Carolina had ratified the Constitution, repealed all acts ratifying amendments to the same, and declared the union between South Carolina and other states dissolved. After the ordinance was passed, South Carolina was declared by the president, D. F. Jameson, to be an independent sovereignty, and the convention proceeded to the organization of her government as such.

Meanwhile, a resolution providing for the sending of commissioners to each slave state was adopted by the convention. The commissioners to Alabama, Mississippi, Louisiana, and Arkansas were elected on January 2, 1861. No one received a majority of the votes cast for the missions to Georgia and Texas, and those commissioners, together with those to Florida and North Carolina, received their appointments at a later date.[44] The commissioners were instructed to proceed to the states to which they were accredited and present a copy of South Carolina's ordinance of secession to the highest constituted authorities of such states. They were to offer, to such states as might secede, the Constitution of the United States as a basis for a provisional government in the formation of a Southern confederacy. The committee on relations with slaveholding states, in recommending the existing constitution as a workable basis for a provisional government, declared it to be the work of master minds and sufficient as to details if interpreted honestly and administered impartially. Many people of the South held a veneration for the instrument, were familiar with its provisions, and would feel safe under it as construed by the South. The committee further felt that no better in-

[44] *Journal of . . . the Convention of the People of South Carolina . . . 1861*, 36-37, 103-104.

strument could be devised in the short time allowed by circumstances for the formation of a provisional government. They felt that it would allay any suspicions of selfish designs on the part of South Carolina; and believed that Europe would regard such a form of government as "competent to produce a prompt organization for internal necessities, and a sufficient protection of foreign commerce." [45] The commissioners met in Charleston the day following their appointment, and agreed upon the first Monday in February as a date to propose to other states for holding the Southern convention. [46]

The first step in the movement for Southern independence and the formation of a confederacy had been accomplished with but little opposition. Meanwhile, the legislatures in Georgia, Florida, and Louisiana had provided for state conventions.

The Georgia legislature assembled in regular session at Milledgeville, November 8, 1860. Governor Joseph E. Brown recommended retaliatory legislation against the Northern states. His plan was for the legislature to enact laws authorizing the seizure of property of any citizens of states responsible for loss incurred by Georgia's citizens, and provide a tax of 25 per cent on all goods from states which refused to repeal their unfriendly legislation. He believed that this procedure would strengthen rather than weaken the Union by destroying the sectional controversy and narrowing the issue to a contest between states. He defended the right of peaceable secession, and expressed the opinion that if the Southern states would meet in convention and withdraw as a unit there would

[45] Convention of South Carolina, *Report and Resolutions from the Committee on Relations with Slaveholding States.*
[46] A. P. Calhoun, "Address to the Alabama Convention, January 8, 1861," in Smith, *op. cit.,* 33.

be no war. He urged the legislature to call a convention as soon as it was ascertained that the Republicans had won the presidential election, and asked for an appropriation of $1,000,000 for military purposes.[47]

Excitement in the state was intense, but the legislature was far from unanimous on any course of procedure.[48] Alexander H. Stephens, his brother, Linton Stephens, Benjamin Hill, and Herschel V. Johnson were the foremost leaders against separate state action. Senator Robert Toombs, T. R. R. Cobb, and Governor Joseph E. Brown were their most powerful antagonists. The contest in the legislature reached its climax in the struggle between Toombs and Stephens over the question of immediate secession or delay and coöperation. Toombs addressed an assembly of the two houses on November 13, advocating immediate action. It was a magnificent defense of Southern rights. He believed that the Northern people had subverted the fundamental principles of the federal government, and closed the door to all compromise and conciliation; that the ultimate object of the Republican party, foreshadowed by many acts of hostility, was the abolition of the institution of slavery; and that guarantees from men who had already violated their plighted faith to uphold the Constitution were worthless.[49] The following day Stephens delivered one of the greatest speeches

[47] Governor Joseph E. Brown, "Message to the Legislature of Georgia," in the *Weekly Mississippian*, November 21, 1860; see, also, Fielder, *A Sketch of the Life and Times and Speeches of Joseph E. Brown*, 168-169.

[48] The political classification of the two houses of the legislature was uncertain, but on joint ballot the Constitutional Democrats had approximately 200; the Constitutional Unionists, 80; and the Douglas Democrats, 25.

[49] "Speech of Hon. Robert Toombs delivered before the Legislature of Georgia," in the *Daily Missouri Republican*, December 20, 1860.

of his career in answer to Toombs. He did not deny the right of secession, but hoped that it would not be necessary. His plan was to call a state convention, coöperate with the other Southern states in attempting to secure a repeal of the unfriendly statutes of the Northern states, and resist the first unconstitutional act of the incoming administration. Stephens was standing upon the Georgia platform; and the difference between Toombs and himself was not essential so far as the action of the legislature in calling a convention was concerned. Toombs wanted immediate action, and was quite willing to have the legislature take the state out of the Union. Stephens felt that there was no immediate danger, because Congress would be controlled by the opponents of Lincoln; that there was some slight hope of adjusting the difficulties; and, above all, that whatever action was taken should be by a state convention. Stephens had faith in a convention; Toombs was afraid of it.[50] Three days later the legislature definitely decided upon an aggressive policy, and appropriated $1,000,000 to arm the state. At the same time it passed an act providing for an election, January 2, of delegates to meet in convention on January 16, 1861. The act gave to the convention the power "to consider all grievances impairing or affecting the equality of rights of the people of Georgia as members of the United States, and to determine the mode, measure, and time of redress." [51]

In none of the other states of the lower South was there any difficulty in securing provision for state conventions except in Texas, where the refusal of Governor

[50] "Speech of Hon. A. H. Stephens, delivered in the Hall of the House of Representatives of Georgia, Wednesday Evening, November 14, 1860," in the *Daily Missouri Republican*, November 26, 1860.
[51] "The Georgia Convention Bill," in the *Weekly Mississippian*, November 28, 1860.

Houston to convene the legislature forced extra legal procedure on the part of the secessionists.[52]

The program outlined and put into operation by the governors of Alabama, Mississippi, and South Carolina created actual working majorities of immediate separate state secessionists in all of the cotton states, and left little for the opposition to contend for except methods of procedure. Sanguine of something being accomplished in Congress, they urged that secession ordinances be made effective as of March 4, or that they be submitted to the people for ratification. They were not seeking by dilatory tactics to prevent Southern action. That point can scarcely be overemphasized. They were seeking a sense of security with respect to persons and property, the loss of which in the Union was responsible for the existing agitation at the South, and without which no new government could long survive. The action of South Carolina was regarded by many as overhasty, perhaps eccentric, but as a typical manifestation of the prevailing sentiment in the cotton states.

[52] For the attitude of Houston, see Crane, *Life and Select Literary Remains of Sam Houston of Texas*, II, 60. The details of the method by which a convention was secured are given in *Journal of the Secession Convention of Texas, 1861*, 9-14.

# CHAPTER VIII

## FIRST EFFORTS AT COMPROMISE

WHEN Congress assembled on December 3, 1860, many believed there was still a possibility of saving the Union. The country was in the midst of political revolution; and American statesmanship was confronted with the task of restoring internal peace to a nation split asunder over the question of the rights of slavery under the Constitution.

The majority of the people in the lower South had despaired of securing definitive amendments to the Constitution and were preparing to assert the sovereignty of their states and withdraw from the Union. Some of them had faith in the ultimate success of a new nation. Thousands believed it the only possible method of assuring an adjustment of the difficulties and looked to a future reconstructed Union on what they believed to be sound principles of equity and justice.[1] They wanted peace, but

[1] *The New Orleans Bee,* January 10, 1861, said: "Among the advocates of secession it is safe to say there are many thousands who believe that the decided position assumed by the South is the only practicable means left of bringing the free States to a recognition of our rights and of their constitutional obligations. It is thought that when once the act of separation will have been consummated by a large segment of the South, the North will be thoroughly convinced of its past errors; that an overpowering popular reaction will occur; that Black Republicanism will be overthrown, and that

they were reconciled to the horrors of war if there were no escape from it. Their entire position on this point was summed up by Benjamin in the last trying days at Washington when all hope of compromise was gone:

We desire, we beseech you, let this parting be in peace. I conjure you to indulge in no vain delusion that duty or conscience, interest or honor, imposes upon you the necessity of invading our States or shedding the blood of our people. You have no possible justification for it. I trust it is in no craven spirit, and with no sacrifice of the honor or dignity of my own state, that I make this last appeal, but from far higher and holier motives. If, however, it shall prove vain, if you are resolved to pervert the Government framed by the fathers for the protection of our rights into an instrument for subjugating and enslaving us, then, appealing to the Supreme Judge of the universe for the rectitude of our intentions, we must meet the issue that you force upon us as best becomes free men defending all that is dear to man.

What may be the fate of this horrible contest no man can tell, none pretend to foresee; but this much I will say: the fortunes of war may be adverse to our arms; you may carry desolation into our peaceful land, and with the torch and fire you may set our cities in flames . . . but you never can subjugate us; you never can convert the free sons of the soil into vassals, paying tribute to your power; and you never, never can degrade them to the level of an inferior and servile race. Never! Never! [2]

Men of this mind controlled the seven states of the lower South. They refused to make advances in Congress. They considered themselves the representatives of sovereign states and believed in the right of a sovereign state to judge the extent of its grievances and determine the

the people of the free States will, with one accord, invite the South to reconstruct the Union upon a satisfactory basis of immutable constitutional guarantee." See, also, *ibid.*, December 22, 1860.
[2] *Cong. Globe*, 36 Cong., 2 Sess., I, 217.

nature of redress. The states which they represented having provided for conventions to consider their future
status in the Union,[3] they declared that it would be im-
politic as well as impossible to state in advance the nature
of guarantees which would be deemed acceptable. They
expressed a willingness to transmit to their constituents
any proposals for compromise the North chose to offer,
but further than that they refused to go.[4]

Others favored a final effort to secure an assurance of
safety for their institutions by constitutional methods,
through an appeal to the representatives of the Northern
people. They constituted the minority in the remaining
slave states, in which they were likely to become a majority at any time; and they included in their number such
statesmen as Stephens and Johnson of Georgia, Soulé of
Louisiana, and governors Ellis of North Carolina, Letcher

| [3] State | Convention Bill Passed by Legislature | Date of Election of Delegates | Date Conventions Were to Assemble |
|---|---|---|---|
| Alabama ........ | Feb. 24, 1860 | Dec. 24, 1860 | Jan. 7, 1861 |
| South Carolina ... | Nov. 10, 1860 | Dec. 6, 1860 | Dec. 17, 1860 |
| Georgia ......... | Nov. 18, 1860 | Jan. 2, 1861 | Jan. 16, 1861 |
| Florida ......... | Nov. 28, 1860 | Dec. 18, 1860 | Jan. 3, 1861 |
| Mississippi ...... | Nov. 29, 1860 | Dec. 20, 1860 | Jan. 7, 1861 |
| Texas .......... | Dec. 3, 1860 | Jan. 8, 1861 | Jan. 28, 1861 |
| Louisiana ....... | Dec. 11, 1860 | Jan. 7, 1861 | Jan. 23, 1861 |

[4] Davis, Remarks in the Senate, December 5, 1860, *ibid*, 12;
Clingman, Remarks in the Senate, December 3, 1860, *ibid*, 4; Singleton, Jones, Clopton, Miles, and Gatrell, Remarks in the House of
Representatives, December 4, 1860, *ibid*., 7. They were supported
in this attitude by a large portion of the Southern press. The *Richmond Semi-Weekly Examiner*, January 22, 1861, said: "The appeal
for a compromise committee in Congress came from the wronged
and endangered South. It was granted, and that and every successive
proposal for adjustment coming from the South lowered the tone, we
think misrepresented the purpose of the Southern people, and rendered the achievement of Southern security more precarious, if not
impossible. Not one of those plans should have come from the South
as a matter of policy." See, also, *The New Orleans Bee*, December
21, 1860.

of Virginia, Magoffin of Kentucky, Harris of Tennessee, and Jackson of Missouri.

Still others, regarding the Republicans as a Northern minority and as disposed to adopt a pacific attitude during the crisis, were in favor of remaining in the Union until —and this was their ultimatum—the incoming administration attempted to subjugate any state which had interposed its sovereignty in defense of its constitutional rights. Bell of Tennessee, Morehead of North Carolina, Tyler of Virginia, and Breckinridge of Kentucky were among their number.

United with these two groups of Southerners in an effort to secure some sort of definitive amendments to the Constitution as a means of saving the nation from dismemberment was a large portion of the Douglas Democrats of the Northwest, represented by Douglas, McClernand, and Logan of Illinois, Fitch of Indiana, and Pugh and Vallandigham of Ohio. As a party they had nothing to lose and much to gain by assuming the leadership in urging conciliation. Their political fortunes were on the decline. Many of them had been defeated at the last election and others were in line for defeat at the next election. A successful consummation of their efforts at compromise would have placed them in a strategic position and shattered the party organization of their chief opponents.

At the other extreme were the Republicans, equally as reticent as the Southern-rights men, though probably for a different reason. They were, in December, 1860, without a well-defined policy and lacked stability in party organization. Having but recently won the presidential election, not yet in control of the national government, and recognized as a sectional and minority party, they sought to avoid any action tending toward dissension and disintegration within the party. To admit the moral right of the Southern demands for constitutional safeguards would have been a tacit admission of party designs against Southern institutions. No man, not even Lincoln, was established firmly enough as a party leader to be able to define party policies, other than to express surprise at the unusual political excitement. Unhappily, irresolution in the crisis constituted a definitive attitude, because the party controlled the legislatures of the Northern states; and because in Congress the adoption of constitutional amendments depended upon its active support. Congress was powerless to act unless the Republicans were willing to have it do so. Likewise, the people of the free states were powerless to register their sentiments on the question of compromise, unless they gave their approval to the calling of state conventions.

Constitutional amendments were imperative as the only means of quieting the tense political situation; and whether they were to be secured in the usual manner or through the medium of a national convention the coöperation of the Republican party was essential. By this method alone the sense of the people relative to the existing controversy could be secured. The strongest argument of those Southerners who opposed secession was that the principles of the Republican party were neither the principles of the majority of the Northern people, nor of the people of a majority of the states. The question was, would the people, with whom all sovereignty rested, be allowed to speak in the crisis. Proposed amendments in Congress presented an opportunity of ascertaining the willingness of the Republican party to define its position.

Men of all parties and from all sections of the country urged immediate action. Herschel V. Johnson, vice presidential candidate on the Douglas Democratic ticket, and opponent of immediate secession in Georgia, said that any one was laboring under a great delusion who thought that the South was divided on the question of submitting to a federal administration along the lines of the Chicago platform. He predicted that unless the personal liberty laws were immediately repealed, and the claims to Congress of the power to prohibit slavery in the territories and the interstate slave trade were abandoned, no power on earth could save the Union. He said further: "The great mass of the Southern people believe in the right of secession, and they will not receive patiently its negation by the Federal Executive." He pleaded for the Northern legislatures to take some immediate, positive action toward repealing their obnoxious laws, and for Lincoln or some one authorized to speak for him to disclaim all "intention to use the power of Congress against slavery anywhere, under any pretext, for any purpose. . . . Lincoln would not violate the dignity of his position, nor act unworthy a patriot and statesman, by making or causing the announcement above suggested even before his inauguration. The emergency is great. The peril to the Government imminent. The interests at stake are incalculable." [5]

Cobb of Alabama said in the House of Representatives, December 11, "If anything is to be done to save my State, it must be done immediately. . . . My prayer is that something may be done by which that State may remain in this Union upon constitutional and equal principles. I am not a secessionist. I desire peace. But, sir, I desire

[5] Herschel V. Johnson to August Belmont, November 27, 1860, in *Daily Missouri Republican*, St. Louis, December 12, 1860.

that my State may be awarded her rights under the Constitution." [6]

Ex-Governor Neill S. Brown of Tennessee, leader of the most conservative party of the state, declared that "if the people of the United States have so far lost their love of country that they could not, in a spirit of conciliation, adopt such amendments, or any amendments necessary to heal the present breach and restore harmony, then indeed may it be truly said that the Union cannot be preserved, and is not worth preserving." [7] Senator Crittenden declared that if the members of Congress had not come to Washington in a spirit susceptible to solemn consideration of the disturbing questions before the country, they were not fit for the positions they occupied. [8] Senator Powell of the same state emphatically stated that "every impulse of honor, duty, and patriotism demands that we, without delay, exhaust every constitutional means within our power to restore harmony and quiet the country, and preserve a wise and just Constitutional Union." [9]

Dixon, Republican senator from Connecticut, regarded further crimination and recrimination as dangerous; asserted that "if it be possible, the first thing should be to restore the fraternal spirit which once existed, ought to exist, and may still exist"; and declared that he knew no other way to do it except "by cheerfully and honestly assuring to every section of the country its constitutional rights. No section professes to ask more; no section ought

[6] *Cong. Globe*, 36 Cong., I, 59.

[7] Ex-Governor Neill S. Brown to A. Milman, A. C. Beech, E. Cunningham, W. S. Cheatam, and others, December 10, 1860, in the *Republican Banner*, Nashville, December 13, 1860.

[8] Crittenden, Remarks in the Senate, December 4, 1860, *Cong. Globe*, 36 Cong., 2 Sess., I, 5.

[9] Powell, Remarks in the Senate, December 10, 1860, *ibid.*, 24.

to offer less." [10]  Senator Pugh of Ohio maintained that ninety-nine hundredths of the people of the entire country "are anxious this day to redress all outrages and all causes of reasonable complaint"; that if the American people could not arrange their difficulties in a satisfactory manner there was no hope for mankind anywhere; and that if South Carolina "cannot be retained by the bonds of affection, or, if estranged, cannot be brought back to us by the arts of kindness, why, then, in God's name—horrible as I esteem such an alternative—let her depart in sorrowful silence." He favored a convention in each state, followed by a national convention, "in order, if possible, to lay more deeply, more broadly, and, I trust, more wisely, the foundation of our common liberty and security and happiness." [11]

Douglas urged the members of the Senate to lay aside party feuds until they had saved the country.[12]  Sickles of New York asserted that "the Southern representatives on this floor cannot, if they would, no matter what personal sacrifices they may deem it their duty to make, arrest the movement which has already enlisted the support of the great masses of the Southern people . . . the responsibility of dealing with the existing state of things and the power to deal with it effectively rest alone on the Republican leaders. . . . Let the representatives of the aggressive States at the other end of the Capitol and here speak to their people. Let the legislatures of the Northern States be convened and let them act." [13]  The *Missouri Republican* declared that Lincoln could do more than any other

[10] Dixon, Remarks in the Senate, December 10, 1860, *ibid.,* 32.
[11] Pugh, Remarks in the Senate, December 10, 1860, *ibid.,* 34.
[12] Douglas, Remarks in the Senate, December 10, 1860, *ibid.,* 28.
[13] Sickles, Remarks in the House of Representatives, December 10, 1860, *ibid.,* 40.

man to quiet the country if he would but recommend the repeal of the personal liberty laws and assure the South of pacific intentions.[14] Vallandigham of Ohio was indefatigable in his efforts to avert a disruption of the Union. "The time is short," said he, "the danger imminent; the malady deep-seated and of long standing. Whatever is to be done must be done at once, and it must be done thoroughly. . . . Let there be no delays, no weak inventions, no temporizing expedients. Otherwise, not secession of a few States only, but total and absolute disruption of this whole Government is inevitable." [15]

The central theme of the President's message was that the Union could and ought to be saved by peaceable methods. He denied the right of the Southern states to justify resistance on any ground but the right of revolution, which "ought to be the last desperate remedy of a despairing people, after every other constitutional means of conciliation had been exhausted." He denied, likewise, the right of the federal executive or of Congress to make war upon the people of any state, holding that the Union was based upon public opinion, and that "if it cannot live in the affections of the people, it must one day perish. Congress possesses many means of preserving it by conciliation, but the sword was not placed in their hands to preserve it by force." Explanatory amendments to the Constitution, definitely settling the disputed points, ought to be adopted by Congress or by a national convention called for that purpose; and Congress and the state legislatures should assume the responsibility of restoring peace and harmony between the states. As to the nature of the amendments which should be adopted, he suggested: first,

[14] The *Daily Missouri Republican*, November 15, 1860.
[15] Vallandigham, Remarks in the House of Representatives, December 10, 1860, *Cong. Globe*, 36 Cong., 2 Sess., I, 38.

a recognition of the right of property in slaves in the several states where it existed; second, provision for the protection of slavery in the common territories; and third, recognition of the right of the slave owner to the restoration of fugitive slaves, together with a definite statement of the unconstitutionality of the personal liberty laws.[16] The message was suited admirably to the exigencies of the moment, but was criticized severely by the extremists of both sections.[17] For Buchanan to have asserted the right of the executive department to precipitate civil war, when the predominant sentiment of the country was believed to be in favor of pacification, and previous to the assembling of Congress and the state legislatures upon whom the responsibility of effecting peaceable adjustment rested, would not only have been a lack of statesmanship, it would have been sheer madness. Whether there was a possibility of preserving the Union by peaceable means no man certainly could know, and no one can yet say positively because of the mass of conflicting testimony. The people of those states about to assert their independence had refrained wisely from armed collision with the federal government. They did not want war, and war was inevitable if the federal government assumed an aggressive attitude.

In the House of Representatives a resolution of Boteler of Virginia was adopted on the second day of the session, providing a special committee of one from each state to consider that part of the President's message relating to the critical situation. The vote on the adoption of this resolution and the appointment of members to the com-

[16] Buchanan, Fourth Annual Message to Congress, December 3, 1860, *ibid.*, II, Appendix, 1-7.

[17] See the *Richmond Semi-Weekly Examiner*, December 7, 1860, for a hostile Southern attitude.

mittee were ample evidence of what was to be expected. The resolution was adopted by a vote of 145 to 38. The thirty-eight votes in opposition were all Republicans.[18] It is true that the great majority of the Republicans voted for it; but that is not a criterion for judging their attitude toward conciliation. The committee, appointed by a Republican Speaker, included four members who had voted against it: Tappan of New Hampshire, Morse of Maine, Howard of Michigan, and Washburn of Wisconsin. It was, moreover, placed under the chairmanship of Corwin of Ohio, whom the Southerners had thoroughly distrusted since the days of the Mexican War, and whose state delegation had been conspicuous in the vote against creating the committee. Furthermore, wherever it was possible, Republicans were placed upon the committee. Sixteen members of that party were appointed, to the exclusion of the Northern Douglas Democrats, though that party had voted solidly for the committee. The Bell men were given only two places on the committee, and, wherever possible, Southern representation was accorded the Douglas supporters, who were out of harmony with the vast majority of the people in that section. The committee was provided to expedite the framing of a program of possible conciliation, and to eliminate further dissension which would be certain to follow debate in the committee of the whole. Its labors would be worthless if its report were not acceptable to the House. Expediency demanded that its composition be such as to unite all parties, and especially to insure a report upon which the conservative elements of the country might unite. Vallandigham of

[18] The vote against the committee by states was as follows: Ohio 10, New York 8, Pennsylvania 5, Michigan 3, Wisconsin 2, Massachusetts 2, Connecticut 2, Illinois 2, Maine 2, Indiana 1, New Hampshire 1; *Cong. Globe,* 36 Cong., 2 Sess., I, 6.

Ohio most ably said: "If the gentleman from Ohio, the chairman of this committee, would do anything effectively to correct public sentiment in our common State, it is to the two hundred and ten thousand men, not of his own party, together with such others of that party as he may be able to carry over with him, that he is to trust for the vindication of such measures, if any, of conciliation and adjustment which his committee may propose, and the House and the Senate may adopt." [19]

The immediate and most disastrous result was that, while some Southerners regarded it as a mere expedient to gain time and disorganize the South, others accepted it as an indication that the Republicans never would accede to measures of conciliation.[20] Hawkins of Florida and Boyce of South Carolina refused to serve upon the committee after the House had refused them the usual courtesy of being excused upon request.[21] The Republicans were, therefore, in complete control of the committee, and they converted it into a graveyard for every proposal of compromise and conciliation introduced into the House of Representatives.[22]

In the Senate, acrimonious debate was precipitated immediately over that part of the President's message relating to the right of the federal government to assert forcibly its authority in a seceding state. The proceedings during the first three weeks of December present a dreary debate upon the intricacies of constitutional law, while the authority of the federal government was crumbling,

[19] Vallandigham, Remarks in the House of Representatives, December 10, 1860, *ibid.*, 38.
[20] Hawkins, Remarks in the House of Representatives, December 10, 1860, *ibid.*, 36.
[21] *Ibid.*, 22-23.
[22] For the many proposed amendments buried in committee, see *ibid.*, 76-79.

the Union was being disrupted, and conservative men were pleading for peace and conciliation. The Republicans sought to confine all discussion to the question of employing forcible measures to preserve the Union. Hale of New Hampshire foreshadowed the party attitude on the third day of the session when, in debate with Iverson of Georgia, he said the existing state of affairs "looks to a surrender of that popular sentiment which has been uttered through the constituted forms of the ballot-box, or it looks to open war." [23]

Powell of Kentucky introduced into the Senate, December 6, a resolution to submit to a special Committee of Thirteen that part of the President's message dealing with the disturbed condition of the country, with power to offer any recommendation it might think necessary for federal legislation or constitutional amendments. [24] Repeated efforts were made on the part of the Republicans to defeat the resolution, and it was not until December 18 that the committee was finally agreed upon. Upon that committee were placed Senators Powell and Crittenden of Kentucky; Powell, because he was the author of the resolution, and Crittenden because he had devised the most sensible and acceptable scheme for adjusting the sectional dispute by constitutional amendment. Hunter of Virginia completed the representation from the states of the upper South. Toombs of Georgia and Davis of Mississippi represented that party of the South which favored immediate Southern independence. Douglas of Illinois, Rice of Minnesota, and Bigler of Pennsylvania represented the Northern opposition to Republicanism. Seward of New York, Wade of Ohio, Collamer of New Hampshire, Doolittle

[23] Hale, Remarks in the Senate, December 5, 1860, *ibid.*, 9.
[24] *Ibid.*, 19.

of Wisconsin, and Grimes of Iowa represented the Republican party. It was a well-balanced committee both from the standpoint of geographical distribution, political principles, and public leadership.

The Committee of Thirty-three did not meet until December 11, and the Committee of Thirteen did nothing definite until December 22. Meanwhile, Johnson of Tennessee and Crittenden of Kentucky had introduced into the Senate important groups of joint resolutions. The Johnson resolutions, introduced on December 13, proposed the following constitutional amendments: (1) election of United States senators by direct popular vote; (2) division of the several states into electoral districts equal in number to the congressional representation of each state, each of which should cast one vote for President and Vice President; (3) provision for a second election between the two candidates receiving the highest number of votes, in case no one received a majority vote in the first election; (4) choice of the President from the Northern states and the Vice President from the Southern states in 1864, alternating every four years; and (5) division of the Supreme Court into three classes, one third to retire every four years, and each class to be equally divided between the North and South.[25]

Crittenden introduced his famous proposed amendments together with resolutions relative to additional congressional legislation on December 18. The leading provisions of the Crittenden proposals were those which had to do with slavery in the territories. This had been first submitted to the Committee of Thirty-three on December 12 by Nelson of Tennessee and Taylor of Louisiana.

[25] *Ibid.*, 82-83. These resolutions were referred to the Committee of Thirteen and were never brought to a vote either in committee or in the House.

Nelson proposed that the territories be divided along the line of 36 degrees and 30 minutes; that slavery be forever prohibited in the region north of that line; that it might exist, and should be protected by congressional legislation in the region south of that line, so long as it remained under territorial governments; and that, when any new state should be created in the Southern region, the inhabitants thereof should continue or abolish slavery as they might choose. Taylor proposed that the citizens of the several states should be allowed to carry into the territories every species of property recognized by the states from which they came, and be secured in the enjoyment of it until such time as state constitutions were framed preparatory to admission into the Union. Other amendments proposed by Nelson and Taylor would prohibit Congress from interfering with the interstate slave trade and with slavery in the District of Columbia. Each proposed an amendment to allow Congress to provide compensation to slave owners for property lost because of any nullification of the fugitive slave law. Nelson proposed that the President and Vice President should come from opposite sides of the 36 degree 30 minute parallel. Taylor submitted an amendment limiting the franchise to members of the Caucasian race. Whiteley of Delaware suggested extending the presidential term to eight years and the choice of electors by congressional districts. By a solid Republican vote all consideration of these and kindred constitutional amendments was postponed in the committee until December 27; and at that time Nelson substituted the Crittenden proposals for his own.[26]

Meanwhile, every proposition contained in the Critten-

[26] *Journal of the Committee of Thirty-three,* 3-9.

den amendments had been defeated in the Committee of Thirteen, Collamer, Doolittle, Grimes, Seward, and Wade voting against them in their entirety.[27] The same members then voted against resolutions tendered by Crittenden endorsing the right of the slaveholder to the return of his property and recommending the repeal of all state laws nullifying the fugitive slave law. A resolution to amend the fugitive slave law in such manner as to eliminate features objectionable in the North was unanimously adopted, as was a resolution recommending a thorough enforcement of the laws prohibiting the foreign slave trade.[28] On the following day, Douglas placed before the committee a series of proposed amendments which in substance embraced the Crittenden program except for the question of the territories. His proposal was (1) that the status of slavery in all existing territories should remain unchanged until the time of the formation of state constitutions; (2) that no new territory should be acquired except by treaty, two thirds of each House concurring, and the status thereof in respect to servitude remaining as at the time of acquisition; (3) that the area of all new states should be as nearly uniform as possible, not less than sixty thousand nor more than eighty thousand square miles; and (4) no new state to be admitted with less than fifty thousand inhabitants.[29] Again the Republican members voted against every proposition and Douglas's plan was discarded.[30] Crittenden's proposals, submitted to the Committee of Thirty-three by Nelson, met a similar fate and all hope of Congress agreeing upon any substantial measures of adjustment was gone.

[27] *Journal of the Committee of Thirteen*, 4-6.
[28] *Ibid.*, 7.
[29] *Ibid.*, 8-11.
[30] *Ibid.*, 16-17.

Having failed in their efforts to secure the adoption of constitutional amendments by Congress, the conservative forces directed their attention to securing a national convention, and to preventing a collision between the armed forces of the federal government and those of the Southern states until a convention could be assembled. After two weeks of silence on their part, broken only by occasional and noncommittal remarks necessary to defer the adoption of the Powell resolution, the Republican senators had assumed an aggressive attitude on December 17. Wade of Ohio delivered on that day an address which was published in every Southern newspaper of importance, and which did more to advance the cause of immediate secession than any other event thus far in the session.[81] He stated that he had not even been aware of any unusual discontent or political excitement until he reached Washington. He was certain that the complaints against the personal liberty laws had no basis in fact; that there was not a single principle in the Chicago platform injurious to Southern rights; and that whatever apprehensions existed among the Southern people arose from unwarrantable prejudice and nothing else. He knew of no just grievance, and the day of compromise was past. The people had rendered a verdict upon the question of slavery, and "it would be humiliating and dishonorable to us

---

[81] The following editorial comment of *The New Orleans Bee*, December 25, 1860, is typical of the Southern reaction: "Now, Mr. Wade echoes the opinions of Seward, and Sumner, and Chase, and Trumbull, and King, and the whole host of Black Republicans in and out of Congress. They have no idea whatever of receding. They know that such a policy would be suicidal, and they will risk the integrity of the Union rather than shatter their own organization into fragments. Besides, they are fanatics, and fanaticism never reasons. The Black Republicans declare through Senator Wade that the day of compromises is past, and that it is absolutely ridiculous to talk about them. He is right in more than one sense."

if we were to listen to a compromise by which he who has the verdict of the people in his pocket should make his way to the presidential chair. . . . I know not what others may do; but I tell you that, with the verdict of the people given in favor of the platform upon which our candidates have been elected, so far as I am concerned, I would suffer anything to come before I would compromise that away." He denied the right of secession, and plainly intimated that the incoming administration would enforce the federal jurisdiction in any state which attempted to secede. Resistance would place the Southerners in a position of making war upon the government and subject them to punishment for treason. Not satisfied with stating his unwillingness to join in measures of compromise, he remarked that South Carolina was "a small State; and probably, if she were sunk by an earthquake today, we would hardly ever find it out, except by the unwonted harmony that might prevail in this chamber." [2] The Senate immediately adjourned and, on the following day, the Powell resolution was adopted, Crittenden introduced his famous compromise measures, and Lane of Oregon presented a resolution providing for a national convention.

Lane's resolution also requested the Southern states to meet first in convention to determine the nature of guarantees necessary to their security and peace, and instructed the executive department of the federal government to refrain from all acts of violence against the aggrieved states, even to the extent of withdrawing the military forces from the Southern forts, if necessary. [3] The resolution was referred to the Committee of Thirteen where

[2] Wade, Remarks in the Senate, December 17, 1860, *Cong. Globe*, 36 Cong., 2 Sess., I, 99-104.
[3] *Ibid.*, 112.

it was never brought to a vote. A similar proposal, presented by Burch of California, was defeated by a vote of 13 to 16 in the Committee of Thirty-three, every Republican except Corwin of Ohio voting against it.[34]

Whatever hope had existed early in December of arresting the secession movement in the lower South had virtually disappeared.[35] The first prerequisite to the adoption of any plan of conciliation was to admit that the Southern people did have grievances in fact, and that there was a real cause for the distracted condition of political affairs, arising from the apprehensions of further aggression by the incoming administration. This the Republicans refused to admit.

Those who favored conciliatory measures contended that the issue before the American people in December, 1860, was not the same issue which they had been called upon to decide during the presidential campaign. They emphasized the fact that at least ten million citizens, representing a tremendous majority in seven states and a powerful minority in as many more, regarded the results of the election as a direct threat against their future

[34] *Journal of the Committee of Thirty-three,* 39.
[35] "A dissolution of the Federal Union cannot be prevented. South Carolina is gone already! There was but one hope that others would not follow her; and the refusal of the Black Republicans in Congress to make any concessions to the wronged and greatly aggrieved South, the many indications that the dominant party intend to continue their unholy attacks on slavery and the slave States, the war tone of the friends of the President elect throughout the country, have blasted that almost ere it was born." The *Daily Courier,* Louisville, December 27, 1860. "In the face of this deep and ominous agitation of the whole South . . . nothing has yet been done or offered by the ruling minds of the North in the cause of reconciliation to quiet alarms or restore peace. The population grows wilder and the movement rises and spreads, and the master chiefs of the dominant section are dumb, or only speak so as to give new provocations to the excited and new discouragements to the moderate." *The Daily Picayune,* December 27, 1860. See, also, *The New Orleans Bee,* February 6, 1861.

security, and intended to interpose the authority of their state governments for protection. The three alternatives were before the remaining portion of the people: (1) to provide, by legislative enactments and constitutional amendments, guarantees of the rights of a powerful minority sufficient to allay the apprehensions of the Southern people; (2) to arrange for a peaceable separation of the Union; or (3) to withhold all guarantees, refuse to permit a separation of the states, and plunge the nation into civil war. They denied that those issues were decided in the November election. It might well be, although it was extremely doubtful, that a majority of the people in a majority of the states concurred in an endorsement of the slavery provisions of the Chicago platform, when presented with the alternative of endorsing popular sovereignty or congressional protection. It was not certain that, one month later, or at any earlier time, they would have demanded adherence to that platform even to the extremity of subjugating the Southern people by force of arms.

Those who favored conciliation believed that, if the controlling group of Republican congressmen were certain that the Chicago platform represented the principles of the people, they should have been willing to call a national convention; and that, if they had no intention of seizing upon the opportunity presented to initiate a destructive war against the Southern people, they would not have assumed such inflexible hostility toward all the innumerable proposals designed to prevent war. Douglas summarized their analysis of the situation when he said:

For the purpose of removing the apprehensions of the southern people, and for no other purpose, you propose to amend the Constitution, so as to render it impossible, in all future time, for Congress to interfere with slavery in the States where it may exist under the laws thereof. Why not insert a similar amendment in respect to slavery in the District of Columbia, and in the navy-yards, forts, arsenals, and other places within the limits of the slaveholding States, over which Congress has exclusive jurisdiction? Why not insert a similar provision in respect to the slave trade between the slaveholding States? The southern people have more serious apprehension on these points than they have of your direct interference with slavery in the States.

If their apprehensions on these several points are groundless, is it not a duty you owe to God and your country to relieve their anxiety and remove all causes of discontent? Is there not quite as much reason for relieving their apprehensions upon these points, in regard to which they are more sensitive, as in respect to your direct interference in the States, where they know and you acknowledge that you have no power to interfere as the Constitution now stands? The fact that you propose to give assurance on the one point and peremptorily refuse to give it on the other, seems to authorize the presumption that you do intend to use the powers of the Federal Government for the purpose of direct interference with slavery and the slave trade everywhere else, with the view to its indirect effects upon slavery in the States, or, in the language of Mr. Lincoln, with the view of its "ultimate extinction in all States, old as well as new, north as well as south."

If you had exhausted your ingenuity in devising a plan for the express purpose of increasing the apprehensions and inflaming the passions of the southern people, with the view of driving them into revolution and disunion, none could have been contrived better calculated to accomplish the object than the offering of that one amendmert to the Constitution, and rejecting all others which are infinitely more important to the safety and domestic tranquillity of the slaveholding States.

The Republican congressmen denied any intention of making war upon the states which might assert their independence, but insisted that the revenues must be collected and the delivery of the mails sustained. Pugh replied that it was not of the slightest consequence whether they called it "coercion, or collecting the revenue, or defending public property, or enforcing the laws; you know, and I know, that it means war; and that war will follow it." [86]

The action of the Republicans in steadfastly opposing all plans of conciliation brought forward and earnestly endorsed by such eminent men as Crittenden, Douglas, Pugh, and others stimulated the secession movement. Viewed from the standpoint of the Southerners this refusal to do anything to restore harmony and friendly relations between the sections, combined with the evident intention to discountenance the right of Southern independence, was especially irritating. Many Southerners believed that the party had carried the election because of the division in the ranks of their opponents; that their elevation to power rested upon accidental circumstances and not upon popular endorsement of their principles; and that the party leaders knew it, and dared not appeal to the people for an endorsement of their position. The refusal to allow the various amendments to the Constitution to be reported from the congressional committees that they might be discussed in open debate, and the refusal to call a national convention substantiated that interpretation of the Republican attitude. Those Southerners, therefore, who had urged that the secession movement be delayed until an opportunity could be presented to the Northern people of defining their attitude, rapidly became secessionists because they believed the Northern people would never be given an opportunity to speak in the

[86] Pugh, Remarks in the Senate, December 20, 1860, *Cong. Globe*, 36 Cong., 2 Sess., II, Appendix, 33.

crisis.[37] The attitude of Hale, Wade, and other Republican congressmen left no ground for the leaders of the minority in the lower South to stand upon. Stephens, Johnson, Taylor, and others like them were attempting to stem the tide of secession, not because they denied that right, but because they believed the immediate secessionists had incorrectly judged the strength of the radical Republican party in the Northern states; because they believed that if secession could be delayed, guarantees of Southern rights would be granted. Had the Republicans, therefore, deliberately sought the most efficient method of furthering the secession movement they could have found none better than their refusal to listen to methods of conciliation, and the haste with which they threatened South Carolina and other states which might follow her with violence. It was a course which, from the very start, crystallized Southern sentiment, broke down all differences of opinion, and united the two great parties in the lower South. While conservative Southern men were exerting every effort to delay immediate action, the Republicans in the North were fighting the battle for the unconditional secessionists.

On the other hand, it must be remembered that the Crittenden proposals were the most moderate emanating from the South. Their adoption by Congress, unless

[37] *The New Orleans Bee,* January 16, said: "We believe that with the possible exception of a few of the New England States, there is not a non-slaveholding Commonwealth of which the people would not accept the Crittenden amendments by an overwhelming majority. Give them but a chance to do so, and our firm conviction is that they would record a sentence of condemnation against Black Republicanism such as it has never received. We are, however, fully convinced that the adversaries of the South will not lend their countenance to any project of ascertaining the will of the people, simply because they are certain in advance of utter discomfiture. They dare not plead their cause before a tribunal from which they would be expelled with ignominy and scorn."

accompanied by a manifestation of approval from the people, would have been interpreted as a concession made on the basis of expediency; and the Southern people were determined to accept nothing less than substantial proof that anti-slavery agitation would not be revived with the passing of the crisis.[38] There were Southerners who believed that slavery would expand to the territories if granted the same protection as other property, and there were some who subscribed to the positive good argument; but it was as a speculative idea upon morals, principles, and the theoretical ideal of state equality that the territorial question loomed large. The Charlottesville *Review,* leading anti-secession paper of Virginia, reached the heart of the issue when it said: "There is a habit of speaking derisively of going to war for an *idea*—an abstraction—something which you cannot see. This is precisely the point on which we would go to war. An idea is exactly the thing that we would fight for. . . . The people who will not fight for ideas will never retain the spirit to fight for anything. Life loses its highest meaning, when opinions become matters of indifference. . . . Therefore, we say, for this *idea* of State honor—for this abstract principle of not bating her just claims upon threat of coercion—we would convulse this Union from centre to circumference." [39] The fact that this was typical of the attitude of conservatives in the upper South makes it extremely doubtful if a compromise of the territorial question would have been accepted. The lower South would not have

[38] *The Daily Picayune,* New Orleans, December 4, 1860; *The Daily Herald,* Wilmington, N. C., January 7, 1861; *Daily Nashville Patriot,* February 19, 1860; *New Orleans Daily Crescent,* February 14, 1861; *The New Orleans Bee,* December 22, 1860; and the *Frankfort Commonwealth,* January 23, 1861.

[39] January 25, 1861. See, also, *The New Orleans Bee,* December 21, 1860.

agreed to constitutional amendments embracing the slavery question, unless additional governmental machinery had been devised giving to the South the exclusive control of the institution of slavery. Finally, no state, after having released its citizens from the authority of the United States Government, would have recognized an amended constitution as other than a basis of negotiation for a reconstruction of the Union; nor would any such have sent delegates to a national convention organized on any other basis than the principles of free consent.[40]

[40] *The Daily Picayune*, New Orleans, February 10, 1861; *Richmond Enquirer*, December 18, 1860.

# CHAPTER IX

## THE RESULT OF THE FIRST FAILURE
## AT COMPROMISE

IMPORTANT events occurred with greater rapidity during the three weeks subsequent to the failure of the Crittenden Amendments in the Committee of Thirteen than at any other period during the secession movement. There were elections in Georgia, Louisiana, and Texas. Conventions assembled in Florida, Alabama, and Mississippi. Three important transfers of federal troops were made: Anderson from Fort Moultrie to Fort Sumter, Slemmer from Barrancas Barracks to Fort Pickens, and Brannan from the mainland to Fort Taylor. The President's Cabinet was disrupted. The reinforcement of Forts Taylor and Jefferson was accomplished and the reinforcement of Forts Sumter and Pickens was attempted. The arsenals at Charleston, Chattahoochee, Mount Vernon, and Baton Rouge were seized by state troops, as were Forts Morgan, Moultrie, Jackson, St. Philip, Livingstone, and Pulaski, and the Pensacola navy yard.

From the beginning of the secession movement there had been an increasing concern over the ultimate disposition of federal property within the limits of the Southern states. As the movement progressed and it became apparent that at least six states would resume their sovereignty, the question of the forts and arsenals became acute. Most

171

of them were in a mediocre state of repair and insufficiently garrisoned; but they contained war supplies of great value. The popular mind was excited. Vigilance committees, companies of minutemen, and home guards were being organized in virtually every locality of the slave states. Mob psychology recognizes no legal restraints, and the danger of irresponsible attacks upon the forts was serious enough to cause governors, mayors, and other executive officers grave concern. There was no clear indication of whether the idea of peaceable separation or that of coercion would gain ascendancy at the North, and until that was ascertained it was highly desirable to avoid a collision between the military forces of the federal government and state troops or irresponsible mobs.

Secession sentiment was as strong in many parts of the South as at Charleston, and in many places the populace was more susceptible to sudden disorder; but unfortunately Fort Sumter was a new fort nearing completion, and the strongest on the American continent. Until it should be ready for occupancy the garrison in Charleston harbor was stationed in Fort Moultrie and Castle Pinckney, both easy of attack from the mainland and near enough for a hostile garrison to destroy the city. The engineers found it difficult to retain reliable workmen at Fort Sumter, and the people of Charleston became excited at every evidence of increased activity at the fort. The garrison at Moultrie chafed under the delay and became more apprehensive with each new hostile demonstration. Acting upon the necessity of having responsible and prudent men in command during the crisis, the government placed Major Anderson in charge of the forts.[1]

[1] Cooper to Anderson, November 12, 1860, *Official Records . . . Armies*, Series I, Vol. I, 72; Special Order, No. 137, November 15, 1860, *ibid.*, 73.

Captain J. G. Foster of the Engineering Department was sent to undertake temporary defensive arrangements at Fort Moultrie and to promote vigorously the work of repairs on Fort Sumter.[2] Meanwhile Governor Pickens tendered a guard of state militia for the arsenal and the offer was accepted by the sergeant in charge.[3] Colonel Benjamin Huger was later sent by the federal government to take charge of the arsenal and the state guard was removed. This action on the part of the federal government at once diminished the popular excitement at that point.[4]

Anderson had been told at the time of his appointment that the policy of the government was to avoid a conflict with the people of the state, and that consequently no attempt had been made to increase the forces at Charleston. His instructions, as orally given and subsequently recorded, were to avoid every act which might provoke aggression; to assume no position "without evident and imminent necessity" which might be regarded as the assumption of a hostile attitude; but to retain possession of the forts, and if attacked to defend himself to the last extremity.[5]

President Buchanan was informed by the South Carolina congressmen, December 8, that in view of the prevailing excitement among the people of the state, any attempt to reinforce the forts would lead to an attack by a lawless mob. They expressed as an honest opinion, however, that the federal forces were in no danger of attack until after the state should secede and send commissioners to treat

[2] Foster to De Russy, November 14, 1860, *ibid.*, 73.
[3] Humphreys to Craig, November 12, 1860, *ibid.*, 72.
[4] Huger to Craig, November 20, 1860, *ibid.*, 74.
[5] Buell, "Memorandum of Verbal Instructions to Major Anderson, First Artillery, Commanding at Fort Moultrie, S. C." (December 11, 1860) in *ibid.*, 89-90.

with the government at Washington.[6] This opinion was substantiated repeatedly by the official reports from Anderson and Foster.

Nothing of importance occurred at Charleston until December 17 when Captain Foster removed forty muskets from the arsenal to Fort Sumter. The state convention was assembling in Columbia, and the removal created intense excitement in Charleston. Secretary of War Floyd ordered the arms returned and the incident might have ended had not Governor Pickens seized the opportunity to force the issue of a surrender of the forts to the state. He sent a special messenger to Washington with a confidential letter to Buchanan. Professing to believe that the forts were being prepared for warfare against the state, he urged that no further work be done, and that no reinforcements be sent. As a palliative for the public excitement, he requested that state troops be allowed to occupy Fort Sumter as had been done previously at the Charleston arsenal.[7]

Buchanan prepared an answer to this letter in which he stated that he had done and would continue to do everything in his power to prevent a collision, and for that reason had refused to send reinforcements to Charleston harbor; that his action had been prompted by repeated assurances that South Carolina would make no attack

[6] "Statement of Messrs. Miles and Keitt of what transpired between the President and the South Carolina Delegation," in *ibid.*, 125. Buchanan to Barnwell, Adams, and Orr, December 31, 1860, *ibid.*, 115-118.

[7] Anderson to Cooper, December 18, 1860, *ibid.*, 94-95; Foster to De Russy, December 18, 1860, *ibid.*, 95-96; Humphreys to Foster, December 18, 1860, *ibid.*, 96; Foster to Humphreys, December 18, 1860, *ibid.*, 97; Foster to De Russy, December 19, 1860, *ibid.*, 97-98; Foster to De Russy, December 20, 1860, *ibid.*, 100-101; Pickens to Buchanan, December 17, 1860, in Nicolay and Hay, *Abraham Lincoln: A History*, III, 2-3.

upon them previous to sending commissioners to treat with Congress; but that he possessed no power to surrender federal property and had not authorized the guarding of the arsenal by state troops. Realizing the seriousness of the situation created by this precipitate action of Governor Pickens, the South Carolina congressmen and Assistant Secretary of State Trescott intervened and secured the withdrawal of Pickens' letter, thus forestalling the necessity of a reply from Buchanan.

Two days after South Carolina passed her ordinance of secession, R. W. Barnwell, J. H. Adams, and James L. Orr were appointed as commissioners to negotiate with the government of the United States concerning the surrender of government property within the limits of the state, an apportionment of the public debt and division of the public property, and arrangements for future peaceable relations between the two governments.[8] The commission proceeded to Washington and obtained an interview with President Buchanan for December 27. Within a few hours, however, news from Charleston was received which terminated negotiations. Anderson had transferred his garrison from Fort Moultrie to Fort Sumter.

The transfer was regarded by South Carolina authorities as an act of war and state troops seized Fort Moultrie, Castle Pinckney, and the arsenal.[9] Buchanan maintained that this was an act of war against the federal government and refused to withdraw the forces from Charleston harbor. The South Carolina commissioners declared that the transfer was an unauthorized act on the part of Anderson, and that Buchanan was under obligation to disavow the

[8] "The State of South Carolina, by the Convention of the People of the said State, to Robert W. Barnwell, James H. Adams, and James L. Orr," in *Official Records . . . Armies,* Series I, Vol. I, 111.
[9] Pickens to Anderson, January 9, 1861, *ibid.,* 135.

act and reassure them of his good faith in the matter by removing the forces before they would continue their negotiations.[10]   Secretary of War Floyd, who was on the eve of dismissal for suspected complicity in the defalcation of a million dollars in Indian bonds, seized the opportunity to make a graceful escape by charging Buchanan with inconsistency, and the War Department was immediately placed under the jurisdiction of Postmaster General Holt.   Meanwhile, Buchanan had notified the South Carolina commissioners that he was willing to communicate to Congress any proposal which they might have to make with reference to future relations between South Carolina and the federal government; but that he possessed no power either to surrender federal property or recognize the dissolution of the Union.[11]

Momentarily, at least, Buchanan was forced to abandon his policy of pacification by the threatened disruption of his Cabinet.   In fact, to prevent the resignation of Black, he was forced to submit to having reinforcements sent to the Southern forts.[12]   The steamship *Star of the West* was loaded secretly with supplies and reinforcements and sent to Charleston harbor.   Orders were sent to Lieutenant Slemmer, who was in charge of the forts in Pensacola harbor, to coöperate with Commodore Armstrong at the Pensacola navy yard in preventing the seizure of the government posts at that place.[13]   Captain Brannan, in command at Key West barracks, was ordered to transfer his command to Fort Taylor and defend it to the

[10] Barnwell, Adams, and Orr to the President of the United States, December 28, 1860, *ibid.*, 109-110.
[11] Buchanan to Barnwell, Adams, and Orr, December 31, 1860, *ibid.*, 115-118.
[12] Auchampaugh, *James Buchanan and his Cabinet*, 160-172.
[13] Lay to Slemmer, January 3, 1861, *Official Records . . . Armies*, Series I, Vol. I, 334.

last extremity;[14] and a force of sixty-two men under the command of Major Arnold was ordered from Fort Independence to Fort Jefferson. Slemmer had anticipated an attempt to occupy the forts at Pensacola and had transferred his company and provisions from Barrancas Barracks to Fort Pickens, an almost impregnable island fortress which commanded the entrance to the bay. The order for Brannan to transfer his forces from the mainland to Fort Taylor did not reach him until January 26, but he had also acted upon his own responsibility and effected the transfer on January 14.[15] The apprehension of the government that an attack was to be made upon Fort Jefferson by an expedition from Charleston was without foundation. Arnold arrived at that post on January 18, and immediately strengthened its defenses with arms secured from Fort Taylor.[16]

The expedition to Charleston harbor failed because the South Carolina military forces fired upon the vessel and forced it to turn back.[17] Anderson immediately notified Pickens that, unless the act was disavowed by him, it would be regarded as a declaration of war; and that he would destroy any vessel of South Carolina which came within reach of his guns. Pickens replied that South Carolina had resumed her independence; that any attempt by the government of the United States to reinforce the

[14] Lay to Brannan, January 4, 1861, *ibid.*, 345.
[15] Brannan to Thomas, January 14, 1861, *ibid.*, 342; Brannan to Deas, January 15, 1861, *ibid.*, 343; Brannan to Thomas, January 31, 1861, *ibid.*, 344.
[16] Arnold to Thomas, January 19, 1861, *ibid.*, 345-346; Arnold to Thomas, January 23, 1861, *ibid.*, 346-347; Arnold to Cooper, January 18, 1861, *ibid.*, 346.
[17] For the various details concerning the expedition, see Scott, "Memorandum of Arrangements," in *ibid.*, 128-129; Thomas to Scott, January 5, 1861, *ibid.*, 131; Thomas to Woods, January 5, 1861, *ibid.*, 132.

troops at Fort Sumter or to resume possession of the other forts within the limits of South Carolina could be regarded in no other light than an attempt at coercion; that the *Star of the West* had been warned to stop by a shot fired across its bow and had disregarded the warning; and that Anderson must judge of his own responsibilities with regard to his threat to fire upon the vessels of South Carolina.[18]

The temporary departure of Buchanan from his previous policy cost him the confidence of the Southern people and accelerated the secession movement. They were fully conscious of the fact that he never had admitted the constitutional power of the people of a state, meeting in convention, to emancipate themselves from the authority of the federal government; and they regarded the sudden activity in the War Department as preliminary to attempted coercion. The news dispatches from Charleston and Washington so increased the popular excitement that only by prompt action on the part of the regularly constituted authorities could the precipitation of bloody collisions be averted. Moreover, the election of a secession majority to the Georgia convention removed any existing doubt concerning the secession of the Gulf states and the formation of a Southern confederacy. State conventions were to assemble in Florida on January 3, in Mississippi and Alabama on January 7, in Georgia on January 16, in Louisiana on January 23, and in Texas on January 28. Elections to the state conventions in the two latter states were to be held on January 7 and January 8, respectively. Prudence dictated that the deliberations of these conventions be free from the influence of the proximity of armed forces of the federal government; and self-preservation

[18] Pickens to Anderson, January 9, 1861, *ibid.*, 135-136.

demanded the removal of hostile forces after the resumption of state independence.[19]

The election of delegates to the Georgia state convention took place on January 2, and Governor Brown immediately ordered the occupation of Fort Pulaski by state troops. He then telegraphed to the governors of Florida, Alabama, Mississippi, and Louisiana concerning the action he had taken, urging them to do likewise. At ten o'clock that night two hundred Alabama troops quietly embarked at Mobile and proceeded to Fort Morgan. They took possession of the post at three o'clock the following morning, its only occupants being an ordnance sergeant and two laborers.[20] At the same time another detachment of state troops proceeded to Mount Vernon arsenal, forty-five miles north of Mobile, and occupied it before the garrison of seventeen men knew of their presence.[21] Florida troops took possession of the arsenal at Chattahoochee, of Fort Marion at St. Augustine, and of Fort Clinch at Fernandina on January 4, concurrently with the seizure of Fort Pulaski in Georgia and of Fort Morgan and Mount Vernon arsenal in Alabama. Because of the geographical location of Pensacola harbor, the reinforcement of the forts at that point was of more serious consequence to Alabama than to Florida. Moreover, the detachment of Florida troops in west Florida was too small to occupy and hold the forts at that point, and Alabama troops could reach them more quickly than troops from east Florida. Governor Perry, consequently, appealed to Gov-

[19] A. B. Moore to Buchanan, January 4, 1861, *ibid.*, 327-328.

[20] *The New Orleans Bee*, January 8, 1861; *The Daily True Delta*, January 6, 1861; Patterson to the Adjutant General, January 5, 1861, *Official Records . . . Armies*, Series I, Vol. I, 327.

[21] *The New Orleans Bee*, January 8, 1861; Reno to Maynadier, January 4, 1861, *Official Records . . . Armies*, Series I, Vol. I, 327.

ernor Moore to occupy those posts with Alabama troops.[22] The inability of the Alabama convention to arrive at a decision prevented immediate action, and Colonel Chase with his detachment of troops did not arrive at Pensacola until January 12.[23] Several hundred Alabama and Florida troops, under the command of Colonel Lomax, surrounded the navy yard at Pensacola on the morning of January 13. Commodore Armstrong surrendered without resistance and was allowed to depart on the revenue cutter *Wyandotte*. Two days later Chase demanded the surrender of Fort Pickens, with the understanding that Slemmer's command would be allowed to return to Barrancas Barracks, and that the fort would be returned to the federal government if the Union should be reconstructed.[24] The demand was refused, and no attempt was made to capture the fort although Mississippi troops had increased the Southern forces to more than seventeen hundred men. Mail deliveries and supplies continued to be received at the fort in the usual manner, and every effort was exerted by both commanders to prevent open hostilities.

On the morning of January 9 Colonel Pickett of the United States Army arrived in New Orleans on his way to assume the position of consul at Vera Cruz. He was the bearer of sealed orders for the commander of the naval squadron at that place; and rumors immediately spread through the city that the squadron was being ordered home for the purpose of blockading the city. On the same day telegraphic dispatches from Boston informed

[22] Maxwell and Perry to Watts, January 8, 1861, in Smith, *op. cit.*, 49; Moore to Brooks, January 8, 1861, *ibid.*, 52.
[23] For the debates in the Alabama convention on the expediency of sending troops outside the state, see *ibid.*, 50-74.
[24] Chase to Slemmer, January 15, 1861, *Official Records . . . Armies*, Series I, Vol. I, 337-338.

the people that the government at Washington had chartered the steamer *Joseph Whitney,* and that it was being loaded with troops and provisions at Fort Independence for reinforcing the forts off the coast of Florida.[25]  Mayor Monroe wired to Governor T. O. Moore that there was no longer doubt of the government's intention to reinforce the fortifications at Tortugas and strengthen the garrisons in the neighborhood of New Orleans. He added that if the forts below New Orleans were strongly garrisoned the commerce of the city could be completely destroyed and Louisiana forced into submission to the federal government; and he emphatically stated that excitement in New Orleans was so intense that only immediate occupation of the forts by state troops would prevent their seizure by irresponsible organizations.[26]  On the morning of January 10, Senators Benjamin and Slidell telegraphed to Daniel W. Adams, chairman of the newly created military board of Louisiana, that the government was continuing its efforts to garrison Southern forts secretly, and there was special danger from the Gulf squadron.[27]  Slidell telegraphed to Governor Moore that the danger was not from St. Louis but from the Gulf.[28]

There were no fortifications above the city of New Orleans, but the people of the city did not fear an attack from that direction. Batteries placed at strategic positions on the banks of the Mississippi, from Cairo to Vicksburg, would be ample protection against the possibility of hostile forces reaching New Orleans. The newspapers boasted that not even the famous steel-plated frigates of

[25] *The New Orleans Bee,* January 10, 1861.
[26] Monroe to Moore, January 9, 1861, in *The Daily Delta,* January 10, 1861.
[27] Benjamin and Slidell to Adams, January 10, 1861, *Official Records . . . Armies,* Series I, Vol. I, 496.
[28] Slidell to Moore, January 10, 1861, *ibid.,* 496.

the French navy could run the gauntlet. There were, however, many approaches to the city from the Gulf. Major Beauregard reported to the War Department in 1859 that there was not a seaport on the continent more easy of approach, and consequently, none more difficult to defend. The water approaches from the Gulf were six in number.[29] A seventh approach, in some respects the best, was by way of the Mexican Gulf Railroad which led directly up from Lake Borgne over the Metairie Ridge into the city.

Orders were issued by Governor Moore during the evening of January 9 for state troops to proceed to Baton Rouge and occupy the federal arsenal. Six companies from New Orleans left immediately by steamer and reached Baton Rouge the following morning. Their number was increased to more than six hundred by forces from other parts of the state, and a demand was made upon Major Haskin to surrender the arsenal.[30] It was useless for the garrison of ninety men to offer resistance to superior numbers led by veteran officers, and the arsenal and barracks were turned over to the state officials. The garrison was given thirty-six hours to leave the state,

[29] The water approaches included: (1) the main channel of the Mississippi, defended by Fort Jackson on the right bank and Fort St. Philip on the left, seventy miles below the city; (2) Barataria Bay, used by the oyster boats, hunters, and fishermen in reaching the New Orleans markets, and defended by Fort Livingstone (half completed) on Grande Terre Island; (3) the Rigolets, a narrow strait connecting Lake Borgne and Lake Pontchartrain, used by the Mobile mail steamers and defended by Fort Pike; (4) the South Pass, also connecting Lake Borgne and Lake Pontchartrain, and defended by Fort Macomb; and (5) bayous Bienvenue and Dupré, emptying into Lake Borgne, and nearly connecting with the Mississippi River a few miles below New Orleans, and defended by Battery Bienvenu and Tower Dupré.
[30] Moore to Haskin, January 10, 1861, *Official Records . . . Armies*, Series I, Vol. I, 490.

and departed by steamer for Cairo.[81]   On January 11 troops from New Orleans took possession of Forts Jackson, St. Philip, and Pike.[82]   Fort Macomb and the quartermaster's stores at New Orleans were not seized until January 28.[83]   Governor Moore, in his message to the legislature on January 23, explained his reasons for ordering the occupation of the forts.   He was convinced by the changing attitude of the federal administration, by the speeches of the Republican members of Congress, and by the official acts of the governors and legislatures of the Northern states, that an effort would be made to preserve the Union by force of arms.   The refusal of President Buchanan to withdraw the troops from Fort Sumter, the attempt to reinforce Forts Sumter and Pickens, and the recall of naval vessels from foreign waters indicated a determination to occupy and hold military posts within the boundaries of states which were about to declare themselves independen: commonwealths.   Secret information indicated the danger of an early attack upon New Orleans; and restlessness within the state made the danger of collision between the federal forces and irresponsible parties a standing menace to law and order.[84]   In order to insure the defense of the state against attacks by way of the upper Mississippi, Moore turned over to Governor

[81] Haskin to Cooper, January 10, 1861, *ibid.*, 489; Haskin to Cooper, January 11, 1861, *ibid.*, 490; "Articles of Agreement between Thomas O. Moore, Governor of the State of Louisiana, and Bvt. Maj. Joseph A. Haskin, U. S. Army, commanding the Barracks at Baton Rouge, La.," *ibid.*, 490.

[82] Smith to Cooper, January 11, 1861, *ibid.*, 491.

[83] Wilber to Cooper, January 31, 1861, *ibid.*, 492; Myers to Cooper, January 28, 1861, *ibid.*, 492-493; details of the various expeditions, by accompanying reporters and participants, are to be found in *The New Orleans Bee*, January 10, 1861.

[84] "Moore to the Louisiana State Legislature, January 23, 1861," *Official Records . . . Armies*, Series I, Vol. I, 493-496; *The New Orleans Bee*, January 24, 1861.

Pettus of Mississippi large quantities of arms and ammunition from the Baton Rouge arsenal. Fort Hill, a short distance above Vicksburg, was occupied by Mississippi troops on January 12, and a battery was planted in position to prevent United States troops from passing down the river.

The unfortunate result of the disruption of the President's Cabinet and the secret attempt to reinforce Southern forts was that the positions of the extremists in both sections of the country were strengthened. Nothing could have been better calculated to promote the purposes of the radicals in the Republican party. They were endeavoring to turn the attention of the country away from compromise of the slavery question by discussing the preservation of the federal authority, and had indicated an intention of justifying civil war on the ground of protecting the federal property. Buchanan had attempted to secure congressional action for a friendly adjustment of the critical political situation. He had successfully avoided an armed conflict until the conservative forces of the country might have time to act. The incidents in Charleston harbor tended to popularize the position of those who had thwarted all attempts at peaceable adjustment by congressional action, and made more difficult future efforts in that direction. It is a grave error, however, to suppose that the issue of civil war turned upon the incidents of those two days. Buchanan had never admitted the right of the executive department to surrender federal property or to acknowledge a separation of the states. The South Carolina commissioners finally would have had to deal with Congress, and would have failed to reach a satisfactory adjustment. It may well be doubted if that body would have entered into negotiation with them, and the forcible seizure of the forts in the Southern states, however delayed, doubtless must have come eventually.

Two days after the *Star of the West* fiasco a state commission endeavored to persuade Anderson to surrender Fort Sumter. He refused to do so and suggested that a joint commission be sent to Washington to lay the proposal before the government of the United States. Anderson's previous instructions would have justified a peremptory refusal to surrender without further negotiation; and the experience of the previous South Carolina commission to Washington should have been sufficient evidence to Pickens that Buchanan would not withdraw the federal forces. Both parties seem to have entered upon the agreement as the only honorable escape from instituting open hostilities, and Attorney General Hayne and Lieutenant Hall left for Washington on January 12. Hayne was the bearer of a letter to Buchanan in which Pickens made a formal demand for the surrender of Fort Sumter, with a pledge to fully compensate the federal government for the value of the property.[35] After Hayne had held an informal conversation with Buchanan, but before he had presented the communication from Pickens, the senators from the six Gulf states intervened to prevent its delivery. These senators impressed upon Hayne the fact that the states they represented had also asserted their independence or were about to do so, and would unite their destiny with that of South Carolina.[36] They argued that they ought to be consulted in any action which might tend to alter the possibility of peaceful relations between their states and the government of the United States. They

[35] Pickens to Buchanan, January 12, 1861, *House Ex. Docs.*, 36 Cong., 2 Sess., IX, Doc. 61, 13-14.

[36] Four states had resumed their independence at the time this letter was written: South Carolina, Florida, Mississippi, and Alabama.

admitted that the continued occupation of Fort Sumter by federal forces was a just cause for apprehension on the part of South Carolina; but they claimed to have substantial evidence that the fort was being held as property which Buchanan felt it was his duty to protect, and not with any unfriendly purpose toward South Carolina.

They proposed, therefore, that President Buchanan and South Carolina enter into an agreement to maintain the existing status in Charleston harbor until a new Southern confederacy, which was certain to be formed early in February, might "devise a wise, just, and peaceable solution of existing difficulties." They offered to submit their proposal to Buchanan and urged Hayne to do the same with regard to Governor Pickens.[87] Hayne agreed to the plan, and the correspondence between the senators and Hayne was submitted to Buchanan by Slidell, Fitzpatrick, and Mallory.[88] Buchanan replied, through Secretary Holt, that he was obliged to protect the public property and could enter into no agreement, nor give any assurance that reinforcements should not be sent to Fort Sumter. He admitted that no necessity existed for sending reinforcements immediately, but stated emphatically that if future necessity required it they would be sent. He stated, furthermore, that Congress possessed the power to make war and he had no right to say that they would not exercise that power against South Carolina. In conclusion, he said:

Major Anderson is not menacing Charleston; and I am convinced that the happiest result which can be obtained is, that both he and the authorities of South Carolina shall re-

[87] Wigfall, Hemphill, Yulee, Mallory, Davis, Clay, Fitzpatrick, Iverson, Slidell, and Benjamin to Hayne, January 15, 1861, *House Ex. Docs.*, 36 Cong., 2 Sess., IX, Doc. 61, 2-3.
[88] Hayne to Wigfall, Hemphill, etc., January 17, 1861, *ibid.*, 3-4; Slidell, Fitzpatrick, and Mallory to Buchanan, January 19, 1861, *ibid.*, 4-5.

main on their present amicable footing, neither party being bound by any obligations whatever, except the high Christian and moral duty to keep the peace, and to avoid all causes of mutual irritation.[39]

Hayne replied that the presence of a garrison in Fort Sumter placed it in greater jeopardy than if it were surrendered to South Carolina with a pledge of full compensation; that the occupation of a fort by armed forces with guns trained on every part of the harbor, and under the orders of a government whose authority was no longer recognized, was not conducive to the preservation of peace; and that the continued occupation of the fort was the worst possible means of securing a "peaceful solution of existing difficulties short of war itself." He assured the senators, however, that their suggestions would carry great weight with the authorities of South Carolina.[40] He expressed similar sentiments in a communication to Buchanan, together with the statement that the security of his state required a definition of the President's position.[41]

This communication evoked a further statement from Holt in which he reiterated his previous contention that the President had no constitutional power to sell or otherwise dispose of public property. He stated further that Fort Sumter was a military post, held by the federal government for the purpose in which it had been constructed: the defense of Charleston against a foreign enemy. The garrison was small, under orders to act upon the defensive, and "the government and people of South Carolina

[39] Holt to Slidell, Fitzpatrick, and Mallory, January 22, 1861, *ibid.*, 5-6; *Official Records . . . Armies,* Series I, Vol. I, 149-150.
[40] Hayne to Wigfall, Yulee, and others, January 24, 1861, *House Ex. Docs.,* 36 Cong., 2 Sess., IX, Doc. 61, 8-9.
[41] Hayne to Buchanan, January 31, 1861, *ibid.,* 8-14.

must well know that they can never receive aught but shelter from its guns, unless, in the absence of all provocation, they should assault it and seek its destruction." [42]

The government of the Confederate States, in the process of formation at the time of this last communication from the War Department, took over the responsibility of negotiating with the government at Washington concerning the forts and other public property, and friendly relations continued in Charleston harbor. The garrison in Fort Sumter continued its regular purchases of meat, vegetables, etc., in the Charleston markets. Anderson was again cautioned to use the utmost care to prevent a collision, and both sides strengthened their position in the forts which they respectively held. [43]

[42] Holt to Hayne, February 6, 1861, *ibid.*, 14-17; *Official Record . . . Armies,* Series I, Vol. I, 166-168.
[43] See, especially, Holt to Anderson, February 23, 1861, *ibid.*, 182-183; Anderson to Pickens, February 13, 1861, *ibid.*, 171-172; and Foster to Totten, February 13, 1861, *ibid.*, 172-173.

# CHAPTER X

## THE SECESSION OF THE GULF STATES

THE failure of Congress either to consider seriously the adoption of constitutional guarantees for the security of Southern institutions, or to provide for a national constitutional convention, assured the election of immediate secession majorities to the conventions of the six Gulf states. Every new indication of sectional hostility was given wide circulation by Southern newspapers, and Southern statesmen kept their constituents informed of what was transpiring at Washington.

Howell Cobb, Secretary of the Treasury, was the most influential member of Buchanan's Cabinet and a power in the lower South. He was besieged with anxious inquiries concerning the possibility of compromise and the course the Southern states ought to pursue. Unwilling to refuse an answer to these inquiries, and equally reluctant to subject the administration to unjust criticism by remaining in the Cabinet after a public expression of his convictions, he decided to publish an address to the people of Georgia and resign his position.[1]

Cobb's address was published on December 6, 1860. As to whether Lincoln's election was sufficient justification for a dissolution of the Union, it said that after March 4, 1861, the federal government would "cease to have the slightest claim either upon your confidence or

[1] Howell Cobb to James Buchanan, December 8, 1860, in American Historical Association, *Annual Report, 1911*, II, 517-518.

your loyalty; and, in my honest judgment, each hour that Georgia remains thereafter a member of the Union will be an hour of degradation, to be followed by certain and speedy ruin. . . . Arouse, then, all your manhood for the great work before you, and be prepared on that day to announce and maintain your independence out of the Union, for you will never again have equality and justice in it." This conclusion was based upon an analysis of the principles of the Republican party, and of the prospect of the permanent ascendancy of that party in the federal government. That party had its origin in hostility to slavery and continued hostility was its strongest bond of union. It regarded the institution of slavery as a moral and social evil, unrecognized by the Constitution. It maintained that slave property was not entitled to protection by the federal government, nor to the privileges and rights accorded to other property outside the limits and jurisdiction of the several states. It claimed that Congress should prevent the admission of any more slave states into the Union, and encourage the decline and ultimate extinction of slavery where it already existed. It had secured control of the executive department of the federal government by appealing to the abolition fanaticism of the Northern people. It would never recede from its advanced position.

Cobb denied that the Republican party was likely to disintegrate because internal differences of every kind were subordinated to hostility to slavery. He enumerated many convincing facts to substantiate his denial that the Republican party would surrender its fundamental principles: the substantial majorities in the presidential election; the known faithfulness of Lincoln to principles and personal pledges; the faithful adherence of the party leaders and party press to the doctrine of congressional exclusion;

the avowed reorganization of the Supreme Court; the rapidly increasing numerical majority of the Northern states; and the enlistment of the agencies of the churches and schools in furthering anti-slavery propaganda. He denied that the opposition majorities in Congress were sufficient guarantee against Republican aggression. They were too small, constantly decreasing, and powerless to stem the growing power of the party, repeal the personal liberty laws, override a presidential veto, or control the distribution of patronage. Concluding his analysis with a consideration of the course the South should adopt, Cobb declared that the election of Lincoln could "be regarded in no other light than a declaration of the purpose and intention of the people of the North to continue, with the power of the Federal Government, the war already commenced by the ten nullifying States of the North upon the institution of slavery and the constitutional rights of the South. . . . The issue must now be met, or forever abandoned. Equality and safety in the Union are at an end; and it only remains to be seen whether our manhood is equal to the task of asserting and maintaining independence out of it." [2]

The following day Cobb resigned his position in the Cabinet and returned to Georgia to assist in the promotion of the secession movement.[3] After a strenuous campaign through the mountain districts of the state, he was sent as a delegate to the Montgomery convention, was elected chairman of that body, and was mentioned prominently for the presidency of the confederacy.

[2] Howell Cobb to the People of Georgia, December 6, 1860, *ibid.*, 505-506.
[3] See Howell Cobb to his Wife, December 10, 1860, *ibid.*, 518-519. Thomas R. R. Cobb to Howell Cobb, December 15, 1860, *ibid.*, 522; A. Hood to Howell Cobb, December 19, 1860, *ibid.*, 524.

The second important document, published by Southern statesmen, was an address by thirty congressmen from the slave states to their constituents on December 14, 1860. This address, telegraphed to the newspapers of the Southern states, stated that the Republican congressmen would make no concessions and that all hope of compromise was futile. It was occasioned by the attitude of the Republican members of the Committee of Thirty-three on the preceding day. Rust of Arkansas had offered a resolution to the effect that unrest among the Southern people was not without cause, and that guarantees of their constitutional rights sufficient to allay the discontent were "indispensable to the perpetuation of the Union." The Republican members opposed the resolution of Rust so vigorously that the Southern members accepted as a substitute a resolution offered by Dunn of Indiana. This resolution stated that Southern discontent and hostility to the federal government were "greatly to be regretted"; and whether "without just cause or not, any reasonable, proper, and constitutional remedies, and additional and more specific and effectual guarantees of their peculiar rights and interest as recognized by the Constitution, necessary to preserve the peace of the country and perpetuation of the Union, should promptly and cheerfully be granted." [4] This substitute did not admit that there was just cause for Southern unrest, and that admission was an essential prerequisite of substantial guarantees. The Republican members on the committee from Massachusetts, New York, Connecticut, Rhode Island, New Hampshire, Vermont, Maine, and Wisconsin voted against even this noncommittal resolution. Taken in connection with the vote against the appointment of the committee, the fact that up to that

   [4] *Journal of the Committee of Thirty-three*, 7.

time the Republicans had prevented the appointment of a committee in the Senate, the peculiar composition of the Committee of Thirty-three, and the hostile speeches of King, Hale, and others in the Senate, it was fairly conclusive evidence that all hope of obtaining satisfactory congressional action was gone.[5] Subsequent events fully substantiated the prophecy of the Southern congressmen, and the approaching elections in Alabama and Mississippi justified a report to their constituents which otherwise would have seemed premature.

The day following the publication of the address, Judge William L. Harris, commissioner from Mississippi to Georgia, arrived at Milledgeville and addressed the legislature. This was the same day on which his colleague, C. E. Hooker, reached Columbia and, in conjunction with J. A. Elmore of Alabama, became active in promoting the secession of South Carolina. Harris's address contained none of the convincing logic of Stephens and none of the invigorating enthusiasm of Toombs. It was an eloquent appeal to the vanity and courage of the Georgians. He spoke affectionately of the great governors of other days; of Baldwin, Jackson, Troup. Georgia, he said, "glorious old mother" of Mississippi, had been the "brightest exemplar among the advocates and defenders of State Rights and State remedies." Would she fail now that the safety of the South was threatened? To the Georgians he said: "Mississippi indulges the most confidential expectation and belief, founded on sources of information she cannot doubt, as well as on the existence of causes, operating upon them alike as upon her, that every other Gulf State will stand by her side in defense of the position she is

[5] For a different interpretation, see Rhodes, *History of the United States, 1850-1896*, III, 64-65; and Nicolay and Hay, *Abraham Lincoln: A History*, II, 436-438.

about to assume." [6] To his own state, two weeks later, he reported: "There is but one voice in Georgia as to her secession, *in event that Mississippi, Alabama, and Florida shall have taken that step before the meeting of her convention on the 16th of January.*" [7] Following the address of Harris, the legislature adopted resolutions in favor of the immediate secession of the state from the Union. This indication of the probable action of the state was important. Georgia was the pivotal state of the cotton belt, and was generally spoken of as the "Great Empire State of the South." Thousands of her native sons had migrated westward and were counted among the influential citizens of Mississippi and Alabama. Many looked to the state of their nativity for guidance in the crisis. The first of the elections in the Gulf states were held in Mississippi on the day that South Carolina seceded from the Union and in Alabama four days later. The secession of South Carolina sent a wave of enthusiasm throughout the lower South, but the reaction that would have resulted from success by the coöperationists in Georgia would have been a deathblow to immediate action in the West.

In Mississippi, a competent observer declared as early as November 12, "that nine out of every ten who voted for Breckinridge will vote for direct secession; and I know that most of the Douglas men, to repel the free-soil suspicion their late conduct has subjected them to, are already earnest advocates of secession. Many good men besides, who voted for Bell and Everett, did so in an honest effort to defeat Lincoln, and thus avoid a cause

---

[6] Harris. "Address before the Georgia Legislature, December 15, 1860," in *Journal of the Mississippi State Convention . . . 1861*, 205-207; *Weekly Mississippian*, January 2, 1861.

[7] Harris to Pettus, December 31, 1860, *Journal of the Mississippi State Convention . . . 1861*, 197.

which they think sufficient to justify secession." [8]    One month later the Alabama commissioner to that state, E. W. Pettus, reported that previous party lines had been obliterated. He is authority for the statement that the entire congressional delegation from that state, the governor, the three judges of the supreme court, the auditor, treasurer, attorney general, and all except three of the members of the state legislature were in favor of immediate secession. These men were representatives of public opinion, and there was little doubt as to the outcome of the election. There was, however, a great deal of concern over the ability of Mississippi to maintain a separate national existence because of the lack of a seaport for foreign trade. Most of the commerce of the state passed through Alabama or Louisiana, and had those states been reluctant to take similar action, Mississippi might have shown considerable hesitation. Pettus was there, however, with assurances of Alabama's position. He advised with finality that Alabama would secede, that she would take no part in a conference of states before resuming her independence, and that as soon as possible thereafter she would participate in the formation of a Southern confederacy with other states which might take similar action. Similar assurances as to the course Louisiana would pursue were received from Wirt Adams, commissioner to that state from Mississippi,[9] from the message of Governor T. O. Moore to the state legislature, and from the prompt action of the legislature in providing for a state convention and for arming the state.

So thoroughly did the interstate commissioners do their

[8] Fontaine to Pettus, November 12, 1860, Official Correspondence of Governor John J. Pettus, 1859-1860.
[9] Wirt Adams to John J. Pettus, December 13, 1860, in *Weekly Mississippian*, December 19, 1860.

work in counteracting all tendencies toward discord, and in securing concurrent and harmonious action among the states of the lower South, that the *Weekly Mississippian* was able to declare on the day preceding the election in that state, that the seven states of the lower South would, within sixty days, join in the formation of a new confederacy, that a convention would be held, to which would be sent "men of clear heads, calm judgment, but prompt in action and resolute in purpose"; that the old Constitution, with some slight amendments, would be adopted and referred to the state conventions for ratification; and that the work would be completed before March 4, 1861.

In Mississippi less than a dozen of the sixty counties sent coöperation delegates to the convention.[10] The result was much closer in Alabama, but there was little doubt as to the ultimate action of the state. An analysis of the popular vote is virtually impossible because (1) no contest was made in some counties; (2) the contest in some counties was along personal lines between two sets of secession candidates or two sets of coöperation candidates; and (3) the vote in some counties was very small in comparison to that cast in the presidential contest. These facts make it equally impossible to estimate the popular sentiment from the fact that fifty-four secessionists and forty-five opposition delegates were elected to the convention. The concensus of opinion seems to have been that the popular sentiment was strong for immediate action, and that the opposite would have been true if the Republicans in Congress had shown a disposition to accept the Crittenden amendments.[11] Additional assurance that

[10] For a classified list of the delegates, see *ibid.*, January 2, 1861.
[11] The *Montgomery Daily Advertiser*, December 26, 1860; Hodgson, *The Cradle of the Confederacy*, 491-492; Smith, *op. cit.*, 19-33.

those amendments would not be approved was given to the people of the South by Robert Toombs on the day preceding the election in Alabama.

Toombs had remained in Georgia until the fifteenth, and did not take his seat in the Senate until the nineteenth of that month. Before leaving Georgia he had stated that he did not favor delaying the secession of the state beyond March 4, but that he was perfectly willing to yield the point if active measures for a redress of Southern grievances should be undertaken immediately by the Northern people. He had faith in only one method of securing redress within the Union and that was by constitutional amendment. He regarded all other remedies as "delusions and snares, intended to lull the people into false security, to steal away their rights, and with them the power of redress." He proposed, therefore, that whatever amendments were deemed necessary for the security of Southern rights should be offered in Congress; and, if adopted by that body, secession should be suspended until the several state legislatures could be convened and take definite action.[12] The Senate agreed to create the Committee of Thirteen on December 18, the day before Toombs took his seat. He asked for a place upon that committee and was given it. At the second session of the committee he proposed that the following definitive amendments to the Constitution be recommended: (1) recognizing the right of every citizen to emigrate to the territories with his property (including slaves), and to be protected in its enjoyment until the formation of state constitutions for admission into the Union; (2) guaranteeing the right of protection for slave property equally with

[12] Robert Toombs to E. B. Pullin and others, December 13, 1860, in American Historical Association, *Annual Report, 1911*, II, 519-520.

other property by the federal government; (3) providing for the surrender of fugitives from justice, with the laws of the state in which the act was committed constituting the test of criminality; (4) providing for the punishment of persons aiding and abetting invasion and insurrection; (5) denying the right of *habeas corpus* and trial by jury to fugitive slaves; (6) providing that no law relative to slavery in the states or territories should ever be passed by Congress without the consent of all the states where slavery existed.[13] This was the extreme Southern platform and was not voted upon in committee until December 24, when it was defeated in its entirety. Immediately after Toombs submitted his proposed amendments, however, those of Crittenden were taken under consideration and defeated.[14] The following day, December 23, Toombs telegraphed to the newspapers of the South that the refusal of the Republicans to accept the Crittenden amendments was indicative of their general hostility to all such guarantees and conclusive evidence that hope of constitutional relief was gone. He said in conclusion:

I have put the test fairly and frankly. It is decisive against you; and now I tell you upon the faith of a true man that all further looking to the North for security for your constitutional rights in the Union ought to be instantly abandoned. It is fraught with nothing but ruin to yourselves and your posterity.

Secession by the fourth of March next should be thundered from the ballot-box by the unanimous voice of Georgia on the second day of January next. Such a voice will be your best guarantee for liberty, security, tranquillity, and glory.[15]

There can be no minimizing of the influence of his action.

[13] *Journal of the Committee of Thirteen*, 2-3.
[14] *Ibid.*, 5-6.
[15] Robert Toombs to the People of Georgia, December 23, 1860, in American Historical Association, *Annual Report, 1911*, II, 525.

Many conservative men of the state still hoped for constitutional guarantees from Congress against further interference with slavery. Stephens had rekindled hope in many a doubtful heart in spite of the address of the Southern congressmen to their constituents; but even Stephens gave up hope of compromise thereafter.[16]

The Florida, Mississippi, and Alabama conventions assembled on schedule. There was no question as to the success of the secession movement in any of the three states. In Florida the only opposition came from those who wanted the secession of the state to follow rather than precede that of Alabama and Georgia; and the ordinance was passed on January 9 by a vote of 62 to 7. In the Mississippi convention the immediate secession forces outnumbered those of the opposition by more than four to one; and the opposition members, who had been elected on the coöperation ticket, were not all opposed to secession. Some favored coöperating with the entire South; others wished to make the ordinance ineffective until the other Gulf states had taken similar action; and still others urged that the ordinance be submitted to the people for ratification. The ordinance, as reported on the second day of the session, in addition to resuming all powers previously delegated to the federal government and repealing all ordinances and laws supporting the same, consented to the formation of a new confederation on the basis of the Constitution of the United States. J. S. Yerger of Washington County offered as an amendment (1) that, in the opinion of the convention, Mississippi could no longer remain with safety as a member of the United States unless amendments to the Constitution were

[16] Alexander H. Stephens to J. Henly Smith, December 31, 1860, in *ibid.*, 526-527.

passed granting equality in the Union to the slave states and forever settling the slavery controversy; (2) that the safest and most efficient means of securing such redress was through a convention of all the slaveholding states; (3) that all states willing to unite in such action should be invited to a convention at Lexington, Kentucky, on February 10; and (4) that if such amendments were not secured, this Southern convention should reassemble and form an independent confederacy. This amendment was defeated by a vote of 78 to 20. A second amendment, offered by J. L. Alcorn of Coahoma County, providing that the ordinance should not go into effect until Alabama, Florida, Georgia, and Louisiana also resumed their independence, was defeated by a vote of 74 to 25. A final amendment, offered by Walker Brooke of Warren County, providing for the submission of the ordinance to popular vote on February 4, was defeated by a vote of 70 to 29. Following these defeats, the opposition forces divided. The ordinance of secession was passed by a vote of 83 to 15, and was signed by every member of the convention. The variation between the votes cast for the several amendments and that cast against the ordinance on the final vote is a fair index of the extent to which secession sentiment had gained in strength since the election. Brooke and Alcorn both voted for the ordinance. In explanation of his vote, Brooke said:

I was elected by a large majority, as what is known as coöperationist—which means, as I understand it, one who was in favor of united Southern action for the purpose of demanding further guarantees from the North, or failing in that, the formation of a Southern Confederacy. . . . Previous coöperation, or coöperation before secession, was the first object of my desire. Failing in this I am willing to take the next best, subsequent coöperation or coöperation after seces-

sion. The former is now impossible. I therefore am willing
to adopt the latter. Should I vote against the ordinance after
what has passed, I should consider myself as voting for the
convention to do nothing. Shall the convention adjourn
without action? Should we do so we would make ourselves
obnoxious [sic.] to the scorn and ridicule of the world. The
next breeze from the North, or from the East, may bring to
our ears the clash of resounding arms. Perhaps already the calm
and peaceful waters of Charleston Bay are dyed and tinged
with the blood of our friends and countrymen. . . . Influenced by considerations of this sort which I cannot now fully
express, I therefore feel it my duty, painful as it may be, to
part from those with whom I have heretofore acted, to assume
the responsibility of casting at least one of the votes of
Warren County for the passage of the ordinance as reported.

The fifteen votes cast against the ordinance did not represent factious opposition to it. They were of men who
openly declared that there were no submissionists among
their constituents, but felt that their obligations to them
were not fulfilled until they had registered their votes
against the ordinance.[17]

The relative strength of the immediate secessionists and
the coöperationists in the Alabama convention was 54 to
45. As in Mississippi, the opposition forces represented
various opinions, some favoring coöperation with the
slaveholding states; others favoring coöperation with the
Gulf states; and still others desiring popular ratification
of the ordinance of secession. The leading members of
the opposition resented every implication that they were
submissionists. Smith of Tuscaloosa County said: "It is
true, that it has been ascertained by the elections which
have just been had here, that we are a minority. I am of
that minority; but I do not associate with submissionists!
There is not one in our company. We scorn the prospec-

[17] *Weekly Mississippian*, January 16, 1861.

tive Black Republican rule as much as the gentleman from Calhoun [Whatley] or any of his friends." [18] Similar sentiment was expressed by other members of the group, and, as proof of the unity of the convention with respect to the issue before the country, it passed unanimously on the first day of the session a resolution stating that the state of Alabama could not and would not submit to the administration of Lincoln and Hamlin.[19] A. P. Calhoun, commissioner from South Carolina, addressed the convention on the second day of its session. He invited Alabama to join in forming a Southern confederacy with the Constitution of the United States as a basis for a provisional government; and suggested the first Monday of February as a date agreed upon by the South Carolina commissioners before leaving Charleston.[20] The secession sentiment prevailing in the convention received frequent stimulus from telegrams sent by congressmen and commissioners to other states. Congressmen Moore and Clopton wired from Washington that the Republican party in the House of Representatives had refused to consider the border-state compromise, and had endorsed the action of Anderson in Charleston harbor.[21] Commissioners Hopkins and Gilmer wired from Richmond that the Virginia legislature had passed, by a vote of 112 to 5, a resolution to resist coercion of a seceding state, and urged immediate action by the Alabama convention.[22] Another dispatch from Governor Pettus promised the secession of Mississippi before January 9.

The committee appointed to draft an ordinance of seces-

[18] Smith, *op. cit.*, 26.
[19] *Ibid.*, 30.
[20] Calhoun, "Address before the Alabama Convention, January 8, 1861," in *ibid.*, 31-34.
[21] Clopton and Moore to Watts, January 7, 1861, *ibid.*, 34.
[22] Hopkins and Gilmer to Moore, January 8, 1861, *ibid.*, 34.

sion reported on January 9, the third day of the session. The majority report provided for the immediate secession of Alabama, and for a convention of delegates from all the slaveholding states at Montgomery on February 4 for the purpose of "consulting with each other as to the most effectual mode of securing concerted and harmonious action in whatever measures may be deemed most desirable for our common peace and security." The minority report provided for a convention of delegates from all the slaveholding states at Nashville, Tennessee, on February 22. The Alabama delegates to this convention were to demand as a basis for settlement of the difficulties between the North and South irrepealable amendments to the Constitution providing for (1) a faithful execution of the fugitive slave law, (2) explicit provisions for the surrender of fugitives from justice, (3) a guarantee that Congress should not interfere with the interstate slave trade and slavery in the District of Columbia, (4) protection for slavery in the territories, and (5) the right of transit with slaves through the free states.[88] The report pledged Alabama to resist meanwhile any attempt to coerce a seceding state, and provided that in event of a failure to secure the proposed constitutional guarantees Alabama should look to separation and independent national existence for her future security.

Every provision of the minority report was defeated by a vote of 54 to 45; and the ordinance of secession was adopted 61 to 39. By voting for the minority report, certain of the coöperationists felt that they had fulfilled their obligation to their constituents. They then voted for the ordinance because they were unwilling to give any basis for a claim that Alabama was divided on the ques-

[88] *Ibid.,* 78-80.

tion of resistance to Republican rule.[24] Explaining their position, Clemens said:

> The act you are about to commit, is, to my apprehension, treason, and subjects you, if unsuccessful, to all the pains and penalties pronounced against that highest political crime, or noblest political virtue, according to the motives which govern its commission. Whatever may be my opinion of the wisdom and justice of the course pursued by the majority, I do not choose that any man shall put himself in danger of a halter in defense of the honor and rights of my native State, without sharing that danger with him. I believe your Ordinance to be wrong—if I could defeat it, I would; but I know I cannot. It will pass, and when passed it becomes the act of the State of Alabama. . . . I am a son of Alabama; her destiny is mine; her people are mine; her enemies are mine. Acting upon the convictions of a lifetime, calmly and deliberately, I walk into revolution. Be its perils—be its privations—be its sufferings what they may, I shall share them with you, although as a member of this Convention I opposed your Ordinance.[25]

More than half of those who voted against the ordinance voluntarily pledged themselves to devote their energies in peace or in war to the support of the state.[26] Northern newspapers stated that the convention was far from unanimous, and that a large part of the state was decidedly opposed to extreme measures. On the other hand, Hodgson states, in his *Cradle of the Confederacy,* that if secession had required every vote in convention the ordinance would have passed. Apparently neither was correct. Thirty-three members of the convention refused to sign the ordinance and published an address stating their reasons for not signing it. They refused (1) because it was not submitted to the people for rati-

[24] Crumpler, Remarks in the Convention, *ibid.,* 78-80.
[25] *Ibid.,* 117-118.
[26] *Ibid.,* 93-118.

fication, and (2) because Alabama did not consult with the other slave states before taking action. But the address also stated that "in refusing to sign the Ordinance of Secession, the undersigned are actuated by no desire to avoid the responsibilities that now attach, or may hereafter attach, to the act by which the State withdrew from the Federal Union. Not only will they share these responsibilities alike with those who sign the Ordinance, but if it shall appear that the public interest or expediency require the affixing of their signatures, they will unhesitatingly and cheerfully do so. . . ." [27] Thirteen of the thirty-three members who joined in the address were among those who had pledged their lives to the support of the state; and no doubt can exist concerning the sincerity of those who affixed their signatures to it.

On the same day that the convention passed the ordinance of secession, it passed a resolution inviting the delegates of all slaveholding states to meet in Montgomery on February 4 for the purpose of forming a Southern confederacy. A further resolution strongly urging this action upon the states was passed on January 14, following the receipt of a report from J. L. M. Curry and J. L. Pugh at Washington concerning the action of the Committee of Thirty-three. This report declared hope for compromise to be losing ground in the upper South, and sentiment in the North to be against coercion. It urged the immediate formation of a confederacy to influence the states of the upper South and deter any thought of coercion.[28] The election in Georgia had resulted in a substantial victory for the immediate secession forces; and the events which transpired between the time of the

[27] *Ibid.*, 445-447.
[28] Pugh and Curry to Brooks, *Official Records . . . Armies,* Series IV, Vol. I, 46-47.

assembling of the convention on January 16 did much to weaken the strength of the opposition. Among the members of the convention were Robert Toombs, Alexander H. Stephens, Herschel V. Johnson, Benjamin H. Hill, Henry L. Benning, and other influential men of the state. J. L. Orr, commissioner from South Carolina, addressed the convention on the first day of its session. He urged the acceptance of Alabama's invitation to a convention at Montgomery, and recommended the Constitution of the United States as a basis for the formation of a provisional government.[19] The test of the relative strength of the secession and opposition forces came on the second day of the session. E. A. Nesbit introduced a resolution declaring that in the opinion of the convention Georgia should secede from the Union and coöperate in the formation of a Southern confederacy.[20] Herschel V. Johnson offered as an amendment that "whilst the State of Georgia will not and cannot, compatibly with her safety, abide permanently in the Union without new and ample security for future safety, still she is not disposed to sever her connection with it precipitately, nor without respectful consultation with her Southern Confederates." His resolution provided for a conference of the slaveholding states at Atlanta on February 16, and named the following as conditions on which Georgia would remain in the Union: (1) that Congress should have no power to prohibit slavery in the territories; (2) that slaveholders should be compensated for all losses incurred through nullification of the fugitive slave law; (3) that heavy penalties should be provided for enticing slaves away from their masters;

[19] Orr, "Address before the Georgia Convention, January 16, 1861," *Journal of the Convention of the People of Georgia . . . 1861,* 305-306.
[20] *Ibid.,* 15.

(4) that slave property should receive equal protection with all other property by the federal government; (5) that Congress should not interfere with the interstate slave trade; (6) that slaveholders should enjoy the right of transit with their property; and (7) that negroes should never be allowed to hold federal offices. The resolution further stated that Georgia would not remain in the Union unless all personal liberty laws were repealed; that she would join in protecting against coercion any state which might resume its independence; that Fort Pulaski should temporarily remain in the possession of the state; and that, if her demands were refused by the Northern states, the convention should reassemble on February 25 for the purpose of joining other states in forming a Southern confederacy.[31] A direct vote on the Johnson resolutions was prevented by a demand for the previous question, and the resolution offered by Nesbit was adopted by a vote of 166 to 130. A communication from Governor Morgan of New York to Governor Brown was then presented to the convention. It contained resolutions passed by the New York legislature which denounced as treason the action of the South Carolina authorities in firing upon the *Star of the West,* and tendered men and money to be used in enforcing the laws and upholding the authority of the federal government. The convention immediately adopted, by a unanimous vote, a resolution endorsing the action of Governor Brown in seizing Fort Pulaski, and ordered a copy forwarded to Governor Morgan.[32] The incident served to stimulate secession sentiment, and on the following day an ordinance of secession was adopted by a vote of 208 to 89.

[31] *Ibid.,* 15-20.
[32] *Ibid.,* 24-26.

The election of delegates to the Louisiana convention was not held until January 7, and by that time the rapid march of events had neutralized opposing forces. It was of little consequence, so far as secession was concerned, which set of candidates received the majority of votes. The strongest arguments of the opponents of immediate secession had lost their validity. The attitude of the Republicans in Congress had eliminated the possibility of securing definitive constitutional amendments. The incidents in Charleston harbor, followed by the sending of reinforcements to Southern forts, served to increase the danger of delay in withdrawing from the Union. The election of large secession majorities in Florida, Georgia, Alabama, and Mississippi, together with the certain knowledge that a Southern confederacy would be formed, established secession as a prerequisite to coöperation. Whatever might have been the prevailing sentiment at an earlier date, the election showed a tremendous majority for immediate secession.

The state convention assembled at Baton Rouge on January 23. The respective strength of the immediate secession and coöperation forces, as shown by the vote for president of the convention, was 81 to 42. Following the organization of the convention, however, party lines were obliterated. The fact that five states had already resumed their independence, and had provided for a convention at Montgomery on February 4, altered the plea for further delay in order to enable coöperation with other states to a plea for immediate secession and the appointment of delegates. Coöperation with the other states of the lower South in the formation of a southern confederacy was urged by Commissioner Manning of South Carolina, and by Commissioner Winston of Alabama.[33] An amendment to the ordinance of secession providing for a convention of the slaveholding states at Nashville, Tennessee, on February 25 was defeated by a vote of 106 to 24.[34] The ordinance of secession was adopted on January 26 by a vote of 113 to 17. A resolution approving Governor Moore's action in ordering the occupation of the federal forts was passed by a vote of 118 to 5. A resolution recognizing the free navigation of the Mississippi River was adopted by a unanimous vote.[35]

The Texas state convention assembled on January 28, and passed an ordinance of secession three days later by a vote of 166 to 8. The same force of circumstances operated in Texas as in Louisiana to eliminate opposition to the ordinance, and it was approved by a popular vote of 46,129 to 14,697. John McQueen, commissioner from South Carolina, addressed the convention and urged Texas to join in forming a Southern confederacy.[36] In a declaration of the causes which impelled the state to secede from the Union, the convention declared: "By the secession of six of the slaveholding States, and the certainty that others will speedily do likewise, Texas has no alternative but to remain in an isolated connection with the North, or unite her destinies with the South." [37]

Secession in the states from South Carolina to Texas was not a triumph of one party over another but rather a

[33] "Address of Ex-Governor Manning of South Carolina," in *The New Orleans Bee*, January 26, 1861; "Address of Ex-Governor Winston of Alabama," in *ibid*.

[34] "Proceedings of the Louisiana State Convention," in *ibid.*, January 27, 1861.

[35] "Proceedings of the Louisiana State Convention," in *ibid.*, January 25, 1861.

[36] *Journal of the Secession Convention of Texas, 1861*, 50-52.

[37] "A Declaration of the Causes which impel the State of Texas to secede from the Federal Union," in *ibid.*, 61-66.

demonstration that the lower South was finally united. The plan for a confederacy, conceived by the South Carolina convention, and advocated by the interstate commissioners, swept many coöperationists into the ranks of the secessionists because they feared a disintegration of the South. The failure of Congress to sanction guarantees for the security of Southern institutions converted those coöperationists who had favored delay because they believed such guarantees could be secured. The apparent inclination of the federal administration to hold the Southern forts as an aid to the enforcement of federal authority, coupled with the ominous silence of the President-elect and the aggressive attitude of Republican congressmen, completed the virtual unity of the lower South.

The Southern convention assembled at Montgomery, Alabama, February 4, 1861. Delegates from South Carolina, Mississippi, Alabama, Florida, Georgia, and Louisiana were present, bearing credentials from the conventions of their respective states, equal in number to each state's former congressional representation. The Texas delegates did not reach Montgomery in time to participate in the work of constructing a provisional government, but they were admitted and affixed their signatures to the constitution on March 2. Four days only were required to frame a constitution for the provisional government of the Confederate States of America. By this the convention was converted into a congress empowered to exercise all the functions exercised by both branches of the Congress of the United States and also to frame a permanent constitution. The provisional president and vice president, to be elected by the provisional congress, were to hold office for one year, unless automatically suspended by the establishment of a permanent government. Each state was created into a separate judicial district, with all powers previously vested in the district and circuit courts, and the several judges were constituted the Supreme Court of the confederacy. The president was to have power to veto any separate appropriation without vetoing the whole bill of which it might be a part. The African slave trade was prohibited. Congress was given the power to prohibit the introduction of slaves from any state not a member of the confederacy. All appropriations were to originate with the cabinet. Members of congress were not forbidden to hold other offices under the provisional government. All reference to capitation taxes and export duties were omitted. States were not forbidden to maintain armies in time of peace. Compensation was provided for slaves lost by abduction. Congress was empowered to amend the constitution by a two thirds vote at any time. The provisional government was required to immediately settle all matters of property and debts arising from the separation of the states. Montgomery was chosen as the temporary capital of the confederacy. The constitution was to continue in force for one year unless suspended by a permanent government, and no provision was made for its ratification by the several states.[88]

The two clauses of the provisional constitution of special interest to those slave states which had not yet withdrawn from the Union were those respecting the African slave trade and the introduction of slaves from the states outside the confederacy. The African slave traffic was opposed by the people of the lower South primarily on the ground of public policy. It was generally conceded that any objection to the slave trade on grounds of moral-

[88] "Constitution for the Provisional Government of the Confederate States of America," in *Official Records . . . Armies*, Series IV, Vol. I, 92-99.

ity applied more forcibly to the sale of negroes from the upper South to the lower South than to the foreign traffic. Behind the whole controversy which had raged over the question of the rights of slavery in the territories was the fear of slave increase and greater danger of insurrections. Moreover, Europe and the United States condemned the trade on moral grounds, and maintained a strict surveillance of the high seas to prevent it. Any attempt to reopen the trade would probably provoke hostilities, and the new nation desired and needed peace. On the question of the introduction of slaves from the states of the upper South the confederacy faced a perplexing problem. They feared that, unless it were prohibited, those states which remained in the Union would be inclined to dispose of their slaves in the markets of the confederacy. Those states would then face the same problem of unnatural increase of the slave population that would arise from a reopening of the African trade, and would be paying a much higher price for their slaves. It was also to the interest of the confederacy to keep those states which did not join the confederacy slave states as long as possible.

On February 9, 1861, the congress unanimously elected Jefferson Davis and Alexander H. Stephens as president and vice president respectively of the confederacy. They then authorized the acceptance of one hundred thousand volunteers for twelve months' service in the army, provided for the issue of one million dollars of treasury notes, and passed acts to organize a navy, a postal system, and a court system. A commission headed by Yancey was sent abroad to obtain recognition and negotiate treaties, and commissioners were appointed to treat with the United States Government for the division of the territories and debts, and to arrange for future friendly relations.

## CHAPTER XI

## THE PROPOSED PROGRAM FOR
## RECONSTRUCTION

DURING the early stages of the secession movement the majority of the people in the states of the upper South were coöperationists. Many advocated a conference of the slave states and a united demand for a redress of grievances. Many others advocated a determined effort to secure constitutional amendments as a means of preserving the Union, but wanted the existing status maintained until a positive act of aggression should be committed. The sequence of events which produced a fusion of parties in the lower South, however, wrought profound changes in sentiment among the people of the remaining slave states. The issues presented to them when the state legislatures met early in January were strikingly different from those which previously had occupied their attention.[1] There was no longer a question as to whether the elevation of the Republican party to power in the federal government justified a dissolution of the Union. The

[1] The legislature of Arkansas met in regular session on November 15, but took no action in the premises before the year's end. The legislatures of Missouri and Delaware met in regular session on December 31 and January 2, respectively. Governors Harris of Tennessee and Letcher of Virginia summoned the legislatures of their states to assemble in extra session on January 7; and the legislature of North Carolina reassembled on that date, having recessed for the Christmas holidays. Governor Magoffin of Kentucky did not call an extra session of the legislature until induced to do so on December 27 by Commissioner Hale of Alabama. It was to assemble on January 17.

213

Union was dissolved already by the withdrawal of several states, and all intelligent observers knew that a Southern confederacy would be formed. There was no longer a possibility of preventing a disruption of the Union by securing constitutional guarantees of Southern rights. The question was, Could something be done to reunite the states in a new confederation on a more permanent basis? Congress had failed to preserve the Union by conciliation, the majority party being apparently content to witness the development of a situation in which they would be forced to choose between acknowledging the existence of a Southern confederacy and waging a war of conquest. The upper South deprecated that dilemma, which meant death to the Union of accord; and its leaders undertook a direct appeal to the states on a program of reconstruction. However much men might deplore the separation of the states, or reproach the more Southern states for hasty and precipitate action, the right of the remaining states to coerce them into submission was denied. Men who had been schooled in the doctrine of state rights, and men who regarded civil war as the greatest evil which could befall a free people, united in a determination to resist any attempt of the federal government forcibly to assert its authority.[2]

[2] "A Constitutional Union is the only one worth preserving, and the only one that can be preserved in the affections of the American people. A Union of *force*, cemented and kept together by *force*, and perhaps by blood, is not the Union of the Constitution. And the effort to maintain such an Union will end, either in a degrading and oppressive despotism or a final and violent disruption of the Confederacy." *North Carolina Standard*, Raleigh, September 12, 1860. Speaking of the duty of Tennessee, the *Daily Nashville Patriot*, April 24, 1861, said: "Let her make no account either of blood or treasure, but arm to the teeth, and sooner than shrink from duty, sooner than sacrifice her honor, her liberty, or her rights, give up everything else. It is these only for which free men live; without these life itself is intolerance. Let but the great cardinal principle of free consent be

Added to this was the question of their own future security and welfare. The states of the upper South were more intimately connected, geographically, socially, and economically, with the lower South than they were with the North. They were, moreover, united by virtue of a common institution, sufficiently vital to their existence to cause apprehension over remaining as a hopeless minority under a government about to be controlled by a party hostile to that institution. They could not lose sight of the fact, in the course of their deliberations, that they soon must choose between joining their natural allies in a Southern confederacy, and remaining in a Union without protection for their institutions, without hope of political privileges, and without markets for their slave surplus. With a quarter of a million slaves, which could not be disposed of in the markets of the lower South, laboring under the pressure of a high protective tariff and the influence of a dominant anti-slavery party, emancipation would be certain to follow.

It was inevitable that the people of the upper South should disagree over the course their respective states ought to pursue. A substantial minority had favored secession from the time of the November election, and their number was daily augmented as war approached. The majority, who have been recorded in history as Union men, believed that the Union could be saved and the rights of the South preserved; and they endeavored to reconstruct the Union on a basis acceptable to that section. They seized upon the Crittenden amendments and urged

---

overturned and freedom is at an end." See, also, *ibid.*, April 17, 1861; *Richmond Semi-Weekly Examiner*, November 23, 1860; *The Daily Herald*, Wilmington, December 28, 1860; *The Review*, Charlottesville, January 4, 1861; *The Daily Picayune*, New Orleans, January 15, 1861.

their adoption, not because they represented their own previous convictions of the proper margin of safety for the South, but because they recognized them as an approach toward the peaceable adjustment of a dangerous issue, upon a basis of honor and justice to all concerned. They condemned the states of the lower South for refusing to participate in a Southern conference, and interpreted their action as indicating a desire to prevent a settlement; but at all times they insisted upon peaceable separation if reconstruction should fail. Some of them favored joining the Southern confederacy in the event of final separation. Others favored union with the lower South if the federal government undertook coercion. A few advocated armed neutrality in order to prevent hostilities.

Govern Hicks of Maryland, of all the governors of the upper South, denied the constitutional right of secession or coöperation by the slave states. Those who favored secession were estopped from taking legal action by his refusal to convene the legislature, despite widespread remonstrance and appeals from the interstate commissioners. A strong combination of circumstances, including a long non-slaveholding frontier and the location of the national capital, militated against revolutionary action within the state; and the direct appeals to the people by Commissioners Curry of Alabama and Handy of Mississippi produced no tangible results.[3]

In Delaware the legislature and not Governor Burton prevented coöperation with the other Southern states. Burton believed that the majority of the people favored a national convention, and would support the South in

[3] Curry to Hicks, December 28, 1860, *Official Records . . . Armies,* Series IV, Vol. I, 38-42; Handy to Pettus, January 10, 1861, Official Correspondence of Governor John J. Pettus, 1859-1860.

event of a dissolution of the Union; but the legislature, in reply to an address by Commissioner Dickinson of Mississippi, expressed an "unqualified disapproval" of secession.[4] On January 17, it passed resolutions endorsing the Crittenden amendments, and strongly urged their approval by Congress.[5]

Governor Henry M. Rector of Arkansas had informed the legislature early in their session that unless they provided for a convention to consider the state of the Union he would call an extra session for that purpose. On the evening of November 22, four aspirants for the United States Senate addressed the legislature. Every one of the four acknowledged the right of secession, and Burrows advised immediate action. The following night Congressmen Hindman and Gantt spoke and both favored secession, Hindman advising a three hundred thousand dollar appropriation for arms. A debate in the committee of the whole, November 24, over a bill to provide a death penalty for any who should steal or inveigle slaves was interpreted by Judge B. F. Boone, representative of the largest county of the state, as indicating strong secession sentiment in the house. Boone said in a letter to Judge Howry of Mississippi: "My convictions are, that overt acts will soon be made to wrest from us the rights we have guaranteed to us under the Constitution, and that sooner or later dissolution must come."[6] The proximity of strong Indian tribes introduced a peculiar complication in Arkan-

[4] Clopton to Burton, January 1, 1861, *Official Records . . . Armies,* Series IV, Vol. I, 34-38; Clopton to Moore, January 8, 1861, *ibid.,* 33-34; Dickinson to Pettus, January 10, 1861, Official Correspondence of Governor John J. Pettus, 1859-1860.

[5] "Resolutions of the Legislature of the State of Delaware approving the Crittenden Resolutions" in *House Mis. Docs.,* 36 Cong., 2 Sess., Doc. 21.

[6] Boone to Howry, November 24, 1860, Official Correspondence of Governor John J. Pettus, 1859-1860.

sas, the counties bordering upon the Indian country being reluctant to secede while those tribes remained under the control of the government of the United States. On December 22, the house passed a convention bill by a nearly unanimous vote. The bill was delayed in the senate and did not finally become a law until January 16, in a modified form. It submitted the question of calling a convention to the vote of the people to be cast when electing delegates on February 18.

Claiborne F. Jackson, elected governor of Missouri to succeed R. M. Stewart, belonged to that group of men who favored coöperative action for a redress of grievances. Some time after the election but before his inauguration, he wrote to General Shields that the time had come for a complete and final adjustment of sectional differences. He had no faith in a repeal of the personal liberty laws, because the states probably would reënact them. On the other hand, he did not regard the election of Lincoln as justification for a disruption of the Union. He advocated definitive amendments to the Constitution and penalties for the violation of Southern rights by the people of the Northern states. He would have convened the legislature if he had been acting governor, and would have sent commissioners to the other states to secure coöperative action for some remedy within the Union. He was in favor of secession if sufficient guarantees were not secured, and of resistance to coercion.[7] Governor Stewart, on the last day of his term in office, informed Commissioner William Cooper of Alabama that the people of Missouri were opposed to immediate secession, but that they were prepared to unite with the South in the

[7] Jackson to Shields, *Official Records . . . Armies,* Series IV, Vol. I, 26-28.

formation of a confederacy if terms of a fair adjustment were not secured from the non-slaveholding states.[8] Governor Jackson in his inaugural address urged the legislature to call a convention and to provide appropriations for arming the state. A convention bill was passed on January 16. The election was to be held on February 18, and the convention was to assemble on February 20. Two days later Commissioner A. R. Russell of Mississippi addressed the legislature, the state officials, and judges of the state supreme court. He declared that the Union would never be restored and that war was inevitable; and he urged Missouri to join with the other Southern states in defense of their rights.[9] The final act of the legislature previous to the date of the election of convention delegates was to pass resolutions, January 28, declaring that Missouri would withdraw from the Union if the federal government attempted to coerce any state which had seceded.

Governor Harris of Tennessee, in his message to the legislature, January 7, insisted that a united South must either secure its constitutional rights within the Union or maintain them in a Southern confederacy. He had despaired of securing constitutional guarantees, because two months had passed without a single proposal emanating from the aggressive party of the North; and because the Republican congressmen had voted down every project of that nature without protest from their constituents. He denied the right of coercion as "untrue to the example of our fathers and the glorious memories of the past; destructive of those great and fundamental principles of civil liberty, purchased with their blood;

[8] Cooper to Stewart, December 26, 1860, *ibid.*, 23-25; Stewart to Moore, December 30, 1860, *ibid.*, 25.
[9] Snead, *The Fight for Missouri*, 47.

destructive of state sovereignty and equality; tending to centralization, and thus subject the rights of the minority to the despotism of an unrestrained majority. Widely as we may differ with some of our sister Southern States as to the wisdom of their policy; desirous as we may be that whatever action taken in this emergency should be taken by the South as a unit; hopeful as we are of finding some remedy for our grievances consistent with the perpetuity of the present confederacy, the question, at last, is one which each member of that confederacy must determine for itself; and any attempt upon the part of the others to hold, by means of military force, an unwilling sovereignty as a member of a common Union, must inevitably lead to the worst form of internecine war, and if successful, result in the establishment of a new and totally different government from the one established by the Constitution—the Constitutional Union being a Union of consent and not of force, of peace, and not of blood—composed of sovereignties, free, and politically equal. But the new and coercive government, while it would 'derive its powers' to govern a portion of the states 'from the consent of the governed,' would derive the power by which it governed the remainder from the cannon and the sword, and not from their consent—a Union, not of equals, but of the victors and the vanquished, pinned together by the bayonet and congealed in blood." [10]

T. J. Wharton, commissioner from Mississippi, had arrived at Nashville several days before the legislature convened, had consulted with the governor and other prominent officials, and had addressed the legislature on January 8. He avoided a discussion of the theory of

[10] Harris to the Legislature of Tennessee, January 7, 1861, in *The Daily True Delta*, January 13, 1861.

secession, but presented the issue on practical grounds. He spoke of the 18,000 secession majority returned by the voters of Mississippi, and of the large majority in the state convention for prompt action. He defended the states of the lower South in not asking for a conference by saying that all such plans fostered delay, and delay was dangerous. Devotion to the Union was as strong in Mississippi as it could possibly be in Tennessee, but "her honor and her constitutional rights she may not, dare not surrender." Lincoln, as shown by his utterances, was devoted to the ultimate extinction of slavery, and his ominous silence since the election was pregnant with meaning. The hope that abolition sentiment would abate was a vain delusion, for "never, in the history of nations, has such a spirit paused or taken a step backward." Whether the people of Tennessee condemned the action of South Carolina as ill-advised and unfair to the other states, or approved it, the fact remained that she had acted, and "we may find ourselves borne along by the current of events, and forced to defend what we might be unwilling to aid in producing." [11]

L. P. Walker, commissioner from Alabama, addressed the legislature on the following day; and an act, submitting the question of calling a convention to the people, February 9, was passed immediately afterward. The convention, if approved, was to meet on February 25, and its action was to be submitted to the people for their ratification. [12]

[11] Wharton, "Address before the Tennessee Legislature, January 9, 1861," in *Journal of the Mississippi State Convention . . . 1861*, 150-161.

[12] "An Act providing for a Convention of the People of Tennessee," in the *Nashville Union and American*, January 20, 1861. Walker meanwhile wrote to Governor Moore of Alabama: "I beg to report as the result of my mission that there is, in my opinion, no

The Tennessee legislature passed, January 20, a joint resolution condemning the New York resolutions as an "indication of a purpose upon the part of the people of that State to further complicate existing difficulties by forcing the people of the South to the extremity of submission or resistance; and . . . whenever the authorities of that state shall send armed forces to the South for the purpose indicated in said resolutions, the people of Tennessee, uniting with their brethren of the South, will, as one man, resist such invasion of the soil of the South at all hazards and to the last extremity." [13] The following day it passed a joint resolution requesting a convention of all the slaveholding states at Nashville on February 4, "to digest and define bases upon which, if possible, the federal Union and the constitutional rights of the slave states may be preserved and perpetuated." The resolutions requested the following amendments to the Constitution: (1) that all slaves should be regarded as property in the slave states, in all places under the jurisdiction of the federal government, within the limits of the slave states, in the territories south of 36 degrees

---

doubt that Tennessee will unite with the Gulf States in forming a Southern Confederacy. The right or wrong of secession is not the question submitted for their determination. That may very well be pretermitted in that State. The Union is dissolved without their action, and the practical question for them to decide is, Shall they go with the North or with the South? And in deciding this question the result is obvious. There is a geographical necessity that Tennessee shall unite with the South . . . her natural sympathies are stimulated by her commercial necessities and make her drift quietly and surely into the union of the Southern States. I consider this result as absolutely certain." Walker to Moore, January 16, 1861, *Official Records . . . Armies*, Series IV, Vol. I, 56.

[13] "Resolutions of the Legislature of the State of Tennessee relative to the Resolutions of the Legislature of the State of New York tendering Men and Money to the General Government to be used to coerce certain sovereign States into Obedience to the General Government," *House Mis. Docs.*, 36 Cong., 2 Sess., Doc. 22.

30 minutes, in the District of Columbia, in transit, and when fugitive from their owners; (2) that all territory, then owned or thereafter acquired, should be regarded as divided on the line of 36 degrees 30 minutes, all south of that line to be formed ultimately into slave states, all north to be formed into free states, and slavery to be protected in all territory south of that line; (3) that Congress should have no power to abolish slavery in the District of Columbia so long as it existed in either Maryland or Virginia, nor without compensation; (4) that Congress should have no power to prohibit the interstate slave trade; (5) that the owner of fugitive slaves should receive compensation for losses incurred through the failure of a state to abide by the provisions of the fugitive slave law; (6) that the slaveholder should enjoy the right of transit with his property; and (7) that these amendments should be perpetual. The resolution further pro-vided that after the Southern convention had agreed upon a satisfactory basis of adjustment, it should be submitted to a national convention at Richmond, Virginia; and that, if guarantees of Southern rights thus formulated were not adopted by the requisite number of states, a new confederacy should be formed excluding those states which refused to ratify the demands.[14]

Governor Magoffin of Kentucky had appealed to the slave states, December 9, to join in a Southern convention in order to present a united demand for constitutional guarantees. Ten days later he assured W. S. Featherstone, commissioner from Mississippi, that the majority of the people of Kentucky were thoroughly Southern in their sympathies; that, in the event of the permanent dissolu-

---

[14] "Resolutions of the Legislature of the State of Tennessee, relative to the present Condition of National Affairs and suggesting certain Amendments to the Constitution," *ibid.*, Doc. 27.

tion of the Union, the state would join a Southern confederacy; but that the then prevailing sentiment was unquestionably in favor of exhausting every honorable means of securing their rights within the Union.[15] He did not summon the legislature into extra session until persuaded to do so by Stephen F. Hale, commissioner from Alabama, December 27. He stated, in his communication to Hale, that "the rights of African slavery in the United States, and the relations of the Federal Government to it, as an institution in the States and Territoreis, most assuredly demand at this time explicit definition and final recognition by the North." He urged a conference of the Southern states in the belief that the demands of the South would be conceded, and a stronger Union perpetuated; that the sentiment of the Southern people would be crystallized into a unit by coöperative action; and that the support of conservative Northern men would be secured for the South if compromise failed.[16]

In his message to the legislature which assembled on January 17, Magoffin asked it to express an approval of the Crittenden amendments, to appropriate funds for arming the state, and to declare, by suitable resolutions, an unconditional remonstrance against the employment of force in any form to coerce the seceding states. He

[15] Featherstone to Pettus, January 22, 1861, Official Correspondence of Governor John J. Pettus, 1859-1860.

[16] Hale to Moore, January 3, 1861, Official Records . . . Armies, Series IV, Vol. I, 4; Magoffin to Hale, December 28, 1860, ibid., 11-15. That he actually had little hope of preserving the Union, however, and was chiefly concerned with the hope of a peaceable separation of the states, is shown by his further statement: "So far as the policy of the incoming Administration is foreshadowed in the antecedents of the President elect, in the enunciations of its representative men, and the avowals of the press, it will be to ignore the acts of sovereignty thus proclaimed by Southern States, and of coercing the continuance of the Union. Its inevitable result will be civil war of the most fearful and revolting character."

suggested the propriety of calling a state convention to determine the future relations of the state with the federal government and the seven states which were certain to secede, and urged that everything possible be done to restore fraternal relations between the states.[17] On January 25 the legislature passed resolutions applying to Congress for a national convention, urging the other states to take similar action, and recommending the Crittenden amendments as a basis for settlement of the existing difficulties.[18]

Governor Letcher of Virginia in his message to the legislature, January 7, 1861, advocated a national convention of delegates from all the states. He had relinquished all hope of preserving the Union and assumed the position that Virginia must have ample guarantees of peace and security irrespective of whether she remained with the North or joined in the formation of a Southern confederacy. He opposed a state convention and suggested that a commission be sent to each of the Northern states, except those of New England, to urge the repeal of the personal liberty laws. He regarded New England as too completely committed to Republican principles to listen to reason and justice. As guarantees necessary to secure the continued adherence of Virginia to the federal Union, he mentioned: (1) non-interference with slavery in the District of Columbia; (2) the right of the slaveholder to transmit through all states and territories with his property; (3) full compensation from any state whose citizens obstructed the recovery of a fugitive slave; (4) non-interference with the interstate slave trade; (5)

---

[17] "Magoffin to the Kentucky State Legislature, January 17, 1861," in the *Daily Missouri Republican*, January 20, 1861.

[18] "Resolutions of the Legislature of Kentucky, applying for a Call of a Convention for proposing Amendments to the Constitution of the United States," *House Ex. Docs.*, 36 Cong., 2 Sess., Doc. 55, 2.

stringent laws for the punishment of any person undertaking to incite slaves to insurrection; and (6) guarantees that the federal government would not appoint to local office within the slave states any person hostile to Southern institutions. To what extent he actually hoped to secure such guarantees it is impossible to say; but he was very positive in his declaration that any attempt to send federal troops through Virginia for the purpose of coercing a Southern state would be regarded as an invasion of the sovereignty of the state, and would be resisted to the last extremity. In spite of Letcher's opposition to a state convention at that time, and of his denunciation of the haste with which South Carolina had withdrawn from the Union, there can be little doubt of his Southern sympathies. In addition to his official documents, which are hostile to Republican supremacy, we have a letter of a prominent officer of the Knights of the Golden Circle, which said: "Our Governor you can trust; place all confidence in him—I am assured by many gentlemen, who know him well, and are placed in daily communication with him, that there is no truer man in the South, and when the time comes for Virginia to move, that he will be found in the front ranks of our Southern Governors." [19] Letcher was reflecting in his official message the prevailing sentiment, that Virginia must delay until better prepared for armed resistance. E. C. Burks, member of the legislature and of the two important committees on federal relations and military affairs, said: "If we are to fight (God grant we never may!) it will take a *long* time to get ready. Virginia needs *delay*—she *must* have it, or I fear all is lost. . . . *Immediate* secession

[19] Colonel V. D. Grover, K.G.C., to Pettus, December 6, 1860, Official Correspondence of Governor John J. Pettus, 1859-1860.

therefore *in my opinion* would be fatal. . . . That is the opinion of some of the coolest and clearest heads here— Democrats, too, who acknowledge the *right* of secession, but look to it as the last resort." [20]

On the second day of its session the legislature adopted resolutions, by a vote of 112 to 5, promising the resistance of Virginia to any attempt by the federal government to coerce a seceding state. A bill providing for a state convention was introduced into the house on January 9, providing for an election on February 4 of delegates who were to meet on February 11. The bill passed both houses of the legislature on January 14, amended to postpone the assembling of the convention until February 13. A. F. Hopkins, commissioner from Alabama, addressed the legislature on January 16. The following day the house passed a bill appropriating one million dollars to arm the state. The bill was delayed in the Senate for two months by the opposition of the members from the western part of the state, and did not become a law until March 14. On January 19 the legislature passed a resolution inviting all the states to send delegates to a conference at Washington, February 4, "to unite with Virginia in an earnest effort to adjust the present unhappy controversies in the spirit in which the Constitution was originally formed and consistently with its principles, so as to afford to the people of the slaveholding States adequate guarantees for the security of their rights . . . and, if practicable, agree upon some suitable adjustment." The resolutions provided that, if the conference should agree upon a plan of adjustment requiring constitutional amendments, they should be submitted to Congress for the pur-

[20] Burks to Buford, January 20, 1861, in *The American Historical Review*, xxxi, 87.

pose of having them ratified by the states according to
the form of the Constitution. As a basis for the adjustment of the political controversy, the resolutions suggested the Crittenden amendments, so altered as to apply
to all territory "now held or hereafter acquired," to provide for effectual protection for slavery in the territory
south of 36 degrees 30 minutes, and to secure to slaveholders the right of transit through non-slaveholding
states and territories. The resolutions appointed Ex-
President Tyler as commissioner to confer with President
Buchanan, and Judge John Robertson as commissioner to
the states which had seceded, and instructed them both
to request abstention from all acts "calculated to produce
a collision of arms between the States and the Government
of the United States," pending the action of the convention.[21] Two days later the legislature adopted a resolution which stated that in the event of a failure to effect
a reconstruction of the Union "every consideration of
honor and interest demands that Virginia shall unite her
destiny with the slaveholding states of the South."[22]

Thus the legislatures of all of the states of the upper
South had provided, before January 19, for state conventions or for submitting the question of calling a convention to the people, with the exception of North Carolina,
Delaware, Maryland, and Kentucky. North Carolina
passed a convention bill on January 30; and the failure
of the Kentucky legislature to do so was due in part to
the fact that the Virginia program was outlined two days
after it assembled. Every state, with the exception of

[21] "Joint Resolutions inviting the other States to send Commissioners to meet Commissioners on the part of Virginia, and providing
for the Appointment of the Same," *Official Records . . . Armies,*
Series IV, Vol. I, 90-91.

[22] "Joint Resolution Concerning the Position of Virginia in Event
of the Dissolution of the Union," *ibid.,* 77.

Maryland, had passed resolutions endorsing the Crittenden amendments or proposing other amendments of a
similar nature, and had emphatically denied the right of
coercion and indicated a determination to resist such a
policy.

The program outlined by the Virginia legislature
rivaled the removal of Anderson to Fort Sumter in its
influence upon subsequent events. The success of the
proposed measures of reconstruction was contingent upon
the elimination of innumerable obstacles. It was imperative that military collision be prevented. The efficacy of
the proposal was dependent upon a favorable response to
the invitation by a sufficient number of states to lend
dignity to its proceedings. The commissioners appointed
to the conference must agree upon some basis of compromise acceptable to the two hostile sections, to Congress,
and subsequently to the state legislatures or conventions.
It was an impossible program, but the entire course of
the secession movement in the states of the upper South
was altered by it.

The disruption of Buchanan's Cabinet, followed by the
sending of reinforcements to the Southern forts, and by
the *Star of the West* fiasco, had been interpreted both at
the North and at the South as indicating a determination
on the part of the administration to enforce federal
authority in the seceding states. The importance of this
interpretation has already been indicated as a factor in the
secession of the states of the lower South. The Republican legislatures of the Northern states and the Republican
majorities in both houses of Congress took advantage of
the opportunity to force the issue to a conclusion under
the Buchanan administration. The New York resolutions
evoked immediate response from the states of the upper

South, and clearly indicated the result which would attend any attempt at coercion. How long conservative sentiment in such states as Virginia, North Carolina, and Tennessee would have prevailed under repetitions of the New York resolutions by other Northern states must be purely a matter of conjecture, for the invitation to a peace conference acted as a palliative to counteract their effect, and as they were received by the legislatures of the Southern states they were put aside without further response.

The Ohio resolutions, January 12, stated "that the General Government cannot permit the secession of any State without violating the obligations by which it is bound, under the compact, to the other States and to every citizen of the United States . . . and that the entire power and resources of Ohio are hereby pledged, whenever necessary and demanded, for the maintenance, under strict subordination, to the civil authority of the Constitution and laws of the general government by whomsoever administered." [23]

The Ohio resolutions were followed, January 18, by those of Maine, which summarized the secession movement as "an extensive combination . . . of evil-disposed persons, to effect the dissolution of the federal Union and the overthrow of the government," assured the President of the loyalty of the people of Maine, and pledged the resources of the state to the defense of the Constitution and the Union. [24] The Wisconsin resolutions, January 21, interpreted the seizure of the federal forts in South Carolina, Georgia, Alabama, and Louisiana as an indication of hostile intentions, and the attack upon the *Star of the*

[23] "Resolutions of the Legislature of the State of Ohio, on the State of the Republic," *House Mis. Docs.*, 36 Cong., 2 Sess., Doc. 18.
[24] "Resolutions of the Legislature of the State of Maine relating to existing national Affairs," *ibid.*, Doc. 26.

*West* as a declaration of war. They denounced those congressmen who defended these treasonable acts, and pledged the resources of the state to the use of the President in enforcing the laws and upholding the federal authority.[25] The legislature of Minnesota, January 22, passed resolutions which stated that, since the rule of the constitutional majority was one of the vital principles of free government, the right of secession could not be acknowledged under any circumstances; that the secession of any state amounted to the precipitation of civil war; and that the election of Lincoln did not justify a disruption of the Union. They stated that "we have heard with astonishment and indignation of the recent outrages perpetrated at Charleston, South Carolina, by firing upon an American steamer, sailing under the flag of our country, and that we expect of the General Government the strongest and most vigorous effort to assert its supremacy, and to check the work of rebellion and treason." They tendered the full resources of the state for that purpose, and said: "We can discover no other honorable or patriotic resource than to test, both on land and ocean, the full strength of the Federal authority under our National Flag." [26] The legislature of Pennsylvania, January 24, denounced "all plots, conspiracies, and warlike demonstrations against the United States" as treason, called upon the President to suppress them without hesitation, and offered the resources of the state for that purpose.[27] The legislature

[25] "Joint Resolutions coöperating with friends of the Union throughout the United States," Official Correspondence of Governor John J. Pettus, 1859-1860.

[26] "Joint Resolutions of the Legislature of the State of Minnesota, on the State of the Union," *House Misc. Docs.*, 36 Cong., 2 Sess., Doc. 33.

[27] "Resolutions of the Legislature of the State of Pennsylvania, relative to the Maintenance of the Constitution and Union," *ibid.*, Doc. 24.

of Michigan, February 2, resolved, "That concession and compromise are not to be entertained or offered to traitors," and tendered the military resources of that state to assist in maintaining the authority of the federal government.[28]

Meanwhile, the withdrawal of the senators and representatives of the seceding states from Congress had given the Republican party a majority in both houses, and there was a clear indication that they intended to force Buchanan's hand, if possible. Crittenden's amendments had been defeated in both houses, but he reintroduced them into the Senate, with a further provision for a national convention, and was devoting his effort to bring them to a vote. Finally, January 16, they were definitely disposed of by the adoption of an amendment, offered by Clark of New Hampshire, which stated "that the provisions of the Constitution are ample for the preservation of the Union, and the protection of all the material interests of the country; that it needs to be obeyed rather than amended; and that an extrication from our present dangers is to be looked for in strenuous efforts to preserve the peace, protect the public property, and enforce the laws, rather than in new guarantees for particular interests, compromises for particular difficulties, or concessions to unreasonable demands." [29] It was clear that the Republican party was determined to resist all measures of conciliation, and to oppose peaceful separation.

The country was dangerously near to civil war when Ex-President Tyler arrived at Washington and presented the Virginia resolutions to Buchanan on January 24. Every federal military post of importance in six states of

[28] "Joint Resolutions of the Legislature of the State of Michigan, relative to the State of the Union," *ibid.*, Doc. 38.
[29] *Cong. Globe*, 36 Cong., 2 Sess., I, 404, 409.

the lower South had been occupied by state troops with the exception of Forts Jefferson, Taylor, Sumter, and Pickens. A temporary armistice had been entered into between Anderson and Governor Pickens, and Attorney General Hayne was in Washington to negotiate with Buchanan for the surrender of Fort Sumter. The federal forces at Pensacola remained in possession of Fort Pickens, but the fort was besieged by superior forces under the command of Colonel Chase who had supervised its construction. The intercession of Mallory, Slidell, and other Southern senators at Washington had delayed the delivery of the formal demand upon Buchanan for the surrender of Fort Sumter; and it may be safely asserted that, when Virginia passed her resolutions on January 19, those senators stood alone between the country and certain war. Five states were already out of the Union, and two more were certain to follow before February 4. Eight Northern states had passed resolutions endorsing a policy of coercion and had offered their resources to the federal government. Congress had refused to call a national convention, and had voted down the only proposal which offered a possibility of peaceable reconstruction. The majority of the states of the upper South were on record as unalterably opposed to coercion and in favor of the amendments which Congress had rejected. The President was misunderstood by every section of the country. Only a person of the most sanguine temperament could have hoped to avert the impending crisis.

Tyler had favored a convention of the border states in a public letter on January 17.[30] The following day he said: "The course of the Pennsylvania and Ohio Legisla-

[30] Tyler, *The Letters and Times of the Tylers,* II, 579. The border states were: Delaware, Maryland, Virginia, Kentucky, Tennessee, Missouri, New Jersey, Pennsylvania, Ohio, Indiana, Illinois, and Iowa.

tures, made known to me on yesterday, leaves but little hope of any adjustment. . . . The fate of Crittenden's project, I suppose, will nearly conclude matters." [31] One day later the legislature adopted its resolutions and Tyler hastened to Washington and presented them to Buchanan, January 24, previous to the departure of Hayne. Buchanan refused to enter into an agreement to refrain "from any and all acts calculated to produce a collision," as requested by Virginia, holding that he had no constitutional power to agree not to do what Congress might at any time compel by legislation. Four days later he sent a message to Congress earnestly requesting it to pass no hostile legislation pending the proceedings of the Washington Conference.

Before Tyler arrived at Washington, the *Brooklyn* had been ordered South with troops and supplies from Fortress Monroe, January 21. Commissioner Robertson wired Tyler from Charleston, January 25, to ascertain if the expedition was intended to reinforce Fort Sumter. Stanton and Black were in conference with Tyler at the time, having called at the request of Buchanan to explain the reason for the delay in transmitting his communication to Congress. Tyler inquired of them whether the orders to the *Brooklyn* had been issued since his arrival in Washington and, neither having any knowledge of the matter, Stanton carried a note of inquiry from Tyler to Buchanan. The latter replied that Fort Sumter was not the destination of the *Brooklyn,* and that the expedition was one of "mercy and relief." Tyler forwarded this assurance to Robertson. [32] Meanwhile, news of the expedition reached Pensacola, and former Senator Mallory wired to Slidell,

. [31] John Tyler to Robert Tyler, January 18, 1861, *ibid.,* 578-579.
[32] Tyler, *ibid.,* 589-590; Tyler to Robertson, January 5 (26), 1861, *Official Records . . . Armies,* Series I, Vol. I, 253.

Hunter, and Bigler that no attack upon Fort Pickens was contemplated; that it was the desire of the besieging forces to preserve the present status and avoid bloodshed; but that attempted reinforcements would lead to immediate war. He concluded, "I am determined to stave off war, if possible.[33] This message from Mallory was transmitted to Buchanan and orders were sent by telegraph and by special messenger to prevent the landing of troops from the *Brooklyn*. Slemmer was also instructed to act strictly on the defensive and avoid, if possible, a collision with the Southern forces concentrated at Pensacola. This action on the part of Buchanan was strictly in accord with his previously defined policy with regard to Fort Sumter, and was prompted by his desire to preserve peace until after the deliberations of the Washington conference convention should be completed.[34] Whatever may have been his previous aversion to an agreement, this was understood to be a solemn compact by the Southern military leaders. Chase abandoned the erection of a battery, February 12, upon protest from Slemmer, saying: "I am determined to make good the assurances that I have given, that no attack shall be made on Fort Pickens, and . . . desiring to avoid all actual or implied preparations for an attack, I will give orders for the discontinuance of the erection of the battery." [35] As late as April 3 General Bragg allowed a favorable opportunity to capture Fort Pickens to pass, because he was uncertain about the continued force of the "agreement of 29th January." [36]

[33] Mallory to Slidell, January 28, 1861, *ibid.*, 354.
[34] Holt to Slemmer, January 29, 1861, *ibid.*, 355; Holt and Toucey to Glyn, Walker, and Slemmer, January 29, 1861, *ibid.*, 355-356.
[35] Slemmer to Chase, February 11, 1861, *ibid.*, 359; Chase to Slemmer, February 12, 1861, *ibid.*, 359.
[36] Bragg to Walker, April 6, 1861, *ibid.*, 456-457.

This agreement, having been made previous to the formation of a Southern confederacy, applied only to the posts at Pensacola, and the situation at Charleston was still disquieting. Hayne sent his final communication to Buchanan on February 1, and left for Charleston three days later. Robertson had meanwhile gone to Montgomery, and had submitted the Virginia resolutions to Governor Moore, with the following statement:

Looking with deep concern at the menacing attitude in which the seceded States, and the Government at Washington stand towards each other, the state of Virginia appeals to both parties to abstain from all acts of a hostile tendency, until a farther effort shall be made to terminate existing differences, by an honorable and peaceful adjustment.[37]

Moore expressed appreciation for the friendly mediation contemplated by Virginia, and assured Robertson that, in resuming her independence and occupying the forts and arsenals within the limits of the state, Alabama intended no hostility to the federal government; that the only object had been to protect the rights and interests of the state without disturbing peaceful relations; and that this would continue to be the policy of the state unless the government at Washington resorted to a hostile demonstration against the seceding states. He promised to transmit the Virginia resolutions to the Alabama legislature, but with the statement that he did "not feel authorized to indulge the least hope that concessions will be made affording such guarantees as the seceding States can or will accept." [38] Roberston was invited to address the legislature on February 7, but he declined on the ground that his commission limited the scope of his activi-

[37] Robertson to Moore, February 3, 1861, in the *Montgomery Daily Advertiser*, February 7, 1861.
[38] Moore to Robertson, February 3, 1861, in *ibid*.

ties to communications with the executive authorities of the several seceding states.[39] Meanwhile, Tyler had been elected chairman of the Washington conference and was serving in that capacity in addition to performing his duties as commissioner to the federal government. On February 7, he telegraphed to Robertson that Hayne had returned to Charleston, and urged him to prevent a collision at that point.[40] At the same time he sent the following telegram to Governor Pickens:

> Can my voice reach you? If so, do not attack Fort Sumter. You know my sincerity. The Virginia delegation here earnestly unite.

Two days later he wired Pickens that Buchanan's letter to Hayne was designed to be both respectful and kind; and that Buchanan deeply regretted any offense it may have conveyed. He also inquired of Pickens whether he would give an assurance not to attack Fort Sumter if Buchanan would consent not to attempt to send reinforcements.[41] At this point in the negotiations the formation of the Confederate States government intervened to relieve the officials of the state governments from further responsibility. The congress of the Confederate States, February 12, assumed the burden of negotiating with the government at Washington for the surrender of the forts and other public property.[42] This action was telegraphed to Governor Pickens, but his reply to Howell Cobb, president

[39] Robertson to McIntyre, Ligon, Walker, Hubbard, and Lyon, February 7, *ibid.*, February 8, 1861.

[40] Tyler to Robertson, February 7, 1861, *Official Records . . . Armies,* Series I, Vol. I, 253.

[41] Tyler to Pickens, February 9, 1861, *ibid.*, 254.

[42] *Acts and Resolutions of the First Session of the Provisional Congress of the Confederate States,* 1861, 5.

of the provisional congress, was a clear indication that there was still danger of an attack by the forces of the state.[43]

Meanwhile, the Washington conference convention assembled on February 4, in accordance with the Virginia program; and the continued influence of Tyler, together with a judicious handling of the situation by President Davis and Secretary of War Walker, prevented the outbreak of war during its deliberations.[44] The importance of the convention lies principally in its influence upon the elections of delegates to the conventions of the states of the upper South.[45] A correct understanding of the situation, however, requires an investigation of the nature and composition of the convention.

[43] Pickens to Cobb, February 13, 1861, *Official Records . . . Armies,* Series I, Vol. I, 254-257.

[44] Tyler to Pickens, February 18, 1861, *ibid.,* 257; Tyler to Pickens, February 21, 1861, *ibid.,* 257; Pickens to Davis, February 27, 1861, *ibid.,* 258-259; Walker to Pickens, March 1, 1861, *ibid.,* 259-260.

[45] Dates of elections: Virginia, February 4; Tennessee, February 9; Missouri, February 18; Arkansas, February 18; North Carolina, February 28.

# CHAPTER XII

## THE WASHINGTON CONFERENCE CONVENTION

THE proposed Washington conference was the last expedient of the border slave state conservatives to arrest revolution and political distintegration. Three months had passed since the November election. They had first proposed a conference of the slave states to consolidate Southern demands into a concerted program. The immediate secessionists rejected their plea, suspected their fealty to Southern rights, and frequently assailed them as submissionists. They coöperated with the conservatives of the border free states in an effort to conquer partisanship in the proceedings of Congress and procure definitive amendments to the Constitution. In this case the response from the Southern-rights men was favorable, but the rejection of every proposal by the majority party, representing Northern sectionalism, thwarted the hopes of the most conservative. Convinced that an unwilling Congress would adopt no remedy sufficient to counteract the trend toward separation, they asked for a national convention as the only constitutional means of referring the question to the sovereign people. This proposal was likewise rejected by the Republican party in Congress. Finally, after two months had passed without a single assurance of an adjustment of the national difficulties, the legislatures of five states turned their attention to the interests of their own constituents, and made provision for state conventions.

At this particular moment a new probability was thrust into the midst of the already distracting situation, which demanded the exercise of superior judgment and fortitude, the imminence of civil war. The men who had carried the burden of attempted conciliation and reconstruction, who had been equally misjudged as submissionists by the immediate secessionists and as unconditional Unionists by the Republicans, remained loyal to their constitutional obligations as they understood them, but with a determination to defend their constitutional rights and the sovereignty of their states.[1] They regarded the burden of proof as resting upon the federal government in its relations with the states, and were determined to resist coercion as subversive to liberty and the eternal principles of free government. The threatened collision between the federal troops and those of the Southern states, followed by the hostile resolutions of the Northern state legislatures, presented to the conservatives of the upper South an issue which they had not expected to arise until after the inauguration of Lincoln if at all. The Washington conference was their response to a new and dangerous

[1] "So limited is the understanding of Southern principles that the North is wholly insensible to the truth that there is no Union party in some ten or more slaveholding States. It confounds Coöperationists with Unionists, and is possessed with the fallacious idea that because many high-minded and sincere Southerners believed it would be more expedient for the Cotton States to act in concert than to withdraw separately, they are all anxious to preserve the Union, albeit at the price of submission to the administration of Abraham Lincoln. This is a wild and absolutely baseless notion. Seven-eights of the Coöperationists are heartily in favor of secession." *The New Orleans Bee*, January 22, 1861. See, also, *The Daily South Carolinian*, December 9, 1860; *The Daily Herald*, Wilmington, March 8, 1861; *The Daily True Delta*, New Orleans, February 15, 1861; *Louisville Daily Journal*, January 5, 1861; *The Daily Picayune*, New Orleans, December 28, 1860.

situation. Its object was threefold: (1) to arrange some plan of conciliation (not necessarily of reconstruction), and to urge its adoption by Congress with all the moral force arising from its endorsement by the representatives of powerful constituencies; (2) to force from the governments of the Northern states some indication of their attitude toward compromise and conciliation; and (3) to counteract the drift toward civil war and allow time for a conservative reaction to develop.

The first objective was defeated before the conference met, because of the nature of the invitation. Virginia had requested a response from all states, "whether slaveholding or non-slaveholding, as are willing to unite with Virginia in an earnest effort to adjust the present unhappy controversies, in the spirit in which the Constitution was originally formed, and consistently with its principles so as to afford to the people of the slaveholding States adequate guarantees for the security of their rights . . . and, if practicable, agree upon some suitable adjustment." [2] Twenty-one of the thirty-four states were represented. Delegates from six states of the lower South met on the same day at Montgomery for the purpose of forming a Southern confederacy, and these sent no commissioners to Washington. All the remaining states were represented except Texas, Arkansas, Michigan, Wisconsin, Minnesota, California, and Oregon. The slave states of the upper South would doubtless have been able to arrange some tangible agreement along the lines of the Crittenden amendments, if they had adhered to their original plan of a conference of Southern states for coöperative action; but the appointment of commissioners

[2] *Official Journal of the Conference Convention held at Washington City, February, 1861*, 3.

by the ultra-Republican states of New England introduced elements into the conference too heterogeneous to coalesce. Most of the Northern state legislatures professed a desire to prevent the impending strife, but they differed from the people of the slave states over the validity of grievances, and consequently over the nature of remedies. They sent commissioners to the conference, moreover, for the avowed purpose of obstructing the early consummation of its deliberations. This was in accord with the tactics previously employed in both houses of Congress.

The legislature of Ohio, in conformity with this policy, appointed commissioners to Washington with instructions to use their influence to secure an adjournment until April 4, being "fully satisfied that the Constitution of the United States as it is, if fairly interpreted and obeyed by all sections of our country, contains ample provisions within itself for the correction of all evils complained of . . ." [3] The Indiana commissioners were directed to take no action until at least nineteen states were represented, to refrain from final action upon any proposed amendments until after referring the matter to the legislature, and to insist upon an adjournment until all the states should have time to appoint commissioners. [4] The legislature of Illinois appointed commissioners, because of an "earnest desire for the return of harmony and kind relations . . . and out of respect to the Commonwealth of Virginia," but with the statement that constitutional amendments were not necessary to secure adequate guarantees of Southern

[3] "Joint Resolutions of the General Assembly of the State of Ohio, relative to the Appointment of Commissioners to the Convention to meet in Washington on the 4th of February, proximo," in *ibid.*, 88.

[4] "A Joint Resolution authorizing the Governor to appoint Commissioners to meet those sent by other States in Convention on the State of the Union," in *ibid.*, 88.

rights, and that the appropriate way to act upon the grievances complained of was by a national convention, as
provided for in the Constitution. The Pennsylvania resolutions expressed the opinion that "no reasonable cause
exists for this extraordinary excitement which now per-
vades some of the States, in relation to our domestic institution, and . . . the people of Pennsylvania do not desire
any alteration or amendment of the Constitution of the
United States." [5] Expressions of this nature from the
legislatures of the several states indicate the predominance
of that wing of the Republican party which refused to
admit the claims of the South for additional guarantees,
denounced secession as treason, and was willing to combat
it with military force. Their presence in the conference
served only to hamper the efforts of the representatives
from the upper South. Beyond a question some of the
commissioners from the Northern states were willing to
acknowledge that the South was not altogether wrong and
preferred compromise to civil war; but in every case they
constituted the minority in their state delegations and were
helpless because of the second peculiar feature of the
convention.

Virginia did not specify in her invitation the basis for
representation in the conference, and there was no uniformity in this respect. Delaware, Illinois, Indiana, Missouri, North Carolina, and Rhode Island followed the
example of Virginia and appointed five commissioners to
the conference; but Connecticut, Iowa, Maine, Vermont,
and Tennessee sent delegations equal to their electoral
votes. Maryland, Massachusetts, Ohio, and Pennsylvania
appointed seven commissioners. Kentucky sent six, New

Hampshire three, New Jersey nine, New York eleven, and Kansas four. The result was that the New England states, with a combined electoral vote of forty-one, were represented by thirty-four commissioners; the remaining free states, with an electoral vote of sixty-nine, were represented by forty-five commissioners. Whatever may have been the plan of procedure expected by those who conceived the idea of the convention, this irregularity of numbers compelled the conference to resort to the doubtful expediency of voting by states; and the seven slave states were at a tremendous disadvantage in securing the adoption of satisfactory recommendations.

A third factor militating against the success of the conference was the fact that it was held in Washington, where a partisan struggle of unusual proportions was being waged, during the last days of the Democratic administration, for the control of the federal offices and the distribution of $100,000,000 in patronage. The congressional leaders of the Republican party were hostile to any proposal which might tend to disorganize their party. Their one hope of permanent ascendancy rested upon an inflexible adherence to the Chicago platform; and whatever tendency the Republican members of the conference might otherwise have shown toward a willingness to make concessions was counteracted by the overpowering influence of party control.

Unpropitious as were these circumstances, they were completely overshadowed by the influence of the elections in Virginia and Tennessee. Their people were staking everything on the success of the Washington conference, and the response of the Northern states to the invitation of Virginia produced a conservative reaction against immediate secession. As a result, very few immediate secessionists were elected to the Virginia convention, February 4; and in Tennessee, five days later, the question of calling a convention was defeated by a popular vote of about 69,000 to 59,000. H. P. Bell and W. C. Daniell, commissioners from Georgia to Tennessee and Kentucky, respectively, arrived in Nashville on the day of the election, and held an extended conference with Governor Harris and Henry S. Foote. They explained the vote as indicative of a widespread belief that the Washington conference would be successful and that the purpose of the seceding states was to return eventually to the Union on a favorable basis granted by the North.[6]

Unfortunately, the successful party in these states was known as the Union party, and the term "Union" had one meaning in Virginia and Tennessee and quite a different meaning in the Northwest and in New England. Nothing can be more certain than the fact that, although few secessionists favoring immediate action were elected to the Virginia convention, there were still fewer unconditional submissionists elected, and that the latter party was in a hopeless minority in Tennessee. The Republicans, however, accepted the term "Union," as used in these states, to mean inflexible opposition to the course adopted by the lower South, interpreted the results of the elections as an indication that those states would not join with the lower South under any circumstances, and became less inclined than before to accede to any proposal capable of reconstructing the Union or of preventing the defection of the remaining slave states. The fallacy of this interpretation is clearly shown by the anti-coercion resolutions passed, by almost unanimous votes, in the leg-

[6] Walker to Moore, January 16, 1861, *Official Records . . . Armies,* Series IV, Vol. I, 56; Daniell, "Report," in *Journal of the Convention of the People of Georgia . . . 1861,* 365-366.

islatures of both states early in January.[7] The Northern legislatures thoroughly misunderstood them. The legislature of Minnesota, in resolutions denouncing secession as treason and tendering military assistance to the federal government, expressed gratitude to the "patriotic citizens of the Southern States, who have nobly and manfully exerted their utmost efforts to prevent the catastrophe of dissolution." [8] The legislature of Wisconsin resolved "that the Union-loving citizens of Delaware, Maryland, Virginia, North Carolina, Kentucky, Missouri, and Tennessee, who labor with devoted courage and patriotism to withhold their States from the vortex of secession, are entitled to the gratitude and admiration of the whole people." [9]

[7] The fallacy of the Northern interpretation is also shown by the following statements from two Nashville papers which did not advocate secession until after Lincoln's war proclamation. The *Daily Nashville Patriot*, February 10, 1861, said: "We would not have the people of the Free States misunderstand our position, and we take this occasion to remind them that the continued loyalty of Tennessee to the existing Government will depend upon the spirit with which her earnest and patriotic efforts to save that Government are received by them. They must not suppose . . . that the majority are for coercion . . . that that majority have any purpose of submitting to the Republican electioneering dogma that the people of the Southern States are to be excluded by legislation from the privilege of settling in the Territories with their slaves." *The Republican Banner*, February 19, 1861, said: "We find journals in the North which pretend to believe that the election of the 9th was an expression of unqualified adherence to the Union . . . such is not the case. We mean to push the experiment of adjustment and settlement of this controversy to the last honorable and reasonable limit, and when we have done so unsuccessfully, we will set up for ourselves in a lawful way, and accept the consequences, whatever they may be." See, also, *The Daily Herald*, Wilmington, February 6, 1861; *Louisville Daily Journal*, January 5, 1861; and Remarks of Caruthers and Smith, in Chittenden, *A Report of the Debates and Proceedings in the Secret Sessions of the Conference Convention . . . 1861*, 214.

[8] "Joint Resolutions of the Legislature of the State of Minnesota, on the State of the Union," *House Mis. Docs.*, 36 Cong., 2 Sess., Doc. 33.

[9] "Joint Resolutions, coöperating with Friends of the Union

Delegations from fourteeen states only were present when the Washington conference completed its organization, and it was not until February 9 that the last of the twenty-one delegations presented its credentials. Many men of national prominence were present, including David Wilmot, John Tyler, J. Motley Morehead, James Guthrie, F. K. Zollicoffer, Alexander W. Doniphan, Salmon P. Chase, John E. Wool, and Reverdy Johnson. Ex-President Tyler was elected chairman of the convention, and James Guthrie was appointed chairman of the committee on resolutions. Every precaution was taken to keep the proceedings secret, and members were forbidden to give out any information whatever, except by special permission to their respective state conventions, legislatures, or governors. The resolutions committee did not report until February 15, and the conference did not adopt any recommendations until February 27. The proposed constitutional amendments adopted at that time were not explicit, nor were they satisfactory to the slave states. The first of these provided (1) that involuntary servitude should be prohibited in all territory north of 36 degrees 30 minutes; (2) that south of that line the "status of persons owing service or labor as it now exists shall not be changed by law while such territory shall be under a territorial government; and neither Congress nor the territorial government shall have power to hinder or prevent the taking of said territory of persons held to labor or involuntary service, within the United States, according to the laws or usages of the State from which

---

throughout the United States," in Official Correspondence of Governor John J. Pettus, 1859-1860. See, also, "Resolutions of the Legislature of the State of Ohio, on the State of the Republic," *ibid.*, Doc. 18.

such persons may be taken, nor to impair the rights arising out of said relation, which shall be subject to judicial cognizance in the federal courts, according to the common law"; and (3) that when the population of any territory should become equivalent to the then existing federal ratio of representation, it should be admitted as a state, with or without involuntary service or labor as its constitution might provide.[10]

This proposed amendment differed very essentially from the Crittenden amendment dealing with the territorial question. In substance, it excluded the slaveholder from four fifths of the common territories and subjected his rights in the remainder to the decisions of federal judges to be appointed by a Republican President. The fundamental principles of the party were that slavery was not based on the common law; that neither Congress nor a territorial legislature possessed the constitutional right to establish slavery in the territories; and that slavery had no legal existence outside the jurisdiction of state governments. Judicial decisions arising from disputes over the rights of the slaveholder would inevitably be predicated upon those principles. The amendment was adopted by a vote of 9 to 8, only five of the fourteen Northern states supporting it, and North Carolina and Virginia voting against it.[11]

[10] *Official Journal of the Conference Convention . . . 1861*, 22-23.

[11] *Ibid.*, 71-72. Illinois, Ohio, New Jersey, Pennsylvania, and Rhode Island voted for the proposition, with Meredith and Wilmot of Pennsylvania, Cook of Illinois, Chase and Wolcott of Ohio dissenting. Ruffin and Morehead of North Carolina, and Rives and Summers of Virginia were willing to support the measure; but Clay and Morehead of Kentucky and Totten of Tennessee opposed it. Field of New York was absent when the vote was taken. His absence left the delegation divided and it did not vote. He was opposed to the proposal and but for his absence it would not have passed.

The second amendment offered by the committee provided that no further territory should be acquired except by treaty, and by the consent of four fifths of all the members of the Senate. It was amended to provide that no territory should be acquired "except by discovery, and for naval and commercial stations, depots, and transit routes," with a majority of all senators from the slave states and a majority of all senators from the free states concurring; or by treaty, with the vote of the majority of the senators from each section constituting a part of the two thirds majority necessary for treaty ratification. This proposal was carried by a vote of 11 to 8. Indiana, New Jersey, Ohio, Pennsylvania, and Rhode Island supported it, and North Carolina voted against it.[12]

The third amendment, as finally voted, provided that Congress should not regulate, abolish, or control involuntary service in the states or territories; nor abolish it in the District of Columbia without the consent of Maryland or without compensation; nor abolish it in places under the exclusive control of the United States within states where it was recognized; nor prohibit the removal of persons held to labor or involuntary service from one state to another or to the territories; nor place a higher rate of taxation on persons held to labor than on land. It was adopted by a vote of 12 to 7, Illinois, New Jersey, Ohio, Pennsylvania, Rhode Island, and all the slave states supporting it.[13] The fourth amendment was that the "third paragraph of the second edition of the fourth article of the Constitution shall not be construed to prevent any of

[12] *Ibid.*, 72. New York and Kansas were divided. Meredith and Wilmot of Pennsylvania, Ruffin and Morehead of North Carolina, Tyler of Virginia, Clay of Kentucky, Hackleman and Orth of Indiana dissented.

[13] Clay of Kentucky, Cook of Illinois, Slaughter of Indiana, Chase and Wolcott of Ohio dissented.

the States, by appropriate legislation . . . from enforcing the delivery of fugitives from labor to the person to whom such service or labor is due." It was intended to prevent Congress from interfering with the surrender of fugitive slaves, rather than to provide for a more strict enforcement of the fugitive slave law; but it was opposed by Iowa, Maine, Massachusetts, and New Hampshire. It was approved by a vote of 15 to 4, New York and Kansas being divided and not voting.[14] The fifth amendment prohibited the foreign slave trade, and imposed upon Congress the duty of preventing the "importation of slaves, coolies, or persons held to service or labor, into the United States and the Territories from places beyond the limits thereof." It was adopted by a vote of 16 to 5, Iowa, Maine, Massachusetts, North Carolina, and Virginia opposing.[15] A final amendment providing for compensation for fugitives from labor lost through intimidation of officials, and providing that the acceptance of compensation should preclude the owner from further claim to the fugitive, was adopted by a vote of 12 to 7.[16]

Maine, New Hampshire, Vermont, Massachusetts, Connecticut, and Iowa voted against every important amendment. New York was divided and did not vote on the six major proposals. The result of these votes, together with the fact that Michigan, Wisconsin, and Minnesota failed to send commissioners to the conference, was added proof that the North, with the possible exception of Rhode Island and the border states, would sanction no effort

[14] *Ibid.,* 74.
[15] The following commissioners dissented from the vote of their states: Baldwin of Connecticut; Clay of Kentucky; Ruffin and Morehead of North Carolina; Chase and Wolcott of Ohio; Hackleman and Orth of Indiana.
[16] *Ibid.,* 75. Connecticut, Iowa, Maine, Missouri, North Carolina, Vermont, and Virginia voted in the negative.

whatever toward conciliation. It substantiates, moreover, the fact that aside from Rhode Island, the New England states sent commissioners to the conference for no other purpose than to prevent the successful consummation of its efforts.[17] Additional evidence of this is to be found in two letters written by Senators Bingham and Chandler of Michigan to Governor Blair of that state. Chandler wrote, February 11, "Governor Bingham and myself telegraphed you on Saturday, at the request of Massachusetts and New York, to send delegates to the peace or compromise Congress. They admit that we were right and that they were wrong; that no Republican State should have sent delegates; but they are here and cannot get away. Ohio, Indiana, and Rhode Island are caving in, and there is danger of Illinois; and now they beg us, for God's sake, to come to their rescue, and save the Republican party from rupture. I hope you will send *stiff-backed* men or none." Four days later Bingham wrote Blair that if Michigan and Wisconsin would "send delegations of true, unflinching men, there would probably be a majority in favor of the Constitution as it is, who would frown down rebellion by the enforcement of laws." [18]

Following the final vote on the several proposed amendments, a resolution was offered by Franklin of Pennsylvania which denied the constitutional right of a state to secede from the Union or to absolve its citizens from their allegiance to the government of the United States.

[17] Delegates from these states occupied the time of the convention in seeking to confine its efforts to advising a national convention, denouncing the convention as revolutionary, and of dangerous precedent, condemning Virginia's anti-coercion resolutions, and in a useless rehash of the historical basis for principles enunciated in the Chicago platform. See Chittenden, *op. cit.,* 59-74; 98-102; 161-189; 219-243.

[18] Chandler to Blair, February 11, 1861, and Bingham to Blair, February 15, 1861, in *Cong. Globe,* 36 Cong., 2 Sess., II, 1247.

A motion to lay this on the table was defeated by a vote of 9 to 12. Ohio and New Jersey were the only Northern states which voted in the affirmative, and it appeared that the conference was about to dissolve over the question of coercion. Sober counsels prevailed, however, and the resolution was indefinitely postponed. Rhode Island united with Ohio, New Jersey, and the slave states, and New York, New Hampshire, Vermont, and Kansas refused to vote.[19] The conference then agreed to submit the result of its deliberations to Congress with the request that they be transmitted to the states as amendments to the Constitution. Its recommendations were received by the Senate, February 27, and referred to a special committee composed of Crittenden, Bigler, Thompson, Seward, and Trumbull. A motion to make the committee report the special order of business for the following day was carried by a vote of 26 to 21. Every senator from Maine, New Hampshire, Vermont, Massachusetts, New York, Michigan, Wisconsin, and Iowa voted against it.[20] The majority of the committee, consisting of Crittenden, Bigler, and Thompson, presented the conference recommendations unchanged, with a resolution to submit them to the states as amendments to the Constitution.[21] Seward offered as a substitute a resolution requesting the state legislatures to take under consideration the question of calling a national convention and to report their desires to Congress. An effort to substitute the original Crittenden amendments for the conference report was defeated by a vote of 14 to 25. The resolution offered by Seward was defeated by the same vote; and the amendments pro-

[19] *Official Journal of the Conference Convention . . . 1861,* 76-77.
[20] *Cong. Globe,* 36 Cong., 2 Sess., II, 1255.
[21] *Ibid.,* 1270.

posed by the conference convention were rejected by a vote of 3 to 34. Speaker Pennington withheld them from the House of Representatives, and the thirty-sixth Congress passed out of existence without providing for reconstructing the Union either by conciliation or coercion.

The recommendations of the Washington conference would not have been acceptable to Tennessee, Virginia, Arkansas, and North Carolina, even if Congress had adopted them.[22] Its failure resolved the issue before the country into the single alternative between separation and civil war; and it left the states of the upper South to face in a short while a choice of allegiance. Meanwhile, interstate commissioners had been industriously advocating the cause of the Confederate States. The importance of their activities can be measured only by the manifold character of the duties they had to perform. They were primarily engaged in awakening the people to the dangers which threatened Southern institutions. Their work was the culmination of the efforts of the minority who had seen in abolitionism, at the beginning of the slavery controversy, a rising tide of fanaticism which would eventually sweep over and destroy the institution of slavery. They believed that war was inevitable unless the entire South could be united, and they sought to awaken the people of the upper South to the crisis before the opportunity passed.

[22] See "Speech of Mr. Davis at Thalian Hall—The Peace Conference and its Failure," in *The Wilmington Journal*, March 4, 1861; "Mr. Davis' Speech," in *The Daily Herald*, March 4, 1861; and "Minority Report of William O. Butler and James B. Clay, Commissioners to the Peace Convention," in *Louisville Daily Journal*, March 26, 1861. See, also, *New Orleans Daily Crescent*, February 19, 1861; *Richmond Enquirer*, March 14, 1861. For a statement of the Kentucky commissioners who supported the conference report, see "Majority Report of Messrs. Wickliffe, Morehead, Bell, and Guthrie, Commissioners, to the Governor of Kentucky," in *Louisville Daily Journal*, March 26, 1861.

From the speeches and writings of the commissioners, as nowhere else, one may realize the depth of feeling and the lack of sympathy between the two sections of the country. Vividly denunciatory of a party pledged to the destruction of Southern institutions, almost tragic in their prophetic tone, and pleading for unity of allied interests, they constitute one of the most interesting series of documents in American history. Their theme was, in every case, a complete arraignment of the Northern people, and especially of Republican sectionalism raised to a position of authority in the government. They emphasized the cleavage of the churches, the conflict of political principles, and the contrast of social systems as evidence of a condition which would not yield to compromise. Built upon the principle of hatred for slavery, the Republican party must, as an assurance of future success, become progressively hostile to the institution. It betokened hatred for the slaveholder, desire for the social and political equality of the races, and contempt for the economic weaknesses of the South. The aims and ideals of the abolitionists were so deeply rooted as to be beyond the power of modification. This general indictment was not universally accepted by the people of the upper South; and the work of the commissioners was a final effort to secure its acceptance in the wavering states to the point where active participation in the cause of secession would result.

Persuasions toward secession involved the question of possible reconstruction; and the commissioners labored to convince the people that the lower South would never again willingly consent to live in a Union with Northern abolitionists. "Our separation is final and irrevocable," said Commissioner Hall of Georgia to the North Carolina legislature, February 13.[22] "We ask no compromise, and we want none," said Fulton Anderson of Mississippi before the Virginia convention, February 18. "We know that we should not get it if we were base enough to desire it, and we have made the irrevocable resolve to take our interests into our own keeping." [24] To the same convention on the following day John S. Preston of South Carolina said:

Leaving out of consideration the fact that the acquiescence, which originally founded the Union, was enforced by necessity rather than free consent, the truth seems evident, to every mind which dares to speculate advisedly on the manifest principles of that revolution we are now enacting, that they do involve fundamental and irreconcilable diversities, between the systems on which slaveholding and non-slaveholding communities may endure. We believe that these repellent diversities pertain to every attribute which belongs to the two systems, and consequently that this revolution . . . is not only a revolution of actual material necessity, but it is a revolution resulting from the deepest convictions; the ideas, the sentiments, the moral and intellectual necessities, of earnest and intelligent men.[25]

Next to the hope of securing guarantees from the Northern states which would secure their own safety in the Union, and the fainter hope of being able to reconstruct the Union, the question of the probable future rights of the slave producer in the markets of the lower South was the most important factor in influencing the subsequent action of the remaining slave states. The constitution of the Confederate States forbade the African

[22] Hall, "Address before the Legislature of North Carolina, February 13, 1861," in *Journal of the Convention of the People of Georgia . . . 1861*, 362-363.
[24] *Addresses delivered before the Virginia State Convention . . . 1861*, 12.
[25] *Ibid.*, 51-59.

slave trade, and gave to Congress the power to exclude slaves from the United States. Unless the states of the upper South joined the confederacy, their slave markets were gone forever; but they were afraid that the African trade would eventually be reopened, and they resented the latter clause of the Constitution as a cleverly devised trick to drag them out of the Union. The task of quieting their apprehensions on these points devolved upon the commissioners. Speaking before the North Carolina legislature, Hall of Georgia said:

> Appeals have been made to your fears—you have been urged to resist this natural and homogenous alliance for the reason that it was the design of the Cotton States to reopen the foreign slave trade. . . . No considerable portion of our people have ever favored the policy of reviving it, while many of them have been opposed to the federal legislation upon that subject, for the reason that they regarded it as the exercise of powers not delegated, and because of the stupidly cruel and severe penalties inflicted upon an act not intrinsically wrong, but only rendered so by politic considerations. Go on, and continue to raise the supply of labor, and we will provide for our wants in your market. We could have influenced your action by prohibiting the introduction of your slaves into our midst. We could have increased them in your borders by restrictive policy, until they would have become worse than valueless to you. We were unwilling to constrain the action of a free people.[26]

Meanwhile, Benning of Georgia had urged Virginia to join the Confederate States because their share of the territories would be thrown open to slavery, and the value of Virginia's slave property would be increased. He denied that the clause of the Constitution giving Congress the power to prevent the introduction of slaves from the

[26] Hall, "Address before the Legislature of North Carolina, February 13, 1861," in *Journal of the Convention of the People of Georgia . . . 1861,* 363-364.

United States was in the nature of a threat. "Its object was not to threaten you, but to save ourselves. If you should join the North, the mere instinct of self-preservation dictates that we ought to do all in our power to keep you a slave State as long as possible. And the best way to do that would be to prevent your citizens from selling their slaves to ours. And, I have no doubt, that they would be prevented from doing so." [27]

Two powerful and conflicting forces, therefore, were influencing the people of the upper South during the month preceding the inauguration. The one, appealing to their devotion to the old Union, centered around the activities of the Washington conference and tended to counteract immediate secession sentiment. The other, operating upon their sense of personal security and somewhat upon their economic interests, grew out of the formation of the Southern confederacy, and was the natural trend toward coöperation by people possessing similar political and social institutions. The calling of the Washington conference and the sending of delegates by the Northern states probably prevented the immediate secession of most of the remaining slave states during January. It certainly delayed secession in Virginia, Tennessee, Arkansas, and North Carolina, and prevented it in Kentucky and Missouri. The people of Tennessee defeated the calling of a convention by only ten thousand votes, and the people of North Carolina by less than one thousand. The election in the latter state occurred the day following the adjournment of the Washington conference, but before the news of its failure could reach the rural districts. Commissioner Hall of Georgia reported

[27] *Addresses delivered before the Virginia State Convention* . . . *1861*, 41.

that misleading dispatches were sent into the central part of the state, stating that the conference had agreed upon a settlement which was certain to be accepted by Congress. The vote was 46,672 for a convention and 47,323 against it. Hall claimed that the result would have been reversed if the people had known the truth concerning the Washington conference. The commissioners upon their return from Washington announced that all hope of reconstructing the Union was gone, and a reaction in favor of immediate secession swept over the state.[28]

The Washington conference had been in session only a few days when Lincoln left Springfield for Washington. Traveling leisurely, he spoke in many cities along the route. His first speech, at Indianapolis, February 9, rendered futile the efforts then being made to effect conciliation and evoked bitter response from the few remaining anti-secession newspapers of the upper South. Every speech thereafter fanned the fierce fires of resistance in the loyal slave states. Somewhat facetious and evasive, they nevertheless contained a political philosophy which, if established in practice, would destroy state lines and establish the rule of an unrestrained majority in a consolidated nation. He denied that there was just cause for political unrest at the South, and pledged faithful adherence to the Chicago platform. The Nashville *Patriot* spoke of him as a "narrow-minded Republican partisan," and of his speeches as disclosing "sentiments which, if meant as an indication of the policy of his administration, show that he will surely have need of prayer, and a great deal of it." The New Orleans *Bee* could not find in his speeches "a trace of enlarged and comprehensive statesmanship"; and the Wilmington *Journal* regarded them as

[28] See the *Wilmington Journal*, March 16, 1861.

a "specimen of such consolidation doctrine as few men would have dared to utter, and none of any party at the South can possibly sustain." [29]

Lincoln's inaugural address reached the people of the slave states about the same time as the reports of their commissioners to the Washington conference. His assertion that all national governments are intended to be perpetual, and his further contention that no state could escape from an association of states without the consent of all, are too familiar to need repetition. They were an express denial of the right of secession. His position, to that extent, was in accord with the sentiment of many Union men in the slave states. His additional statement, however, that he intended to enforce the laws, collect the revenues, and deliver the mails in those states which had seceded was a heavy blow to their expectations. They had ardently worked for reconstruction, and had believed that Lincoln would adopt a pacific policy and look to time and

[29] The *Wilmington Journal*, February 16, 1861; *Louisville Daily Journal*, February 14, 1861; *Daily Courier*, Louisville, February 16, 1861; *Daily Nashville Patriot*, February 15, 16, and 24, 1861; *The New Orleans Bee*, February 27, 1861. These newspapers were representative of the most conservative Southern sentiment. The extreme opinion is indicated by the following statement from the *Daily Delta*, February 26, 1861: "His silly speeches, his ill-timed jocularity, his pusillanimous evasion of responsibility, and vulgar petty-foggery, have no parallel in history, save in the crazy capers of Caligula, or in the effeminate buffoonery of Henry of Valois . . . in profound ignorance of the institutions of the Republic of which he has been chosen chief; in dishonest and cowardly efforts to dodge responsibility and play a double part—in disgusting levity on the most serious subjects, the speeches of Lincoln, on his way to the capital, have no equals in the history of any people, civilized or semi-civilized." The *Richmond Semi-Weekly Examiner*, March 1, 1861, said: "The State which replied to Force bills with those Resolutions which fixed forever Secession to be a right, is now to bend her haughty neck beneath the paw of the Abolition orang-outrang that skulked to Washington the other day from the wilds of Illinois, and who will, in three days more, be propped in the Chair of Washington by the sword of a military dictator."

calm reflection to relieve the sectional enmity and reconstruct the old union of states. This portion of the address was regarded by many as a virtual declaration of war.[30]

That part of the address which dealt with the rights of slavery under the Constitution and with political principles, however, was of far greater significance to the conservatives of the upper South. Taking the context of the passage dealing with the surrender of fugitive slaves in its entirety, and making allowance for Lincoln's proclivity to answer one question by propounding another, they understood him to mean: (1) that the federal government should assume the burden of surrendering the fugitive slaves; (2) that the existing fugitive slave law should be repealed and another substituted which would guarantee the right of *habeas corpus* and jury trial to fugitives; and (3) that the opposition of the Northern states through the medium of personal liberty laws would then cease, since there would no longer be any necessity for those laws. The suggestion that the citizens of each state should be guaranteed the privileges of citizens in the other states by congressional legislation was especially repulsive to state-rights men of the slave states. Aside from the dangerous precedent which such legislation would establish, it would strike at the fundamental principle upon which the institution of slavery rested: the inequality of the races; and the suggestion involved the doctrine frequently expressed at the North that negroes who were recognized as citizens in Northern states should be extended citizenship and equal privileges with all other citizens in the slave states. However, the full significance

[30] *Nashville Union and American*, March 5, 1861; *The Daily Picayune*, New Orleans, March 6, 1861; *New Orleans Daily Crescent*, March 6, 1861; *The Richmond Dispatch*, March 5, 1861; *Richmond Enquirer*, March 5, 1861.

of this suggestion in its influence upon the South is lost unless considered in connection with the additional statement:

All profess to be content in the Union if all constitutional rights can be maintained. Is it true, then, that any right plainly written in the Constitution has been denied? I think not. Happily, the human mind is so constituted that no party can reach to the audacity of doing this. . . . But no organic law can ever be framed with a provision specifically applicable to every question which may occur in practical administration. . . . Shall fugitives from labor be surrendered by national or by State authority? The Constitution does not expressly say. *May* Congress prohibit slavery in the Territories? The Constitution does not expressly say. *Must* Congress protect slavery in the Territories? The Constitution does not expressly say.

From questions of this class spring all our constitutional controversies, and we divided upon them into majorities and minorities. If the minority will not acquiesce, the majority must, or the Government must cease. There is no other alternative, for continuing the Government is acquiescence on one side or the other.

This was taken to imply constitutional construction which in practical application would annihilate all rights of minorities and subject them to the unrestrained will of the majority. It denied the doctrine of the immediate secessionists, that in all cases of dispute between a state and the federal government the state was, in the last analysis, the judge of the extent of its grievances and of the mode and measure of redress. It denied the doctrine of the so-called Unionists of the slave states, that in a similar case the burden of proof was upon the federal government, and that the state might interpose its sovereignty until such time as the people of the several states through delegates assembled in national convention should render a decision. It denied the doctrine of those who regarded the Supreme Court as the final arbiter in all disputes between the federal government and the states. It went farther and implied that, in all cases of dispute over questions of constitutional construction not specifically dealt with in the Constitution, the minority of the people must submit to the will of the majority, irrespective of Supreme Court decisions. "May Congress prohibit slavery in the Territories? The Constitution does not expressly say." Lincoln, thinking of a consolidated nation and of the people as an aggregate whole, said the majority must decide. The Southerners felt that he might well have added: "May Congress abolish slavery within the limits of the States? The Constitution does not expressly say; but the majority must decide." Apparently every power not expressly granted or denied in the Constitution was to be a matter for controversy and subject to the decision of a numerical majority. Coming as a climax to the opposition of the Northern majority to all plans of conciliation, it rendered nugatory the claim that the Southern states had no reasonable cause for apprehension.

The inaugural address was intended to announce the policy of the administration, and from the policy then outlined Lincoln never deviated. Uncertainty and divided counsels prevailed for a time, however, and the entire political situation was confused by the Sumter issue because Lincoln did not take his Cabinet into his confidence. The Union men of the upper South misinterpreted the hesitancy over reinforcing Anderson to be an indication of a peace policy, and were encouraged in their misapprehension by members of the Cabinet. The aggressive policy finally inaugurated by Lincoln was a heavy blow to the remnant who were laboring for peaceable reconstruction.

Some of them felt that their position had been misconstrued by the Lincoln administration; most of them felt that they had been deceived for the purpose of dividing the South. John R. Eakin, one of the strongest opponents of secession in Arkansas up to the time of the issuance of Lincoln's proclamation, said:

We have been deceived. With a knowledge of that came a settled distrust, mingled with that loathsome repugnance with which we always regard those who have tampered with the holiest feelings of our nature. The breach is irreparable. We shall oppose hereafter all efforts to restore the Union. It is no longer desirable. We must be as two people forever.[81]

F. K. Zollicoffer, who had been a member of the Washington conference, and was one of the Southern men who sanctioned the measures proposed by that conference, said: "We all agree in commending the wisdom, the justice, and the humanity of the refusal of our state to furnish men and arms to the President with which to subjugate our brethren of the seceded States. We agree in reprobating a war of coercion upon sister slaveholding States, and in pledging the whole military force of the States, in resistance to a war of humiliation of those who are de-

[81] *The Republican Banner,* April 21, 1861. *The Missouri Republican,* April 19, 1861, said: "Alas! it is becoming not a question of secession and treason, but a question of our own and our children's freedom—a question whether our liberties are secured by laws or whether they are subject to the will, the mere will of despotism." *The Daily Nashville Patriot* expressed similar sentiments, May 2, 1861: "The object of this war is unquestionably to establish the Chicago platform as the paramount rule in the administration of the Government. It involves two of the prime foundation principles of Republican institutions and liberty. It denies the right of property and overturns the idea that all free government is founded on the consent of the people. In yielding to this monstrous aggressive war, we yield both these. Slavery is the pretext, and anti-slavery fanaticism is the motive power; and both are sought to be sustained by a perfidious appeal to a constitution violated and to laws trampled in the dust."

fending rights and interests as dear to us as to them."
The Union Executive Committee of Shelby County, Tennessee, issued an address which said in part:

> In the excited contest through which we have so lately
> passed, we boldly and triumphantly maintained the loyalty
> of our beloved State to the Federal Union. In this we acted
> from honest and patriotic convictions of right. Sympathizing
> with our brethren of the seceded States, yet we could not see
> the necessity of their action, and deplored the course they saw
> fit to pursue. . . . On the other hand, although a sectional
> party that we abhorred had obtained possession of the Govern-
> ment, we still hoped that *even* the President of *its* choice, in
> view of the awful responsibility that rested upon him, would
> be constrained to pursue a conciliatory and pacific policy. . . .
> Our expectations have been disappointed. We have been
> deceived by false and treacherous representations of what
> would be the policy of Mr. Lincoln's Administration. . . . A
> Northern army is to be marched over the territory of the
> Southern States, that have stood loyal to the Union, to subdue
> and chastise our brethren. . . . Mr. Lincoln's government,
> pursuing the course that is indicated, we feel absolved from
> all obligations thereto, and acknowledge fealty alone to our
> own State.[32]

Similar statements were issued by John Bell of Tennessee, Ex-Governor Morehead of Kentucky, Ex-President
Tyler of Virginia, and other men of prominence. The
earnestness with which they had sustained their convictions during the trying period of secession remains as a
rich inheritance too long overshadowed by the results of
the war which followed. They abhorred the thought of
the disintegration of the Union and the horrors of civil
war. They did not believe that the Lincoln administration
would assume the fearful responsibility of attempting to
force the constitutional principles of the Republican party

[32] "Address of the Union Executive Committee of Shelby County,"
in the *Republican Banner,* April 21, 1861.

upon the country by a war of subjugation, without first referring the issue to the people or to their representatives assembled in Congress. Their disillusionment came with Lincoln's proclamation giving the people of the South twenty days in which to submit to the authority of the federal government, and from that time they joined the original secessionists in resistance to what they regarded the tyranny of military despotism.

# APPENDIX

## A

Vote on question to recommit platform.[1]

|  | Yeas | Nays |
|---|---|---|
| Maine ...................... | 3 | 5 |
| New Hampshire ............... |  | 5 |
| Vermont .................... |  | 5 |
| Massachusetts ................. | 8 | 5 |
| Rhode Island ................. |  | 4 |
| Connecticut ................. | 1½ | 4½ |
| New York .................... |  | 35 |
| New Jersey .................. | 4 | 3 |
| Pennsylvania ................. | 16 | 11 |
| Delaware .................... | 3 |  |
| Maryland .................... | 5½ | 2½ |
| Virginia .................... | 14 | 1 |
| North Carolina ............... | 10 |  |
| South Carolina ............... | 8 |  |
| Georgia .................... | 10 |  |
| Florida ..................... | 3 |  |
| Alabama .................... | 9 |  |
| Louisiana ................... | 6 |  |
| Mississippi ................. | 7 |  |
| Texas ..................... | 4 |  |
| Arkansas ................... | 4 |  |
| Missouri ................... | 5 | 4 |
| Tennessee ................. | 11 | 1 |
| Kentucky ................... | 12 |  |
| Ohio ...................... |  | 23 |
| Indiana ................... |  | 13 |
| Illinois .................... |  | 11 |
| Michigan .................. |  | 6 |
| Wisconsin ................. |  | 5 |
| Iowa ...................... |  | 4 |
| Minnesota ................. | 1 | 3 |
| California ................. | 4 |  |
| Oregon .................... | 3 |  |
| Total ............... | 152 | 151 |

[1] *Proceedings of the Conventions at Charleston and Baltimore, 89.*

B

Douglas and Anti-Douglas Strength at Baltimore as shown by the vote on the minority report of the committee on credentials.[1]

|  | *Yeas* | *Nays* |
|---|---|---|
| Maine .................... | 2½ | 5½ |
| New Hampshire ............... | ½ | 4½ |
| Vermont .................... | 1½ | 3½ |
| Massachusetts ................. | 8 | 5 |
| Rhode Island ................. | | 4 |
| Connecticut ................. | 2½ | 3½ |
| New York ................... | | 35 |
| New Jersey ................. | 4 | 3 |
| Pennsylvania ................. | 17 | 10 |
| Delaware .................... | 2 | |
| Maryland ................... | 5½ | 2½ |
| Virginia ................... | 14 | 2 |
| North Carolina ............... | 9 | 1 |
| Arkansas ................... | ½ | ½ |
| Missouri ................... | 5 | 4 |
| Tennessee ................. | 10 | 1 |
| Kentucky ................... | 10 | 2 |
| Ohio ...................... | | 23 |
| Indiana .................... | | 13 |
| Illinois .................... | | 11 |
| Michigan .................... | | 6 |
| Wisconsin .................. | | 5 |
| Iowa ...................... | | 4 |
| Minnesota ................. | 1½ | 2½ |
| California ................. | 4 | |
| Oregon .................... | 3 | |
| Total ............... | 100½ | 150½ |

[1] *Proceedings of the Conventions at Charleston and Baltimore*, 202.

C

| | A | B | C | D | E | F | G | H |
|---|---|---|---|---|---|---|---|---|
| Alabama | 0 | 9 | 9 | 0 | 9 | 0 | 0 | 0* |
| Arkansas | 2½ | 1½ | 1 | 1½ | 1½ | 0 | ½ | 1½ |
| California | 4 | 0 | 0 | 0 | 0 | 0 | 0 | 0 |
| Connecticut | 2 | 4 | 3½ | 1 | 3½ | ½ | 3½ | 4 |
| Delaware | 3 | 0 | 0 | 0 | 0 | 0 | 0 | 3 |
| Florida | 3 | 0 | 0 | 0 | 0 | 0 | 0 | 0 |
| Georgia | 10 | 0 | 0 | 0 | 0 | 0 | 0 | 10† |
| Illinois | 0 | 11 | 11 | 0 | 11 | 0 | 11 | 11 |
| Indiana | 0 | 13 | 13 | 0 | 13 | 0 | 13 | 13 |
| Iowa | 0 | 4 | 4 | 0 | 4 | 0 | 4 | 4 |
| Kentucky | 7½ | 4½ | 0 | 4½ | 3 | 1½ | 3 | 7 |
| Louisiana | 0 | 6 | 6 | 0 | 6 | 0 | 0 | 6‡ |
| Maine | 1 | 7 | 5½ | 0 | 7 | 0 | 5½ | 7 |
| Maryland | 5½ | 2½ | 2½ | ½ | 2½ | 0 | 2½ | 2½ |
| Massachusetts | 8 | 5 | 10 | 0 | 10 | 0 | 5 | 10 |
| Michigan | 0 | 6 | 6 | 0 | 6 | 0 | 6 | 6 |
| Minnesota | 1½ | 2½ | 2½ | 1½ | 4 | 0 | 2½ | 4 |
| Mississippi | 7 | 0 | 0 | 0 | 0 | 0 | 0 | 0 |
| Missouri | 4½ | 4½ | 4½ | ½ | 4½ | 1½ | 4½ | 7§ |
| New Hampshire | 0 | 5 | 5 | 0 | 5 | 0 | 5 | 5 |
| New Jersey | 4½ | 2½ | 2½ | 0 | 2½ | 0 | 2½ | 2½ |
| New York | 1 | 34 | 35 | 0 | 35 | 0 | 20 | 35 |
| North Carolina | 9½ | ½ | 1 | 0 | 1 | 0 | ½ | 1 |
| Ohio | 0 | 23 | 23 | 0 | 23 | 0 | 23 | 23 |
| Oregon | 3 | 0 | 0 | 0 | 0 | 0 | 0 | 0 |
| Pennsylvania | 10 | 17 | 10 | 7 | 10 | 9½ | 10 | 22½ |
| Rhode Island | 0 | 4 | 4 | 0 | 4 | 0 | 4 | 4 |
| South Carolina | 8 | 0 | 0 | 0 | 0 | 0 | 0 | 0 |
| Tennessee | 9½ | 2½ | 3 | 0 | 3 | 0 | 2½ | 3 |
| Texas | 4 | 0 | 0 | 0 | 0 | 0 | 0 | 0 |
| Vermont | ½ | 4½ | 5 | 0 | 5 | 0 | 4½ | 5 |
| Virginia | 12 | 3 | 1½ | 1½ | 3 | 0 | 3 | 3 |
| Wisconsin | 0 | 5 | 5 | 0 | 5 | 0 | 5 | 5 |
| Total | 121½ | 118½ | 173½ | 17 | 181½ | 13 | 141 | 214 |

* Irregular delegates.

† Refused to take their seats but some came into the hall as spectators. All counted.

‡ Irregular delegates.

§ Two joined Maryland Institute convention, seven remained but refused to vote; all counted.

A. Vote represented by absent delegates. In this column are counted those delegates who withdrew from the convention regardless of whether they participated in the proceedings at Maryland Institute. It also includes those who in writing informed the convention that they would no longer participate in its deliberations but remained as spectators.

B. Vote to which remaining delegates were entitled.

C. Vote cast for Douglas on the first ballot.

D. Vote cast for all other candidates on first ballot.

E. Vote cast for Douglas on second ballot.

F. Vote cast for all other candidates on second ballot.

G. Actual strength of Douglas as represented by regular delegates present.

H. Vote counted for Douglas to give him more than two thirds of the total electoral vote.

Compiled from *Proceedings of the Conventions at Charleston and Baltimore; Official Proceedings of the Democratic National Convention held in 1860, at Charleston and Baltimore;* National Democratic Executive Committee, "Address to the Democracy and People of the United States," in *Nashville Union and American, Supplement,* August, 1860, and in *Arkansas True Democrat,* September 4, 1860: Democratic National Executive Committee, *Address to the Democracy of the United States, July 18, 1860.*

## D

Popular vote for President in 1860 [1]

| State | Electoral Vote | Lincoln | Douglas | Breckinridge | Bell |
|---|---|---|---|---|---|
| Alabama | 9 | | 13,651 | 48,831 | 27,875 |
| Arkansas | 4 | | 5,227 | 28,732 | 20,094 |
| California | 4 | 39,173 | 38,516 | 34,334 | 6,817 |
| Connecticut | 6 | 43,792 | 15,522 | 14,641 | *3,291 |
| Delaware | 3 | 3,815 | 1,023 | 7,337 | 3,864 |
| Florida | 3 | | 367 | 8,543 | 5,437 |
| Georgia | 10 | | 11,590 | 51,889 | 42,886 |
| Illinois | 11 | 172,161 | 160,215 | 2,404 | 4,913 |
| Indiana | 13 | 139,033 | 115,509 | 12,295 | 5,306 |
| Iowa | 4 | 70,409 | 55,111 | 1,048 | 1,763 |
| Kentucky | 12 | 1,364 | 25,651 | 53,143 | 66,058 |
| Louisiana | 6 | | 7,625 | 22,681 | 20,204 |
| Maine | 8 | 62,811 | 26,693 | 6,368 | 2,046 |
| Maryland | 8 | 2,294 | 5,966 | 42,482 | 41,760 |
| Massachusetts | 13 | 106,533 | 34,372 | 5,939 | 22,331 |
| Michigan | 6 | 88,480 | 65,057 | 805 | 405 |
| Minnesota | 4 | 22,069 | 11,920 | 748 | 62 |
| Mississippi | 7 | | 3,283 | 40,797 | 25,040 |
| Missouri | 9 | 17,028 | 58,801 | 31,317 | 58,372 |
| New Hampshire | 5 | 37,519 | 25,881 | 2,112 | 441 |
| New Jersey | 7 | 58,324 | * 62,801 | | |
| New York | 35 | 353,804 | *303,329 | | |
| North Carolina | 10 | | 2,701 | 48,539 | 44,990 |
| Ohio | 23 | 231,610 | 187,232 | 11,405 | 12,194 |
| Oregon | 3 | 5,270 | 3,951 | 5,006 | 183 |
| Pennsylvania | 27 | 268,030 | 16,765 | 178,871 | 12,776 |
| Rhode Island | 4 | 12,244 | *7,707 | | |
| South Carolina | 8 | Electors chosen by legislature—vote given to Breckinridge | | | |
| Tennessee | 12 | | 11,350 | 64,709 | 69,274 |
| Texas | 4 | | | 47,548 | 15,438 |
| Vermont | 5 | 33,808 | 6,849 | 218 | 1,969 |
| Virginia | 15 | 1,929 | 16,290 | 74,323 | 74,681 |
| Wisconsin | 5 | 86,110 | 65,021 | 888 | 161 |
| Total | 303 | 1,857,610 | 1,365,976 | 847,953 | 590,631 |

[1] *American Almanac, 1861*, 417.                    * Fusion.

States whose electoral vote would have gone to Lincoln if the popular vote of Douglas, Breckinridge, and Bell had been given to any one of the three.

| | | | | | | | |
|---|---|---|---|---|---|---|---|
| Conn. | 6 | Maine | 8 | New Hampshire | 5 | Rhode Island | 4 |
| Illinois | 11 | Mass. | 13 | New York | 35 | Vermont | 5 |
| Indiana | 13 | Michigan | 6 | Ohio | 23 | Wisconsin | 5 |
| Iowa | 4 | Minnesota | 4 | Pennsylvania | 27 | | |
| | | | | | | Total | 169 |

# BIBLIOGRAPHY

## PRIMARY SOURCES

### UNITED STATES GOVERNMENT PUBLICATIONS

*Congressional Globe,* 31 Cong., 1 Sess.; 33 Cong., 1 Sess.;
35 Cong., 1 Sess.; 35 Cong., 2 Sess.; 36 Cong., 1 Sess.;
36 Cong., 2 Sess.; 37 Cong., 1 Sess.

*House Executive Documents,* 36 Cong., 2 Sess., IX, Docs.
61, 72, 79.

Resolutions relative to the state of the Union and
proposed constitutional amendments by the Kentucky
legislature. Documents concerning the collection of cus-
toms duties and post-office revenues, the seizure of the
New Orleans mint, and important correspondence relating to Fort Sumter.

*House Miscellaneous Documents,* 36 Cong., 2 Sess., Docs.,
15, 19, 21, 22, 23, 26, 30, 31, 32, 33, 38, 41.

Resolutions of the several state legislatures relative
to the advisability of constitutional amendments and a
national convention, stating the nature of acceptable
amendments; and petitions of various workingmen's
organizations urging the adoption of the Crittenden
proposals.

*House Reports,* 36 Cong., 2 Sess., I, II, Reps. 31, 85, 88.

Journal of proceedings and the several reports from
the special Committee of Thirty-three appointed under
the Boteler resolution of December 4, 1860. Report of
committee on military affairs, on forts, arsenals, and
arms. Report of select committee on naval affairs, showing the strength of squadrons, and touching upon resignations. Report of special committee relative to correspondence between President Buchanan and the South
Carolina commissioners. Report of select committee of
five on seizure of federal property.

*Senate Reports,* 36 Cong., 2 Sess., Rep. 288.

Journal of the proceedings and report of the Committee of Thirteen, appointed under the Powell resolution of December 18, 1860, in relation to the distracted condition of the country.

*The War of the Rebellion: A Compilation of the Official Records of the Union and Confederate Armies.* 70 vols., Washington, 1880-1901.

Series I, Vols. I, III, LIII, and Series IV, Vol. I, contain many documents relating to the work of the interstate commissioners, the controversies over federal forts, and correspondence between President Buchanan and various state officials. This collection cannot be relied upon as being complete. Other sources are indicated below.

## STATE PUBLICATIONS

*Addresses delivered by Hon. Fulton Anderson, Commissioner from Mississippi, Hon. Henry L. Benning, Commissioner from Georgia, and Hon. John S. Preston, Commissioner from South Carolina, before the Virginia State Convention, February, 1861.* Charleston, 1861.

A rare and valuable collection of superior expositions. Preston's address is inimitable among the many delivered by interstate commissioners. A member of the convention said of it: "It was perhaps the finest address I ever listened to. It will doubtless read well, but cannot carry the same force as when delivered, accompanied as the delivery was with grace and other attributes of the most finished oratory."

*Communication from the Hon. Peter B. Starke, as Commissioner to Virginia, to his Excellency, J. J. Pettus, with accompanying Documents.* Jackson, 1860.

A collection of documents apparently not preserved in the originals. Together with the Memminger correspondence and address in Capers, *Life and Times of C. G. Memminger,* they furnish the story of attempted coöperation among the Southern states during the early months of 1860.

*Journal of the Constitutional Convention of the State of Alabama, 1861. Ordinances of the State of Alabama, with the Constitution of the Provisional Government of the Confederate States of America.* Montgomery, 1861.

None of the convention journals contains more than a bare record of proceedings. The debates were partially preserved in the following newspapers: New Orleans *Bee, Jackson Mississippian,* Montgomery *Daily Advertiser,* Charleston *Mercury,* Richmond *Examiner,* and *Missouri Republican.*

*Journal of the public and secret Proceedings of the Convention of the People of Georgia, held in Milledgeville and Savannah in 1861, together with the Ordinances adopted.* Milledgeville, 1861.

Especially valuable for the collection of letters, speeches, and reports of Georgia's interstate commissioners.

*Journal of the Mississippi State Convention, and Ordinances and Resolutions adopted in January, 1861, with an Appendix.* Jackson, 1861.

Contains most of the letters and reports of Mississippi's interstate commissioners. Some were not published and are preserved in the Department of Archives and History, State of Mississippi, in Official Correspondence of Governor John J. Pettus, 1859-1860. Others were printed in the *Weekly Mississippian.*

*Journal and Proceedings of the Missouri State Convention, held at Jefferson City and St. Louis, March, 1861.* St. Louis, 1861.

*Journal of the public Proceedings of the Convention of the People of South Carolina, held in 1860–61, together with the Ordinances adopted.* Charleston, 1860.

*Journal of the Convention of the People of North Carolina, held on the 20th of May, 1861.* Raleigh, 1862.

*Journal of the Secession Convention of Texas, 1861.* Austin, 1861.

*Journal of the Acts and Proceedings of a general Convention of the State of Virginia, assembled at Richmond, on the thirteenth day of February, 1861.* Richmond, 1861.

*Official Journal of the Proceedings of the Convention of the State of Louisiana, 1861.* New Orleans, 1861.

SMITH, WILLIAM R.

*The History and Debates of the Convention of the People of Alabama, begun and held in the City of Montgomery on the seventh Day of January, 1861; in which is preserved the Speeches of the secret Sessions, and many valuable State Papers.* Montgomery, Tuscaloosa, and Atlanta, 1861.

The most complete account of debates in any of the state conventions. Also contains the letters, reports, and speeches of Alabama's interstate commissioners. Rare and exceedingly valuable.

## OTHER PRIMARY MATERIALS

*Address of the Democracy of Alabama to the National Democratic Convention at Baltimore, January 18, 1860.* Montgomery, 1860.

AUCHAMPAUGH, PHILIP GERALD.

*James Buchanan and His Cabinet on the Eve of Secession.* Lancaster, Pennsylvania, 1926.

CHITTENDEN, L. E., ed.

*A Report of the Debates and Proceedings in the Secret Sessions of the Conference Convention, for proposing Amendments to the Constitution of the United States.* New York, 1864.

CRALLÉ, RICHARD, ed.

*The Works of John C. Calhoun.* 6 vols. New York, 1853-1855.

DOUGLAS, STEPHEN A.

"The Dividing Line Between Federal and Local Authority," in *Harper's Monthly Magazine,* XIX, 519-537.

HALSTEAD, MURAT.

*Caucuses of 1860. A History of the National Political Conventions of the current Presidential Campaign: being a complete Record of the Business of all the Conventions; with Sketches of distinguished Men in Attendance upon them, and Descriptions of the most characteristic Scenes and Memorable Events.* Columbus, 1860.

*Journal of the Democratic State Convention held at Montgomery, Alabama, February 14, 1848.* Montgomery, 1848.

*Journal of the Southern Rights Convention, held in the City of Montgomery, February 10, 1851; and the Address of The Committee.* Montgomery, 1851.

MOORE, JOHN BASSETT, ed.
*The Works of James Buchanan, comprising his Speeches, State Papers, and private Correspondence.* 12 vols. Philadelphia and London, 1908-1910.

*Official Journal of the Conference Convention, held at Washington City, February, 1861.* Washington, 1861.

*Official Proceedings of the Democratic National Convention in 1860, at Charleston and Baltimore.* Cleveland, 1860. John G. Parkhurst, Recording Secretary, ed.
The proceedings as published by the Douglas Democratic party. Intentionally deleted to the disparagement of the opposition, but accurate as to details included.

*Official Proceedings of the Democratic and Anti-Know-Nothing State Convention of Alabama, held in the City of Montgomery, January 8 and 9, 1856.* Montgomery, 1856.

PHILLIPS, ULRICH BONNELL.
"The Correspondence of Robert Toombs, Alexander H. Stephens, and Howell Cobb," in American Historical Association, *Annual Report, 1911,* II. Washington, 1913.

*Proceedings of the Conventions at Charleston and Baltimore.* Published by order of the National Democratic Convention (Maryland Institute, Baltimore), and under the supervision of the National Democratic Executive Committee. Washington, 1860.

*Proceedings of the Delegates Who Withdrew from the National Democratic Convention at Charleston, in April, 1860.*

*Proceedings of the Democratic State Convention, held in the City of Montgomery, commencing Wednesday, January 11, 1860.* Montgomery, 1860.

*Proceedings of the Democratic State Convention of Alabama, held in the City of Montgomery on the 4th Day of June, 1860.* Baltimore.

*Proceedings of the first three Republican National Conventions of 1856, 1860, and 1864, including Proceedings of the Antecedent National Convention held at Pittsburg, in February, 1856, as reported by Horace Greeley.* Minneapolis, 1893.

WALMSLEY, JAMES ELLIOTT.
"The Change of Secession Sentiment in Virginia in 1861," in *The American Historical Review,* XXXI, 82-101.

### CAMPAIGN DOCUMENTS

BLAIR, FRANK P.
*Speech of, at the Cooper Institute, New York City, Wednesday, January 25, 1860.*

BRECKINRIDGE, JOHN C.
*Speech of, at Ashland, near Lexington, Kentucky, September 5, 1860.* Jackson, 1860.

BROWN, ALBERT G.
*Speech of, at Crystal Springs, Copiah County, Mississippi, September 6, 1860.* Jackson, 1860.

CLAY, JAMES B.
*Speech of, at Elizabethtown, Kentucky, August 1, 1860.* Louisville, 1860.

DOUGLAS, STEPHEN A.
*Letter of, in reply to the Speech of Dr. Gwin at Grass Valley, California.* Reprint from the *Daily National,* San Francisco, September 16, 1859.

DRAKE, CHARLES F.
*Speech of, at Victoria, Jefferson County, Missouri, August 25, 1860.* St. Louis, 1860.

FRELIEGH, J. H.
*The true Position, Interests, and Policy of the South. Union or Secession: which is best?* Memphis, 1861.

GRIFFIN, E. C.
*Speech of, at the City Hall, October 30, 1860, in reply to the Address of William Yancey, delivered at Corinthian Hall, October 17, 1860.* Rochester, 1860.

HALLETT, BENJAMIN F.
*Speech of, in Washington City, June 25, 1860.* Washington, 1860.

*Important Political Pamphlet for the Campaign of 1860.*
Compiled by the *Montgomery Advertiser.*

JOHNSON, REVERDY.
*Speech of, before the political Friends of Stephen A.*
*Douglas at a Meeting in Faneuil Hall, Boston, June 7,*
*1860.* Baltimore, 1860.

MCCABE, JAMES D.
*Facts Versus Fancies. Fanaticism and its Results.* Baltimore, 1860.

*Minority Report of Stephens, Delegate from Oregon, showing*
*the Grounds upon which the regular Southern Delega-*
*tions were entitled to Seats in the Convention at the*
*Front Street Theater, Baltimore.*

REED, WILLIAM B.
*Speech of, on the Presidential Question, delivered before*
*the National Democratic Association. Philadelphia,*
1860.

REPUBLICAN STATE CENTRAL COMMITTEE OF ILLINOIS.
*Political Record of Stephen A. Douglas on the Slavery*
*Question.* Chicago, 1860.

SCHURZ, CARL.
*Douglas and Popular Sovereignty. Speech in Hampden*
*Hall, Springfield, Massachusetts, January 4, 1860.* Wash-
ington, 1860.

SLIDELL, JOHN.
*Address of, to the People of Louisiana, September 25,*
*1860.* Bonnet Carré, 1860.

STEPHENS, ALEXANDER H.
*Speech of, delivered in the City Hall Park, Augusta,*
*Georgia, Saturday Evening, September 1, 1860.* Augusta,
1860.

*The Conspiracy to Break up the Union. Breckinridge and*
*Lane the Candidates of a Disunion Party.* Washington,
1860.

WIGFALL, LOUIS T.
*Speech of, on the pending Political Issues; delivered at*
*Tyler, Smith County, Texas, September 3, 1860.* Wash-
ington, 1860.

*Who are the Disunionists? Breckinridge and Lane the true*
*Union Candidates.* Washington, 1860.

YANCEY, WILLIAM LOWNDES.
*Speech in the Democratic Meeting at Marion, Perry County, May 19, 1860.* Montgomery, 1860.
*Speech of, delivered in the Democratic State Convention of the State of Alabama, held at Montgomery on the 11th, 12th, 13th, and 14th of January, 1860.* Montgomery, 1860.
*Speech of, delivered at Memphis, Tennessee, August 14, 1860, on the Issues involved in the Presidential Contest.* Frankfort, Kentucky, 1860.
*Constitutional Rights Speech of, at Wieting Hall, Syracuse, New York, October 15, 1860.* Syracuse, 1860.

## NEWSPAPERS

BRECKINRIDGE DEMOCRAT
*The Daily Delta*, New Orleans.
*Arkansas True Democrat*, Little Rock.
*Kentucky Yeoman*, Frankfort.
*Southern Kentucky Register*, Madisonville.
*The Charleston Mercury.*
*The Daily South Carolinian*, Columbia.
*The Examiner*, Gallatin, Texas.
*Nashville Union and American.*
*Montgomery Weekly Advertiser.*
*The Florence Gazette.*
*Natchez Free Trader.*
*The Wilmington Journal.*
*North Carolina Standard*, Raleigh.
*Richmond Semi-Weekly Examiner.*
*Richmond Enquirer.*
*Weekly Mississippian*, Jackson.
*Daily Courier*, Louisville.

CONSTITUTIONAL UNIONIST
*The Daily Picayune*, New Orleans.
*New Orleans Daily Crescent.*
*The New Orleans Bee.*
*Frankfort Commonwealth.*
*Louisville Daily Journal.*
*Daily Nashville Patriot.*

*Republican Banner*, Nashville.
*Brownlow's Knoxville Whig.*
*Vicksburg Daily Whig.*
*Montgomery Post.*
*The Savannah Republican.*
*Daily Chronicle and Sentinel*, Augusta.
*The Daily Herald*, Wilmington.
*Richmond Whig and Public Advertiser.*
*The Review*, Charlottesville.

DOUGLAS DEMOCRAT
*The Daily True Delta*, New Orleans.
*Weekly Montgomery Confederation.*
*Daily Missouri Republican*, St. Louis.
*The Daily Constitutionalist*, Augusta.
*Louisville Democrat.*
*The Southern Advocate.*

SECONDARY AUTHORITIES
AMBLER, CHARLES HENRY.
*Sectionalism in Virginia from 1776 to 1861.* Chicago, 1910.
AVERY, I. W.
*The History of the State of Georgia from 1850 to 1881, embracing the three important Epochs: the Decade before the War of 1861 to 1865; The War; the Period of Reconstruction, with Portraits of the leading Men of the Period.* New York, 1881.
BOTTS, JOHN MINER.
*The great Rebellion: its secret History, Rise, Progress, and Disastrous Failure.* New York, 1866.
BOYD, WILLIAM KENNETH.
"North Carolina on the Eve of Secession," in American Historical Association, *Annual Report, 1910*, 165-178.
BROWN, WILLIAM GARROTT.
*The Lower South in American History.* New York, 1903.
BROWNLOW, WILLIAM GANNANWAY.
*Sketches of the Rise, Progress, and Decline of Secession; with a Narrative of personal Adventures among the Rebels.* Philadelphia, 1862.

A vivid contemporary account of the struggle in Eastern Tennessee by an anti-secession exile, compiled for consumption by the North during the early days of the war. May be used cautiously.

CALLAHAN, JAMES MORTON.
*Semi-Centennial History of West Virginia.* Morgantown, 1913.

CAPERS, HENRY D.
*The Life and Times of C. G. Memminger.* Richmond, 1893.

CLAIBORNE, JOHN FRANCIS HAMTRAMCH.
*Life and Correspondence of John A. Quitman, Major General, U. S. A., and Governor of the State of Mississippi.* 2 vols. New York, 1860.

CORWIN, EDWARD SAMUEL.
"Dred Scott Decision," in *The American Historical Review,* XVII, 52-69.

COULTER, ELLIS MERTON.
*The Civil War and Readjustment in Kentucky.* Chapel Hill, 1926.

COX, SAMUEL SULLIVAN.
*Union-Disunion-Reunion.* Providence, 1888.
A contemporary account by a politician who favored conciliation but drifted with the popular current.

CRANE, WILLIAM CAREY.
*Life and select literary Remains of Sam Houston of Texas.* 2 vols. Dallas, 1884.

DAVIS, JEFFERSON.
*The Rise and Fall of the Confederate Government.* New York, 1881.

DAVIS, REUBEN.
*Recollections of Mississippi and Mississippians.* New York, 1889.
An account of Mississippi politics during the troublous years by a strong Southern-rights man, written when age had tempered the bitterness and perhaps dimmed the memory.

DU BOSE, JOHN WITHERSPOON.
"Yancey: A Study," in *Gulf States Magazine.* I, 211-235.
*The Life and Times of William Lowndes Yancey. A*

*History of Political Parties in the United States, from 1834 to 1864; especially as to the Origin of the Confederate States.* Birmingham, 1892.

A collection of reminiscences. Valuable when used in connection with Yancey's many speeches, which have been preserved in pamphlet form.

ECKENRODE, H. J.
*Jefferson Davis: President of the South.* New York, 1923.

FERTIG, JAMES WALTER.
*The Secession and Reconstruction of Tennessee.* Chicago, 1898.

FIELDER, HERBERT.
*A Sketch of the Life and Times and Speeches of Joseph E. Brown.* Springfield, 1883.

FITE, EMERSON DAVID.
*The Presidential Campaign of 1860.* New York, 1911.

FORMSBY, JOHN.
*The American Civil War. A concise History of its Causes, Progress, and Results.* London, 1910.

GARNER, JAMES WILFORD.
"The First Struggle over Secession in Mississippi," in the Mississippi Historical Society, *Publications,* IV, 89-105.

GERSON, ARMAND J.
"The Inception of the Montgomery Convention," in American Historical Association, *Annual Report, 1910,* 179-188.

GIDDINGS, JOSHUA REED.
*History of the Rebellion; its Causes and Authors.* New York, 1864.

A leading abolitionist's memoirs.

GORDON, ARMSTEAD SHEPARD.
*Jefferson Davis.* New York, 1918.

GREELEY, HORACE.
*The American Conflict.* 2 vols. Chicago, 1864-66.

An indispensable account by the Whig-Republican editor of the *New York Tribune,* which enjoyed an exceptionally large circulation in the Northwest.

HELPER, HINTON ROWAN.
   *The Impending Crisis of the South; how to meet it.*
   New York, 1857.
      Styled the Republican Bible by Southerners. Circulated
   by thousands as a campaign document.
HODGSON, JOSEPH.
   *The Cradle of the Confederacy.* Mobile, 1876.
HOWE, DANIEL WAIT.
   *Political History of Secession.* New York, 1914.
HUNNICUTT, JAMES W.
   *The Conspiracy unveiled. The South sacrificed; or the
   Horrors of Secession.* Philadelphia, 1863.
      This account is by a Virginia preacher, unconditional
   Unionist, and self-imposed exile. Valuable for the Vir-
   ginia story.
KING, HORATIO.
   *Turning on the Light. A dispassionate Survey of Presi-
   dent Buchanan's Administration from 1860 to its Close.*
   Philadelphia, 1895.
KONKLE, BURTON ALVA.
   *John Motley Morehead and the Development of North
   Carolina.* Philadelphia, 1922.
MCELROY, ROBERT MCNUTT.
   *Kentucky in the Nation's History.* New York, 1909.
MCPHERSON, EDWARD.
   *The political History of the United States of America,
   during the Great Rebellion.* Washington, 1876.
MUMFORD, B. B.
   *Virginia's Attitude toward Slavery and Secession defined.*
   New York, 1909.
PENDLETON, LOUIS.
   *Alexander H. Stephens.* Philadelphia, 1908.
PHILLIPS, ULRICH BONNELL.
   "The Literary Movement for Secession," in *Studies in
   Southern History and Politics.* New York, 1914.
   *The Life of Robert Toombs.* New York, 1913.
POLLARD, EDWARD ALBERT.
   *The Lost Cause; A new Southern History of the War of
   the Confederates.* New York, 1866.

RAMSDELL, CHARLES WILLIAM.
"The Frontier and Secession," in *Studies in Southern History and Politics*. New York, 1914.

REED, JOHN CALVIN.
*The Brother's War*. Boston, 1905.

REGAN, JOHN.
*Memoirs, with special Reference to Secession and the Civil War*. New York, 1906.

RHODES, JAMES FORD.
*History of the United States, 1850-1896*. 7 vols. New York, 1904.

RUSSELL, R. R.
"Economic Aspects of Southern Sectionalism. 1840-1861," in University of Illinois, *Studies in the Social Sciences*, XI, Numbers 1 and 2.

SHOTWELL, WALTER GASTON.
*The Civil War in America*. 2 vols. New York, 1923.

SNEAD, THOMAS LOWNDES.
*The Fight for Missouri from the Election of Lincoln to the Death of Lyon*. New York, 1888.

STEINER, BERNARD CHRISTIAN.
*Life of Roger Brooke Taney*. Baltimore, 1922.

STEPHENS, ALEXANDER HAMILTON.
*A Constitutional View of the late War between the States; its Causes, Character, Conduct, and Results*. 2 vols. Philadelphia.

STEPHENSON, NATHANIEL WRIGHT.
*The Day of the Confederacy*, in *Chronicles of America Series*. (Alvin Johnson, ed.), XXX. New Haven, 1903.

TEMPLE, OLIVER PERRY.
*Notable Men of Tennessee from 1833 to 1875, their Times and Their Contemporaries*. New York, 1912.

TYLER, LYON GARDINER.
*The Letters and Times of the Tylers*. 2 vols. Richmond, 1865.

VILLARD, OSWALD GARRISON.
*John Brown, 1800-1859. A Biography Fifty Years After*. Boston.

WARREN, CHARLES.
   *The Supreme Court in United States History.* 3 vols.
   Boston, 1922.
WILSON, HENRY.
   *History of the Rise and Fall of the Slave Power in
   America.* 3 vols. New York, 1862.
WOODS, HENRY.
   "A Sketch of the Mississippi Secession Convention of
   1861, its Membership and Work," in Mississippi His-
   torical Society, *Publications,* VI, 91-110.

# INDEX

Adams, J. H., commissioner from South Carolina to federal government, 175.

Adams, Wirt, commissioner from Mississippi to Louisiana, 195.

African slave trade, as a factor in secession debates, 124-125; and Constitution of Confederate States of America, 211-212.

Alabama, Democratic state platform of 1856, 23; platform of 1860, 33; withdrawal of state delegation from Charleston convention, 51; split in Democratic party, 70; Democratic convention of June, 1860, 71; platform of Constitutional Union party, 94-95; early preparation for secession, 136; secession convention, 201-205.

Anderson, Major Robert, Scott's instructions to, 173; transfer of troops to Fort Sumter, 175.

Anderson, Fulton, commissioner from Mississippi to Virginia, 255.

Arkansas, and Alabama platform, 35; split in state delegation to Charleston convention, 53; secession delayed by proximity of Indian tribes, 217-218.

Atlanta conference, proposed by South Carolina, 26; and Mississippi, 28; and Southern opposition press, 31; purpose of, 32.

Baltimore convention, prospect of harmony in, 73-74; report of committee on credentials, 82-

85; withdrawal of state delegations, 87-89.

*Barbarism of Slavery,* circulated as Republican campaign document, 97.

Barnwell, R. W., commissioner from South Carolina to federal government, 175.

Barry, William S., 58.

Baxter, S. S., 76.

Bayard, James A., withdrawal from Charleston convention, 53; admitted to Baltimore convention, 83.

Bell, John, popular vote for, 112.

Bell, H. P., commissioner from Georgia to Tennessee, 245.

Benning, Henry L., commissioner from Georgia to Virginia, 256-**257.**

Benjamin, Judah P., and framing of Kansas-Nebraska Act, 12 n; and schism in Democratic party, 61; speech against coercion, 147.

Bigler, William, member of Committee of Thirteen, 158.

Boteler, Alexander R., author of resolution for Committee of Thirty-three, 155.

Breckinridge, John C., nominated for presidency, 91; popular vote for, 112.

Brown, Joseph E., Governor of Georgia, message to state legislature, 142; and seizure of Fort Pulaski, 179.

Brown, Neill S., remarks in national Constitutional Union